Out With Three:

The Murder and Betrayal

of

Bald Head Island Police Officer
Davina Buff Jones

By

Elaine Buff

ISBN #978-1-4196-8613-5

LCCN # 2007910217

Printed in the United States of America

First Edition

Dedication

This book is dedicated to all the hearing officers who were not intimidated or swayed by political pressures, to all the families of the 13th District in North Carolina who also have suffered from the same type of legal justice as the Buff family, and to all the families of all the dedicated police officers who have given their lives honoring their oath of office. May God bless the memory of each one of these brave heroes.

Acknowledgments

I would like to thank Loy and Harriet Buff and their daughters for allowing me not only access to the materials with which to write Dee's story, but for accepting me into their lives as well. A special thank you goes from all of us to Monty Clark, owner of Clark & Associates, Private Investigative Service. Without his unwavering efforts to wrest the facts from where they had been hidden away, this book could not have been written. To Gigi Dover, we extend our thanks for sharing her talents and love through the song she wrote and performs for her friend and made available to use as the mantra to 'tell all the details.'

For all of those who have made your support known to the family as we have struggled to clear their Davina's name, there are no words to convey how much that encouragement has been appreciated. It enables us to continue the fight for justice with stronger resolve – not just for Davina, but anywhere such injustice has been done. And to the one who has helped in the daily mundane work so the pages could come to life, I could not have done this without you. A heartfelt thanks to God for bringing this task into my life and with it the kinship of this special person whose name I adopted to tell her story. May it do what God wills.

Table of Contents

Everybody Knows
by Gigi Dover ©2006

Come and take a ride down with me
'til 74 dead ends east
air thick as butter
ya barely can breathe
undercurrent flowing like you won't believe

beds are crawlin restless on the reef
footsteps leadin down to the creek
the swamp lies still like a black sheet of water
cicada singing for the middle daughter
Everybody knows but nobody wants to tell –

Cape Fear rise into the waterway
a bitter brew crashin with the local d.a.
a ferryboat ride
October Moon
someone took a life and he holds the proof –

beds are crawlin restless on the reef
footsteps leadin down to the creek
the swamp lies still like a black sheet of water
cicada singing for the middle daughter –

Everybody knows but nobody wants to tell –
tell all the details you've got to tell
let me take it in and judge for myself
out with three on a midnight call
tell me why should she have to take the fall?
Everybody Knows –

for Davina Buff – dedicated with love to her family

gigidover.net

Chapter One

Friday, October 22, 1999

They're out to get you. Run, Dee, run.

Officer Davina Buff Jones shook the thought from her mind and flashed a smile at the woman behind the counter at Hughes Gas and Grocery off Oak Island Drive on Oak Island and plunked down her usual purchase of a 10 ounce Coke and a pack of Basic menthol cigarettes. She voiced her agreement with the clerk's comment about the Carolina fall afternoon. "It is too pretty to go to work. I wish I could think of a good excuse not to go to work today. Maybe I can just hide out tonight."

The six-foot tall clerk smiled down at her regular customer. "You're so little, you could hide out anywhere." The two women often joked about each other's size.

- Wilmington Star News, "Evidence builds case for suicide: Bald Head officer's life is described as troubled." Cece von Kolnitz & Victoria Cherrie. 11/5/99 p. 8A

Dee waved back as she walked out into the coastal afternoon. She took a long swig from her drink before swinging her four-foot eleven-inch ninety pound body up into her silver 1994 Nissan truck. Bald Head Island, playground for the rich and pampered lay just offshore of Southport where she would spend another night as a police officer. She loved the career that she had found after she had turned thirty years old, but the job in such an ideal situation had turned sour within nine months.

"Why is it I can fix other people's problems but not my own? Nope. Stay positive, Dee. Now, how did that oath go again?"

- Dee's journals, nd, np

What was that part of the oath she had taken at graduation that ran through her mind all the time? Something about doing 'the duties of my office as a law enforcement officer according to the best of my skill, abilities, and judgment, so help me, God.' Yes. That's what she tried to do, regardless of how rough things got. She didn't know any other way. That didn't mean it was always easy.

At 33, she had been one of the oldest among the class of seventeen graduates of her Basic Law Enforcement Training, but she had taken that oath to heart. She ran it through her mind sometimes to help her when the going got tough.

They didn't want her over there on Bald Head and she didn't want to be there. What was it but a playground for the wealthy, accessible only by boat, transportation there only by foot, bike or golf cart. The mind set there was 'Do just about whatever you want because you have lots of money.' Until she could find a new position in another police agency, she had to look at every night as a new beginning for her and her babies. Two Australian shepherds, Lord Adam and Precious Queen were the pride and joy of her life. She would get another job from all the applications she had made or would make and she and her babies would start over and look for happiness somewhere else. Where they wanted a police officer to be a police officer. *They're out to get you. Run, Dee, run.*

The daily commute led Dee from her little house deep on Oak Island past the entrance to the golf course home of her parents, across the bridge over the Intracoastal Waterway – if you could look back over your shoulder on the bridge, you could see Old Baldy, the oldest lighthouse in North Carolina off shore. Several miles down the cause way, a right turn at the stop light brought the officer into Southport. Halfway to the Cape Fear River at the foot of town, Dee turned to the right towards Indigo Plantation and the ferry landing.

Paying little attention Officer Jones drove past the elementary school, followed the winding road through the expensive housing development and rounded the hard left turn to the landing. She entered lot A and parked in space 2. A chill was beginning to lace the early evening and it was windy. The 65-degree high of the day was fast disappearing. She pulled on her police officer's jacket before pulling out the drinks for the office and locking her truck.

- Storms, Janet. (10-23-99). *Report: Search of Davina Buff Jones' Nissan truck.*

Crossing the street, she met up with her partner Keith Cain. Sunset would be at 6:30 pm and the wind, which would be quite gusty and strong was already creating high and rough seas measuring 10 – 12 foot swells under a full moon.

- http://www.wunderground.com/history/airport/kswt/1 999/10/22/DailyHistory.html
- Industrial Commission, Crocker Testimony, 2003, p. 252
- Interview with Harriet Buff, 4/20,2006
- Martha Lee email to Karen Grasty, July 24, 2000

They spent most of the twenty minute ferry trip standing up near the wheel house talking with the ship's captain through the door. Dee was in an upbeat mood, so there was a lot of jabbering and joking and laughing. At some point, they looked toward the front left of the boat and saw three men with open beers. They informed the captain. One of the mates got ready to go down and asked if one of them would accompany him to get the beer away from the men.

Dee shrugged. "I'll go. I know it's against the law, but I can't say anything. It's not our jurisdiction, but I'll go." Once the beer had been disposed of without incident, Jones returned topside. At one point she talked briefly inside the passenger area with a retired lawyer and his wife who were returning home from a day trip to Wilmington.

- Statement from lawyer
- Cain interview with Criminal Specialist SD Netherland 10/23/99
- Cain interview with Gene Hardee 11/15/99
- Cain interview with Monty Clark 1/25/2000

Once the ferry docked at Bald Head, the two officers relieved the day watch. Then they proceeded to the police station located at the corner of Edward Teach and Muscadine Streets where they inspected and readied their vehicles for their 6:30 pm to 6:00 am shift. Davina always drove the department's Ford Ranger because she could reach the pedals. Her small size was always causing trouble, the latest of which had been her inability to perform bicycle patrol duty because they had been unable to find a police bicycle small enough for her to ride. Both officers checked the oil, fluids, tires, lights, radio, made sure the vehicle was clean, and readied a clipboard with call sheets.

Once inside the single-wide trailer serving as the police office, Dee chose a large mag flashlight and a radio. Since the polo shirt she wore tonight did not have a shoulder strap, she would have to attach it to the front of her shirt. It should be a slow night since the season was over and most of the wealthy and elite such as William Bennett and Willard Scott who had vacation homes here were gone. Years later the likes of Steelers' coach Bill Cowher and the Burton Brothers of NASCAR would build houses here, but on this night in 1999, there were only several hundred full-time residents on the tiny island.

- Dowell, Susan Stiles. Time Out. *Coastal Living*. Vol. 11, Issue 3. April, 2007. Retrieved 11-26-07 from http://www.baldheadisland.com/downloads/Press/Coastal_Living_april/coastal_living_April2007.pdf

Davina Buff Jones had been a cop only since January and Keith Cain, at 26, had eighteen months experience more than she, having been a truck driver previous to that. He was considered her superior during their duty. He knew that while she didn't mind night duty, she didn't like the dictum that she could no longer write tickets herself nor drive alone because she had made enemies on the island. On her part, she thought a lot of Cain and was glad he was her partner. She preferred working with him over all of the others on the squad; he treated her with more respect and more professionalism than the rest of them did.

For the first part of the evening they patrolled together, doing business and house checks, or keep checks. They went back to the trailer office and Dee worked at a computer on her desk. Around 7:10 they left again to patrol. They received a call about a catering van getting stuck at a house on Middle Island. They investigated but were unable to help get the van free.

A little before 10:30 someone identifying themselves as Jean Krause, the manager from the River Pilot Restaurant, made a call. "We had some guests here tonight who discovered that their golf carts are missing. Can you have our police come down and escort these people?"

"I sure can. And this is reference to larceny?"

"They're just missing. Their golf carts are missing. I'm sure somebody else took them by mistake … and we're getting ready to close so if the police could come as quickly as possible so they'll have a way home."

Dee drove the Ranger followed by Keith Cain in a Blazer. When they arrived minutes later, Dee radioed the 911 dispatcher. "There is no one at the River Pilot Café."

The dispatcher called the number back and got no answer.

Officer Jones said, "10-4 C-COM, thank you."

Jerry Adams and a co-worker were on the porch of a grocery store next door, where they were waxing the floor, so Dee went and asked them if they knew anything about a larceny next door while

Cain asked questions at a neighboring restaurant, Eb and Flo's. Adams suggested that Jones call the captain of the ferry who had just carried off the Pilot's workers. She thanked them and took off in her truck, Cain behind her in the Blazer. Adams said later, "She really peeled rubber." The two men could see her headlights and siren lights on near the lighthouse.

- Wilmington Star News, "Evidence builds case for suicide: Bald Head officer's life is described as troubled." Cece von Kolnitz & Victoria Cherrie. 11/5/99 p. 8A
- Cain interview with Criminal Specialist SD Netherland 10/23/99
- Cain interview with Gene Hardee 11/15/99
- Cain interview with Monty Clark 1/25/2000

The two officers went to the lighthouse because they had earlier seen a golf cart sitting near Old Baldy. The lighthouse sat near a cul-de-sac where a museum was being built on its left. To its right was the Village's conclave of municipal buildings including the post office, town hall, Village Association Building and chapel where many weddings take place. The area is secluded from the general traffic, especially at night, and is dark due to the lack of general traffic and light. The area was accessible by water with a pier out of sight behind the lighthouse, by a cart trail coming from the dock and from two roads coming into the area at right angles to each other. The 1817 Old Baldy's light does not rotate like most lighthouses, but its shaft shoots directly up into the air. At night, pilots can use the light to navigate out to the island and then on out to sea. Once at the lighthouse, Jones got out and took down the cart's registration number. The pair then returned to the station, she returning by North Bald Head Wynd, Cain by West Bald Head Wynd.

Jones had already eaten her dinner prior to this time so she ran information on the computer concerning the golf cart while Cain ate. Then she worked on her resume. Some time after eleven o'clock Dee announced either that she was going for a ride or was going out to smoke a cigarette. Her partner offered to go with her. She declined.

- Cain interview with Criminal Specialist SD Netherland 10/23/99
- Cain interview with Gene Hardee 11/15/99
- Cain interview with Monty Clark 1/25/2000

At eleven thirty Jones made a call from a phone booth at the marina that lasted approximately one minute. Then she was seen walking the area where the ferry docks.

- Monzon, Scott. (2-10-00). *Interview* by Monty Clark.

At 11:45 pm three vacationers were on their way in a golf cart through the darkness from the last ferry from the mainland. They encountered Officer Jones in her truck. She rolled down her window. "You are driving on the wrong side of the road. Get over." She rolled up her window and went on her way towards Old Baldy.

- Canvass Sheet Michelle Baldock 10/24/99
- Canvass Sheet John Ballard 10/24/99
- Canvass Sheet Todd Ballard 10/24/99

Jones entered the area that was the blackest of black. There are no lights in the area where the lighthouse sits hard by the cul-de-sac connected to the marina by a wooded golf cart path.

"C-COM, 4206."

C-COM's dispatcher answered, "4206?"

"10-4. Show me out with three ... Stand by, please." Several seconds later, Jones keyed her portable mike again. "There ain't no reason to have a gun here on Bald Head Island, okay? You want to put down the gun? Come on, do me the favor and put down the gun ..." There was a high pitch frequency squelched sound. "Come on UGU ..."

"C-Com, 4206." The dispatcher repeated the call. Still nothing. "C-COM, 4205 and 6?"

Keith Cain responded on his radio. "C-Com, 4205, did she ever say where she was out at?"

"Negative. She started to advise and said 10-12 and then her radio keyed up and I could hear her advising someone to put the gun down. I did not get a location."

"10-4, C-COM. I'll attempt to locate." Cain had already left the station at his partner's first communication and was frantically trying to locate her.

The dispatcher continued. "C-COM, 4206? C-COM, all units, hold your traffic 'till we can make contact with 4206."

First Keith Cain left Muscadine and headed down South Bald Head Wynd, slowing to look left and right at each intersection, making his way up to the Marina. As he drove, he asked C-COM, "Have you heard anything back from 4206 yet?"

"Negative. Not yet."

Across the overnight parking area, through the cart path leading to the cul-de-sac toward the lighthouse, he saw taillights.

Meanwhile, on the mainland, Randy Robinson was in charge of road traffic for the county for the night. He called in and was apprised of the situation. He advised that he would start heading toward the ferry. Then the dispatcher tried calling Jones again and then Cain.

"C-COM, 4206? C-COM, 4205, any luck?"

"Negative."

Seven minutes from the time of Dee's last transmission, Cain called in that he had arrived on the scene. "C-COM, Located her vehicle. I cannot find her."

"10-4. You're making contact with 3200 (Bald Head Island Fire chief) at this time and also 4200 (Karen Grasty – Bald Head Island Police Chief who was currently out on medical leave)."

- "10-4."Brunswick County 911 Emergency tape 10/22/99

14

- Cain interview with Criminal Specialist SD Netherland 10/23/99
- Cain interview with Gene Hardee 11/15/99
- Cain interview with Monty Clark 1/25/2000

When Keith initially entered the area, he parked his Blazer at a diagonal in the intersection of Ballast Alley and Lighthouse Wynd. He swept her truck with his stinger flashlight. The park lights were on and the engine was running but she was nowhere to be seen. He wondered if she were out chasing someone on foot. He noticed that the lighthouse door had been left open and crossed into the grassy compound around Old Baldy itself. He knew that sometimes teenagers would sneak into the historic structure after dark and drop beer bottles down to the floor below. He shined his light around and listened for noises. Hearing none, he came back out and checked the women's bathroom in what was once the oil house adjacent to the lighthouse. He stopped again, listening, trying to think where she might be.

Retracing his steps, he returned to her truck, glanced inside and saw her flashlight lying in her seat, the lens toward the door. Dee never got out at night without the flashlight. He shined his light in the bed of the truck but didn't see anything. Then he concentrated on the wood line, shining his light around the edges of the cul-de-sac. He saw something dark in the road but went on the sweep the area where a new museum was being built. Seeing nothing there, he began a go over the area before him again.

He took another look into the darkness beyond the trash pile to his right in the distance beyond him. Looking closer, he then realized he had found Dee. At first Cain could not tell until he was about five feet from her that there was blood coming from her head. Her body was face down, her face turned towards her left shoulder, her eyes slightly open. Her legs were straight out but slightly bowed and stretched toward her truck. Her left arm was bent at a forty-five

15

degree angle at her elbow; her mike was lying straight out by her left side about waist high. Her right arm was bent also with her hand just like behind her head. She resembled an upright field goal that had been pushed down. Her weapon, a 40 caliber Glock Model 23 was lying right up under her hand as though she had been holding it some two to three inches from her head.

Cain bent down beside Jones on her left side and checked her pulse on her left arm with his left hand while he watched her chest and head to see if she was breathing. He backed away, returned to her truck, reached inside and turned off the lights and the ignition. Then he repositioned his vehicle for better use of his headlights and take down lights. While he was backing off Cain called in, "C-COM, need rescue ... help ..."

"4205, you're advising you need rescue?"

An officer of the sheriff's department directed, "C-COM, go ahead and start rescue his way. 10-18 (urgent)."

"10-4. C-COM, 4205?"

Cain answered, "Go ahead."

"10-4. Have 4200 by 1021 (phone) also have rescue en route. Can you advise any further?"

The officer's first response was inaudible. "Officer is down. I do not get a pulse at this time."

Darkness as thick as the blood issuing from his partner's head engulfed Cain as he struggled to calm himself. Then it dawned on him. The scene was unsecured. How could emergency vehicles and personnel safely enter the area?

He positioned himself on the passenger side of his Blazer, opening the door and getting into its crease of protection until the Fire Chief, his backup, could arrive.

- Brunswick County 911 Emergency tape 10/22/99
- Cain interview with Criminal Specialist SD Netherland 10/23/99
- Cain interview with Gene Hardee 11/15/99

Brown was the only person authorized to carry a firearm on the island twenty-four hours a day. At the time he entered the scene, he would relieve Keith Cain of command at the scene and is the reason he was summoned by the dispatcher. Until help could arrive from the mainland, the fire chief was the chief police person on Bald Head Island.

At 12:06 a.m. Fire Chief Kent Brown and his wife Trish, also an EMS, arrived, Brown pulling his vehicle parallel to Cain's. Brown's wife stayed in the vehicle. Cain approached them, his gun drawn. The two men crouched between the two vehicles while Cain told Brown where Jones was, that he hadn't found a pulse or signs of breathing. He also reported signs of blood appearing to come from her head but added that he had been trying to check the area around him at the same time and could have missed something in his assessment of her condition.

"I didn't get a pulse, but I may have, you know, maybe I just checked in the wrong place, or ..." Cain was a trained medical responder, but under the circumstances, he couldn't trust his own observations. It is an understandable reaction.

At that point, Brown decided to call in the paramedics. They worked in pairs of two on twenty-four hour shifts. Two minutes later EMS Mike Tripp and EMS Danny Kiser arrived in an ambulance, stopping in the area of the lane coming from the marina to the lighthouse. Because of the dangerous nature of the scene, Brown treated it as a "hot zone' and because Cain had said Dee needed help, ordered the EMS's to do an "in and out." "Get to her!" Cain pleaded.

Brown advanced with Cain. Brown crouched behind the left back of Jones' truck while Cain went down the right side nearer the body by the white picket fence where she lay. Tripp and Kiser, going

17

in without a stretcher, recognized Dee and called her by name. Each grabbed her by a shoulder on each side and the service belt or leg (depending on whose testimony you read), picking her straight up (still face down) and carried her up where the sidewalk now is and straight to the waiting ambulance.

At the back of the ambulance, Kiser noticed a large amount of blood on the back of Jones' head and what felt like a wound. He told Tripp what he had found. "Get her out of here and assess her elsewhere."

Trish Brown sped the ambulance away to the dock while Tripp attended Jones in the back. Brown covered Cain while Cain went back to where Jones had laid to retrieve her gun which had fallen away from her body when she had been snatch up by the EMS'. Cain wanted to secure it, not knowing if there were others nearby in the darkness who could grab it. He carried the gun back to a spot between the two remaining vehicles and placed the gun on the ground.

Almost immediately Kent Brown announced he needed to go to the marina on business and left, taking half of the gun power and protection at the crime scene with him. At that point, Keith moved Dee's gun around to the passenger side of his squad car and placed it inside on the floorboard.

Then he and his unarmed companion EMS Kiser settled in to wait for police to arrive from the mainland. They knew that was likely to take at least twenty minutes. The only protection they had was the passenger side door of his Blazer.

At the marina EMS Tripp had completed a secondary survey that showed no signs of life, no pulse, no breathing, pupils dilated. He noted a gunshot wound to the back of Dee's head. Two EKG's were done and the results relayed to a doctor at Dosher Hospital in

Southport on the mainland. [In the report, the doctor's name is listed as Hilton, but there was no doctor at Southport with that name. The doctor was more likely to have been Doctor Doug Hiltz.]

Whoever the doctor was, they confirmed Asystole x3. Asystole is a medical term that refers to the point where a heartbeat has slowed to become what can be more commonly referred to as 'flat lined.' It is one of the medical conditions necessary for a doctor to pronounce death.

At that point, according to the records, Officer Davina Buff Jones was covered with a sheet. Everyone scattered to do the duties they thought they were bound to do, leaving the fallen officer on the dock. Human silence settled as nature shook the harbor this way and that as the full moon bathed the silvery water in light and white sheet's corners fluttered first one way and then another.

Everyone left Davina as physically as they had left her at every other time in her life when she had needed someone there for her. She laid alone, unguarded in the night, the wind and the moonlight her partners and her companions.

No more would she need to try to get away from the politics and pettiness of Bald Head Island. No more would anyone try to bait her or tell tales to get her into trouble. No more would the black sheep of the Buff family have to worry about measuring up to anyone or anything. It was all over.

She would be leaving on the ferry soon enough.

They're out to get you. Run, Dee, run.

- Cain interview with Criminal Specialist SD Netherland 10/23/99 pp. 1-4
- Cain interview with Gene Hardee 11/15/99 pp. np
- Cain interview with Monty Clark 1/25/2000 pp. 1-53

Out With Three

- Danny Kiser, Ambulance Call Report Narrative 10/23/99
- Kent Brown interview, 10/22/99 pp.1-5
- Kent Brown interview, Monty Clark 2/11/2000

Chapter Two

The Investigation

The first group of law personnel arrived at Bald Head Island twenty minutes after Davina Buff Jones had been confirmed dead over the phone by Dr. Hilton in Southport at Dosher Hospital. Employees from Eb and Flo's had heard the fatal gunshot blast and had been subsequently ordered to come to the ferry landing to leave the island. Upon their arrival, they came upon the body of Officer Jones uncovered on the ambulance gurney, a great amount of blood collected near the right side of her head. The employees left the island on the ferry that brought the police. The rumor of suicide was already growing from that brief unfortunate dockside encounter.

- Calhoun, Terry. (2005, July 13). Former BHI Chief: I know she was murdered. *The State Port Pilot*, A1, A6.
- Danny Kiser, Ambulance Call Report Narrative 23 October,1999
- Skolar, Daniel. (1-18-03). *Hearing officer claim determination. PSOB Case Number 2000-48, p. 27.*
- Grasty, Karen. Letter to Caddell. Nd.

Kent Brown had cleaned out the ambulance and took Lt. Miller, Deputies John Balduc and Allen Britton and Patrolman Brian Wrenn to the crime scene in it. By 12:50 a.m. a crime scene tape cordoned off the area.

- Crocker, David. Investigative report. 23 October, 1999.

Approximately an hour later more officers arrived. At some point the body had been moved to the Bald Head Island Ferry Depot Ticket Office and placed under guard by the Northwest Chief of Police. That is where Lt. David Crocker and Detective Sam Davis began to photograph the body and take a GSR test. Stories of suicide were already beginning to circulate, possibly due to the enormous amount of blood clotted to the side of her head, even EMS Kiser's report already showed a drawing and written description of the wound in the back of her head. Sergeant Randy Robinson had also arrived. Once he had observed the body, he left and proceeded to the crime scene. Interim Bald Head Island Police Chief Gene Hardee also arrived at the crime scene. Sheriff Ronald Hewett and his SWAT team left the Sunny Point Terminal heading toward the island. Dee's training officer Corporal Robert Willis, Inactive Bald Head Island Police Chief Karen Grasty, Detective Roger Harrington and Bald Head Island Officer Dexter Ludlum arrived on the island within the hour.

- Grasty, Karen. (8-29-01). *Interview* by Henry Foy, p. 3.
- Tripp, Michael. (10-23-99). *Ambulance Call Report Narrative Attachment #1*
- Crocker, David. (nd). *Investigative report timeline.* Pp. 1-3.

Grasty requested that Hewett send his assistant Larry Jones to break the news to Davina's parents because Larry was a long-time friend of Loy and Harriet Buff, living not far from them. About two o'clock in the morning, Jones' rap on the front door awoke Harriet, who immediately called out Davina's name, instinctively fearing the worst. She awakened Loy. Shocked, they sat in their night clothes on the steps while Jones told them what little he knew about what had taken place on the island.

- Buff, Loy and Harriet. Interview. By Elaine Buff. 22 October, 2006.
- Grasty, Karen. (10-23-99). *Interview* by Recording officer.

Meanwhile, when Kent Brown returned to the crime scene to take the officers, it was the first time Cain had seen him since he had earlier left. The officers questioned Cain, who basically told them where Jones' body had been, which vehicle had been whose, and where Jones' gun was. Then Robinson told his friend Cain to go to the ferry and let somebody check him. Cain was transported by Mike Tripp to the marina in the passenger seat of the ambulance that had carried his dead partner away earlier.

- Crocker, David. Investigative Report. 22 October, 1999.

Once at the marina, Cain almost stumbled accidentally into the room where Dee's body was, but an officer stopped him. In the captain's quarters of the ferry, Cain was given oxygen. On Bald Head, Cain gave a statement to David Crocker.

By three fifteen Crocker had secured the evidence that had been collected and readied the body for transport. Chief Grasty realized that he was intending to send her over uncovered and alone. She requested a body bag, but none could be found, so she and her husband David, a Topsail Beach policeman, got two sheets and sandwiched the dead officer between them, pinning them together to help protect what evidence might still be left in evidence on the body at this point.

Then the body was placed on the ferry and accompanied on the ferry trip by Rodney Gause, Chief of Shallotte Police Department; Officer David Grasty, Topsail Beach Police Department; and Carey Gaskins, Shallotte Police Department. The ferry bearing the body, the escort, and her partner docked at Indigo Plantation Ferry Landing at 3:55 a.m. Two minutes later Jones' body was loaded into a Southport Police Fire and Rescue Vehicle and transferred to Dosher Hospital by Charles A. Drew, David A. Frye, Tammy A. Drew, and SBI Special Agent Janet Storms.

- Grasty, Karen. (10-23-99). *Interview* by Recording officer.
- *SBI report: crime scene on Bald Head Island.* (10-23-99). Pp. 1-5.

Keith Cain was interviewed by an SBI agent and a GSR test was conducted. They collected his shirt, gun belt and other items, leaving him his tee shirt. A fellow officer Travis Snead collected him and took him home after having him checked out at Brunswick Hospital in Supply near Cain's home.

At 4:01 am Jones' body was met at the Dosher Hospital Morgue by SBI Agent Storms, Coroner Greg White and Southport Police Chief R. A. Gray. White and Charles Drew took the body from the gurney, putting it in a white plastic body bag, placing it onto a holding station. Storms photographed the body. White attached an identification tag on the outside of the body bag and secured the holding station. Doug Hiltz incorrectly noted Jones' height and weight as he completed the Medical Examiner's report, drawing the wound in the wrong place and adding a non-existent exit wound in a diagram. He listed her manner of death as Homicide and added "apparent homicide." White observed the head injury and said he could arrange transport to Jacksonville. The area was secured and locked by hospital security around 5:25 am.

- Hiltz, Douglas. (10-23-99). *Report of investigation by Medical Examiner.*
- *SBI report: crime scene on Bald Head Island.* (10-23-99). Pp. 1-5.

While this was transpiring, more officers were being ferried to the island. Additionally, SBI Agents Pat Daly, Steve Netherland, Tony Cummings, Wayne Johnson, and Aundrea Bridges were aboard. Upon arrival they met Sheriff Hewett at the Bald Head Island Village Hall where Fire Chief Brown had set up a command post.

Sam Davis and David Crocker searched Rescue Unit #4273, the ambulance used to transport Jones, now parked outside the Village Hall for any relevant evidence it might still contain after Brown's cleaning and the transport of all the officers back and forth to the crime scene. SA Daly gathered GSP coordinates of 33.5225 north, 78.0002 west. Lt. Gene Caison, the SBI agents and Chief

Rodney Gause were on the crime scene while Sam Davis of the Brunswick County Sheriff's Department took photographs.

- *SBI report: crime scene on Bald Head Island.* (10-23-99). Pp. 1-5.

On the mainland SBI Agent Storms interviewed the Buffs at their home. Then the Buffs went with Storms to their daughter's home and took Dee's dogs home with them.

- Buff, Loy & Harriet. Interview. By Elaine Buff. 22 October, 2006.

The autopsy of Officer Davina Buff Jones was performed by C. L. Garrett in Jacksonville, N. C. at 10:30 am with Jim Beddard-Dremir and Special Agent Hans Miller present. The procedure described the gunshot wound as an entrance wound depositing heavy soot deposits on the bone. The bullet traveled forward, upward and slightly to the left. A badly deformed lead metal jacketed bullet was removed from the brain and turned over to SBI Agent Miller. The autopsy also revealed that Davina had mild emphysema. She was also having her period.

- Garrett, C. L. (10-28-99). *Preliminary Report of autopsy examination.*

While the autopsy was being completed in Jacksonville, Village Manager Wade Horne had not only asked Sheriff Hewett to help with the investigation even though Karen Grasty had asked that the SBI handle it, he also had asked the Sheriff to serve as the spokesperson and contact for the media. The Sheriff, well-known for his affinity for being in front of the cameras, had earned the nickname "Hollywood." At 11:00 am Hewett, Grasty, Horne and Hardee departed for Indigo Plantation on the mainland for a news conference with Jennifer Miskowitz of WECT-Channel 6, a local television station in nearby Wilmington. Grasty had been out for months with back surgery and Hardee had been the interim chief. On her departure, Grasty ordered that the crime scene be left undisturbed. She placed Bald Head Island Officer Robert Willis in charge of the scene.

By the time the officials finished the news conference and returned to the island, it was after 12:30 pm. Grasty returned to find that in her absence, and against her direct and specific orders, the crime scene had been washed clean and the crime scene tape removed. For the rest of the day, tourists could visit Old Baldy. That afternoon over seventy tourists got to climb to the top of the lighthouse to survey the beautiful island with no thoughts of a murdered police officer to mar their good time. Grasty nor Hardee were ever about to find out who ordered the scene washed down. Fire Chief Kent Brown, whose fire engine washed down the scene, nor Officer Robert Willis, who had been left in charge of the crime scene, could remember or say who had given the order.

- Grasty, Karen. (9-12-00). *Letter* to Loy and Harriet Buff.

By 1:10 pm the last of the seized evidence from the case passed from Sam Davis to Detective Donald Marlow of the Brunswick County Sheriff's Department.

On Sunday, October 24th, the people from the golf cart traveling on the wrong side of the road that Friday night were questions. Sunday morning's newspaper related that investigators had searched the entire island. U. S. Coast Guard and Department of Defense boats from Sunny Point Military Ocean Terminal had patrolled the waters around the island while at one time as many as fifteen SBI and thirty-five Brunswick County Deputies had been searching the island.

They cited officers from Oak Island, Holden Beach, Shallotte, Southport and the North Carolina Highway Patrol assisted. The North Carolina Highway Patrol helicopter had taken aerial photographs of the crime scene as soon as the sun was up on

Saturday morning. The Crake wedding went off without further nasty

inconveniences such as yellow tape complications at the chapel.

- Ramsey, Mike. (10-24-99). Officer dies in Bald Head Island shooting. *The Sunday Star-News* p. 1A.
- SBI Agent Crime scene report via SBI 69-B, 10-23-99, p. 5.

On Monday the village issued a $50,000.00 reward for

information concerning the case. It was said to be one of the largest

ever offered in the state. Monday afternoon a reenactment of the

Friday night events was held with various people in attendance for

varying amounts of time. Assistant District Attorney Marion Warren

represented the DA's office. SBI agent Janet Storms finally made it

to the island along with Hans Miller.

They joined Lt. David Crocker, Deputy Roger Harrington and

Deputy James Christian of the Brunswick County Sheriff's

Department. For whatever reason, Fort Fisher Park Rangers Greg

Snyder and Terry Taylor attended. Bald Head Island officers on hand

included Chief Karen Grasty, Lt. Gene Hardee, Fire Chief Kent

Brown, Officer Robin Wallace, and Officer Robert Willis. A chaplain,

the Reverend James Grasty attended. Stacey Cain accompanied her

husband Keith.

The process began at 2:00 pm with Special Agent Miller

walking over the area with Cain. About 45 minutes later, Miller

outlined in tape the approximate position and location of Jones'

body, assisted by both Cain and Brown. Then Miller photographed

the scene. Once that had been completed, Keith Cain reenacted his

actions while Miller videotaped Cain's movements. By 4:35 pm all of

the reenactment activities were completed. Residents of the island

were not happy to have their daily activities upset by these

proceedings, as we shall see, but finally, most of the activities

dealing with the crime had evaporated from the island by 5:00 pm at

least and everyone was free to let all of the nasty remnants go as freely as the yellow police tape had been swept away on Saturday morning.

- *Buff v. Village of Bald Head Island Police Department, North Carolina League of Municipalities and North Carolina Rescue Workers Cap Death Benefits Act.* North Carolina Industrial Commission. (10-23/24-03). pp. 208-209

Chapter Three

The Memorial Service

One hundred people attended the meeting at the fire station on Tuesday, October 26, 1999. Village council members and residents were in attendance as the death of Officer Jones was discussed. Wade Horne, village manager, had said that officials would not discuss the investigation at the meeting, but that is what the residents wanted to do. Joyce Douglas asked, "Was this a suicide? It sounds selfish, but we need to know if there is a murderer running loose on our island."

- Cherrie, Victoria and Cece von Kolnitz. (10-28-99). Single shot killed officer, autopsy shows. *Morning-Star.* Pp. 1A.

No details were disclosed. Chief Grasty said, "We can't tell you what we don't know." Grasty reiterated that so far there had been no evidence of an intruder. The sentiments expressed during the meeting were that the case needed to be settled quickly and that it needed to be determined a suicide. Both of these conditions were necessary for the best interest of Bald Head Island. The tourist industry would otherwise be adversely affected. Property taxes might go down. It was made clear that residents would prefer to believe a discontented young lady took her own life rather than believe that such an idyllic place could harbor a killer. A neighbor of Dee's remarked "Bald Head is a wealthy little island and people over there don't want to face the idea that a killer might be among them"

- Teague, Matthew. (10-28-99). Police await lab results in death. *The News and Observer.* Np.

The atmosphere and callousness of the meeting caused Chief Grasty to write a letter of protest to the then Village Mayor Kitty

Henson. "I am pleading with you to help in controlling the verbal remarks being made in public concerning the death of Police Office Davina Jones."

- Grasty, Karen. (11-02-99). *Letter* to Kathleen (Kitty) Henson.

Four hours after the contentious village meeting, hundreds of law enforcement officers descended on Peacock-Newman and White Funeral Home in Southport to pay their respects for a fallen comrade. Dee had known the place well, having passed the business every work day on her way to and from the ferry landing at Indigo Plantation.

The officers came from Shallotte, Southport, Ocean Isle Beach, Holden Beach, Oak Island, Wilmington, and Cary Police Departments; New Hanover, and Pender County Sheriff's Departments; North Myrtle Beach, South Carolina Police Department, North Carolina Troopers and wildlife officers. They spilled outside where a long line stood at attention during the service.

Hundreds of flowers surrounded Davina's urn and portrait in the front. During the service Chief Grasty remembered Dee as being ambitious and wanting to be the best police officer she could be. "She may have been small in stature but she had the biggest heart of anyone I've ever met."

Her sisters Tanya and Beverly recalled happier times around 'Beany,' so called due to her fondness was gnawing on raw green beans when she was small. Then they sat in tears as they listened to one of Dee's favorite songs, Diamond Rio's "You're Gone."

- D'Abruzzo, Diana. (10-27-99). 'The biggest heart of anyone ...' *The State Port Pilot*. Pp. 3,5.
- Ramsey, Mike. (10-27-99). Hundreds pay tribute to fallen officer. *Morning-Star*. Pp. 1A, 6A.

Davina's uncle Charles Hale, in a moving eulogy, likened her to a shooting star – "How quickly seen, how soon disappeared and gone, how long remembered!!" He read a poem by Jody Seymour entitled "Your Child First" which included the haunting line "Where were your hands to keep her from harm?"

- Hale, Charles. (10-26-99). *Eulogy for Davina Elaine Buff*.
- Seymour, Jody. (1997) *Your child first* from *Finding God between the lines*. Judson Press: Valley Forge, PA., p. 9.

A color guard of Brunswick County Deputies presented an American flag in traditional military fashion. Sheriff Ronald Hewett offered the flag to Harriet Buff in her daughter's memory. The emotional service ended with a broadcast of 'last call' from the Brunswick County Emergency Service Center Dispatcher, "4206."

Davina had been devoted to her grandparents and liked to go fishing with them at the Yaupon Beach Pier. When her grandfather died, he had been cremated, his ashes scattered from the pier. Dee's ashes, along with her favorite yellow roses, were scattered in the ocean near Yaupon Beach Pier at a later time.

- Funeral. Retrieved 5-31-07 from http://www.officerdavinabuffjones.com/ funeral.htm

Yet her memorial service was tainted by the whispers of suicide moving through the ranks of officers attending, causing them to wonder why they were honoring someone who had killed herself.

On the island, friends tried to remember her there. Her co-workers wore black arm-bands. They wound black ribbons on road signs. People lay wreaths where her body had been found. The village management told the police to remove the arm-bands. The black ribbons were taken

down from the road signs on Bald Head. The flowers were taken away. When Davina's family came to the island on the first anniversary of her death and left flowers, they were removed before the family got back home from the island.

Any that have been left since by anyone have faced the same fate.

Suspects

There were immediate suspects. Three had histories of drug trafficking; two lived on the island; the other worked there and had recently gotten a ticket from Officer Jones for illegal parking. All three men had been on Bald Head Island the night she died. One claimed he had gone to bed early, one was hosting a party, and one was out with his dog. All three supposedly passed polygraph tests taken within several years of the incident.

There is proof of the party host's polygraph test, given over a year later and that of the dog walker. Even though the police said they gave the third man a lie detector test, there was never any documentation. This gentleman still lives on the island.

Other additional suspects were vindicated because they were still incarcerated or passed polygraph tests or were injured and in hospitals in neighboring states at the time. There were as many as fifteen names on the list, including names from citations Jones had issued. They included a strange, un-kept man found on the island and a citation receiver who had once threatened Jones.

The police followed leads including someone from the island who had been selling everything and leaving town, someone in jail who had worked on Bald Head and was said to be anxious for release from jail, and a worker in a Southport marina who supposedly had knowledge of the slayer. There was a sailor on a trip passing through on the Intracoastal Waterway stopping to get gas for his boat. He reported that he had overheard someone on a telephone in a bar saying "He shot her!"

Five or six people were reportedly hiding in a squatter's camp on Bay Creek. A builder who had a record of breaking and entering had fired his whole crew without explanation on Saturday morning after Davina's death. Somebody overheard a supposed girlfriend talking about how her boyfriend had "done in the cop." But that story proved to be the wrong kind of gun, this lead was a story based on a lie for reward, that lead couldn't be proved and such down the list of leads until they were gone.

- Grasty, Karen. (8-29-01). *Interview* by Henry Foy.
- *Buff v. Village of Bald Head Island Police Department, North Carolina League of Municipalities and North Carolina Rescue Workers Cap Death Benefits Act.*
- North Carolina Industrial Commission. (10-23/24-03). Exhibits Part I, Pp. 221, 222, 224, 226, 271, 442-443.
- Noles, Jamie. (10-25-99). Interview by police of record.

Additional suspects included the man named in Dee's pending sexual harassment suit that had been kept from the public's knowledge and Dee's two former boy friends. The man named in the harassment suit was in the middle of working a back-to-back shift on the job and one of the ex-boy friends was an Oak Island policeman who had been working the same shift time Dee had been. These two were eliminated as suspects.

The other gentleman had a military background, had worked as a deputy for the Brunswick County Sheriff's Department in narcotics for five years, and was a relative of the sheriff. He had fallen hard for Davina but she had begun to work at ending the relationship with, beginning to realize the two would only be friends at the most and sometimes even fearing him, avoiding him when he came to her house.

- Atkins, Laura. (10-27-07). *Telephone interview* by Elaine Buff.

This man was known around the sheriff's department as a "loose cannon" and someone capable of doing "just about anything he wants to do without any conscience." He had no alibi for several hours that night. He had been watching television alone at home that night.

- *Buff v. Village of Bald Head Island Police Department, North Carolina League of Municipalities and North Carolina Rescue Workers Cap Death Benefits Act.* North Carolina Industrial Commission. (10-23/24-03). Exhibits Part I. P. 226.

No information concerning suspects or how the case was being conducted really made its way to the general public. Even after the hearings were finished, not much information made its way to print except for the exceptional article. The Buffs were painted as semi-hysterical, money-grubbing people unwilling to face the fact that their daughter killed herself. It was an easy package to pedal when all the information concerning the facts of the case had been carefully kept under wraps.

Loy had several run-ins with first one and then another of the people he saw who he felt had really turned on his daughter – the local police. Friends in the police department stopped talking to him. In the Southport Wal-Mart he ran into one of the Brunswick County drug agents who had worked with Davina and threatened to come after him personally if Loy ever discovered that he had anything to do with her murder.

When Hewett and Gore ran for re-election, Loy was right there on the forefront with signs and words for anyone who would listen. He ran full page ads during the campaigns in the local newspapers whose editors would still deal with him and cancelled his subscriptions with those who won't talk to him any more. When you had the cash money to buy the ad and people refuse to take your money to voice your opinion, Loy figured he didn't need their daily dose of news on his door step.

At one point, he strapped big signs onto his truck and drove through towns around campaign functions, getting surrounded by sheriff's deputies in the public park on Oak Island one time and ending up in a parade in one of the little towns in neighboring Columbus County.

He found himself the lightning rod for many others in the district who called or talked to him on the street about cases where others had suffered the same kind of treatment and judicial action his family was facing. He began to compile names and phone numbers and horror stories from all over the area. It only fuelled the fires burning inside for something to change in the county. How can you fight something so large and out of control and seemingly without any reins to pull it in?

His anger and frustration was hard to conceal – and even harder to survive. Something needed to be done, not only for his own Vanny, but for all of these people he was learning about and wanting now to help. He felt like Scrooge, who, once the Ghost of Christmas Present had showed him the specters of Ignorance and Want, knew he could not forget that they existed. He was coming to know that there were so many other families who had suffered in this district, wanting and needing help. But Loy was powerless to help his own dead daughter, much less anyone else. As a father, he wanted to fix things for his child, and he couldn't. He grew irritable and sleepless and his body ached with new aches and pains.

Harriet handled hers first by withdrawing and then shutting down. Loy wanted to right the wrong done to his daughter; Harriet just longed to hold her daughter one more time. They suffered; their other daughters suffered; the grandchildren suffered from the oppressive, depressive atmosphere. Each one in the family directly was touched by the decisions that had been made in the darkness on the island in 1999 and in the sterile environment of Bolivia's government offices, far removed from the affected family.

But resolve had been at the core of Davina Buff Jones' character. The powers had tried to destroy her and had been forced to kill her to do it. She had gained that resolve from Harriet and Loy Buff. It was in her genes. The Buffs were determined to find out the truth. They never gave up waiting for the truth. On one of her birthday anniversaries following her death, they wrote in the paper: "Someday the truth will be told. One day the guilty will be punished for their sins. And through it all, Dee's light will shine on because through us, she still lives."

- *Davina Buff Jones*. Retrieved on 10-05-07 from http://www.officerdavinabuffjones.com/

The suspects all evaporated, according to the initial police investigations, but the Buff family still felt in the very marrow of their bones that something was still undone, still unsettled, out of kilter, missing.

They knew their daughter too well to believe in their heart of hearts that she had done this grievous thing to herself and to them and they entered each day wondering where they could turn to uncover that one piece of evidence, that one missing link that could get the authorities back on the trail of searching for who might be responsible for the death of their daughter.

They felt like they were operating in a vacuum and later on, they would find they absolutely were. Some of it was by design and some of it is encountered by any family anywhere facing the same intricacies and eccentricities of a murder case.

Death of a child is always a difficult process in and of itself, but when it is violent, it is more difficult. When it comes at the hands of a murderer, it is all the more painful to navigate. Loy Buff only knew his blood pressure began to rise and fall with the mention of each suspect and the announcement of the subsequent dismissal of each name as a viable culprit. The darkness and shadows held possible clues everywhere he looked.

Out With Three
He felt like he was jousting at windmills not even visible to him. Harriet sat in the house, shell shocked, with all of Dee's belongings packed and in the attic or pushed into a bedroom closet.

"Tell all the details you've got to tell
let me take it in and judge for myself."
- Dover, Gigi. (2007). *Everybody Knows*

Autopsy

In North Carolina each jurisdiction has a medical examiner whose job is to certify the cause and manner of death on a death certificate and file a report to the office of the Chief Medical Examiner in Chapel Hill. "Most Medical Examiners (ME) are not pathologists. They may be local physicians, physicians' assistants or even registered nurses."

- Garrett, C. L. (11-25-03). *Deposition. P. 9.*

If it's deemed to be in the interest of the public, the ME can order an autopsy before the death is certified. The ME does not do autopsies; they authorize them. Jones' death was considered "unattended." She died in a place other than a hospital, hospice, or long-term care facility. An autopsy is generally a procedural practice for any unattended death and always for a homicide.

- Garrett, C. L. (11-25-03). *Deposition. P. 9.*
- Ramsland, Katherine. *The medical examiner.* Retrieved on 9/28/07 from http://www.crimelibrary.com/criminal_mind/forensics/crimescene/4.html

At Dosher Hospital Medical Examiner Douglas Hiltz had termed the cause of death as "gunshot wound to head." Probable cause of death was designated "Pending" and at the bottom, "Homicide." He listed Dee's height incorrectly as 65 inches and her weight as 140 pounds when she was 57 inches tall and weighed 90 pounds. He drew the wound to the back of her head behind her right ear.

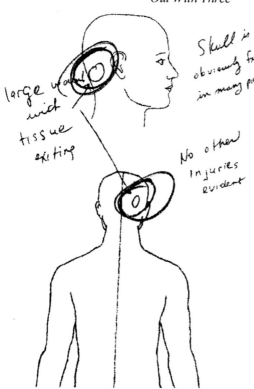

Skull is obviously fr in many pie

large wa with tissue exiting

No other injuries evident

- Hiltz, Douglas. (10-23-99). *Report of Investigation by Medical Examiner.*

When Loy Buff confronted Hiltz later with the Garrett autopsy drawing and Dee's correct height and weight designation, Hiltz replied, "Well, it was 4:30 in the morning and I was tired!"

- Buff, Loy and Harriett. (8-24-07). *Interview* by Elaine Buff.

Present while Hiltz did his job were Storms, County Coroner Greg White and Southport Police Chief Bob Gray. Security Officer Steve Stout secured the morgue and the area was cleared at 7:42 am. Seized items were turned over to BCSD Detective Gene Caison.

- Storms, Janet. (10-23-99). *SBI report: Seizure of personal items from Jones.*

Greg White arranged for the body to be transported to Jacksonville for autopsy. An autopsy is a postmortem medical examination of a corpse to determine manner and cause of death for an official report. In this state, the pathologist takes the facts from the Medical Examiner and performs the autopsy.

On the average an autopsy takes between one and two hours. It takes place in a room with a steel autopsy table equipped for draining away fluids. Next to it is a smaller dissection table for cutting up and examining organs. There is a hanging scale for weighing organs. There also is a large tank on the floor for collecting fluids.

- Ramsland, Katherine. *The medical examiner.* Retrieved on 9/28/07 from http://www.crimelibrary.com/criminal_mind/forensics/crimescene/4.html

There are eleven steps to be completed during an autopsy and there is a road map of sorts to be followed in completing them. It can be said that almost any autopsy is conducted by a standard method following the same procedures as those completed anywhere else. The following steps are standard components of a typical autopsy.

1. Body photographed, both clothed (if clothed when found) and unclothed
2. X-rayed
3. Weighed
4. Finger printed
5. Measured
6. Identifying marks recorded
7. Old and new injuries noted along with tattoos and scars
8. Trace evidence collected: hair, fibers from body and under fingernails before it is cleaned
9. The nails are clipped
10. The wrapping sheet along with clothing and trace evidence is sent for analysis
11. Anything wet from blood must be air dried

A crime scene photographer may take pictures or videotapes during the autopsy and color film is always used. Close-ups are made of all wounds, tattoos, scars or bruises and these are framed with a ruler laid next to the wound or mark. Photographs are taken again after a wound is washed or a body part shaved.

Once the body is clean and free of all hindrances such as clothing and jewelry, it is laid out on its back on the steel table with a stabilizing block placed under the head. The surgeon makes a "Y" incision, a cut into the body from shoulder to shoulder, meeting at the sternum and going straight down the abdomen into the pelvis. The purpose of this incision is to expose the internal organs.

A saw or tree-branch looper is used to cut through the ribs and collarbone so that the rib cage can be lifted away. The surgeon then uses x-rays of injuries or a lodged bullet as a guide. The next step is to take a blood sample to determine blood type. Then the organs are removed and weighed. Samples are taken of the fluids in the organs. The stomach and intestines are split open to examine the contents.

The last step in the process is to examine the head. The eyes are probed for hemorrhages that reveal strangulation. An incision is made in the scalp behind the head and the skin is carefully peeled forward over the face to expose the skull. Using a high-speed oscillating power saw, the skull is opened and a chisel is used to pry off the skullcap. The brain is lifted out, examined and weighed. Tissues from various organs are sent to the lab for further analysis.

- Ramsland, Katherine. *The medical examiner.* Retrieved on 9/28/07 from http://www.crimelibrary.com/criminal_mind/forensics/crimescene/4.html

While the autopsy itself may be completed within several hours, the complete report may take up to three months because reports from all of the lab tests have to return. Once the pathologist collects all the facts, they are returned to the medical examiner.

- Garrett, C. L. (10-28-99). *Preliminary Report of autopsy examination. P. 9.*

A preliminary report is done when time for information is of the essence. Garrett did such a report on October 28, 1999 for Hiltz because of the press for information concerning Dee's death. The autopsy on Jones was done at Onslow Memorial Hospital in Jacksonville, NC beginning at 10:30 am with Jim Beddard-Diener and SBI Agent Hans Miller in attendance. Miller took photographs.

During the process, Garrett recovered "a severely nose deformed lead projectile containing a partial metal jacket." Hans Miller took possession of the bullet. Garrett correctly placed the wound at 4½ "from the top of her head on the posterior midline. The entrance wound was approximately ½" in diameter with 2 3/8" lateral splits and one 3½ " inferior split. There were heavy soot deposits on the bone and multiple ramifying skull fractures. The bullet, after striking the head, "travels forward, upward and slightly to the left." It struck the skull and was reflected back into the brain. The autopsy also disclosed that Dee had mild emphysema.

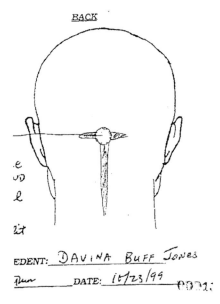

BACK

EDENT: _DAVINA BUFF Jones_

Dun _____DATE: _10/23/99_ P001.

Jones had bad luck again. In drawing the head wound, Garrett drew the head wound upside down. Later he would say that he drew the sketch while the body was face down to him. In the picture on the left, imagine the wound turned pointing upward to understand the kind of wound suffered by the officer. Who would believe a medical examiner and a pathologist

43

could both make mistakes in drawing a head wound? It seems like something from a terribly poor comedy instead of an investigation of the death of a police officer.

- Garrett, C. L. (10-23-99). Autopsy of Davina Buff Jones.

During the procedure, it was noted that the body was clothed in a blue police uniform, black Reebok shoes, police belt (with expandable baton, empty holster, handcuff case, handcuffs, multi-tool with case, badge, empty magazine case, pepper spray case and container of pepper spray). Special Agent Miller noted no indications of tearing, soiling, or other signs of a struggle on the uniform. The measurement from the body's right and left armpits to the tips of the extended respective index finger was approximately 23 inches.

- *Buff v. Village of Bald Head Island Police Department, North   Carolina League of Municipalities and North Carolina Rescue Workers Cap Death Benefits Act.* North Carolina Industrial Commission. (10-23/24-03).

Items taken from the body during the autopsy included:

1. black boots and 2 pairs of socks
2. utility belt with mace, holster, handcuffs, utility knife, baton, badge
3. blue "Police" polo shirt
4. black short sleeve undershirt
5. long light blue underwear shirt
6. pierced ruby birthstone earrings
7. neck chain
8. analog wrist watch with black band
9. silver Indian design ring from middle finger of left hand
10. ruby birthstone ring from right hand
11. cigarette lighter
12. breath spray
13. $1.91
14. white brassiere
15. finger nail scrapings (both hands)
16. 1 Glock Model 23 caliber .40 and clip
17. sample collected from right grip of Glock pistol
18. hair and four (4) fibers removed from Glock pistol

19. SBI sexual assault evidence collection kit
    a. two (2) liquid blood samples of Davina Buff Jones
    b. two (2) vaginal smears
    c. blue panties
    d. four (4) rectal swabs
    e. two (2) rectal smears
    f. four (4) oral swabs
    g. two (2) oral smears
    h. pubic hair combings
    i. known pubic hair sample
20. Known head hair sample
21. Control swabs
22. Blood stains prepared from the blood of Davina Buff Jones (2 liquid blood samples)

- Garrett, C. L. (10-23-99). Autopsy of Davina Buff Jones.

Before the autopsy had even begun in Jacksonville, word spread through Bald Head Island that SBI Agent Miller had called back saying that it looked like Dee's death was a suicide. That was a curious assumption on his part.

The word came before the group of Hardee, Horne, Grasty, and Sheriff Hewett left Bald Head Island to attend the press conference at Indigo Plantation Ferry Landing. Perhaps that information was used to give even more credence to the lack of need to hold the crime scene intact as Chief Grasty had ordered before leaving for the press conference.

If there was a large important wedding taking place the next day and the wedding party wanted to take pictures on Saturday and was pressing the fire department to get the area cleaned, a phone call from an SBI agent saying it was a suicide would certainly give someone license to take the liberty of defying a direct order from a chief of police and washing down – destroying as it were – what was left of a crime scene. It also made it easier to get the scene cleared up quickly if one wanted to get the whole matter out of sight and hopefully out of the minds of people so the whole thing could disappear with a minimum of publicity. Bald Head Island was to be seen as a place to get away from it all, not find more trouble than you had at home when you came to relax. No resident need think they needed to pack up and find a safer place to live either.

Chapter Six

The District Attorney's Decision

One night about six weeks after Davina's death, Assistant District Attorney Marion Warren called Bald Head Island Police Chief Karen Grasty at her home. He told her that while his office was receiving a lot of political pressure to settle the case as soon as possible, District Attorney Rex Gore would wait until Quantico had analyzed the 911 tape to make his announcement as to the nature of Dee's death. He would not reveal the names of those doing the pressuring. He agreed with Grasty that "the case could not possibly be considered anything other than undetermined death due to lack of evidence and the scene being destroyed." Off the record, the comment was made that "Bald Head Island and influential persons weren't partial to having a high profile murder occurring on their island."

- Grasty, Karen. (7-02-00). *Letter* to Loy and Harriet Buff.

Yet that very next morning, Gore's suicide announcement was made public. Davina Buff Jones had died by her own hand. Not all the test results were back. Polygraphs would take years or never occur. Some suspects would not be considered until 2006. But the District Attorney made the decision based on the batch test results. They proved that the bullet came from Dee's gun. The batch test merely proved that the bullet came from the batch of bullets that had been bought by Chief Grasty. All of the bullets being used on Bald Head Island *at that time* came from the same batch.

Gore's decision was based on materials he received from a report from David Crocker, investigator from the Brunswick County Sheriff's Department. Actually, that's not completely true. When Grasty heard about Gore's announcement, she called Warren who told her "that Sheriff Hewett had talked with the press and called the death suicide, putting the District Attorney in a difficult position ... We're going to do whatever the sheriff wants."

- Calhoun, Terry. (7-13-05). Former BHI chief: 'I know she was murdered.' *The State Port Pilot.* Pp. 6A.

Crocker testified "All the leads were closed, we waited for the FBI report on the batch analysis. That, coupled with the medical examiner's office and other reports that the SBI generated about the – the lifestyle of Ms. Jones. This was put in front of the District Attorney, Rex Gore, and he was given an extensive report. He kept if for a *long* (emphasis mine). time before *he* (emphasis mine) finally made a decision and issued a press release as to the results."

- *Buff v. Village of Bald Head Island Police Department, North Carolina League of Municipalities and North Carolina Rescue Workers Cap Death Benefits Act.* North Carolina Industrial Commission. (10-23/24-03). P. 267.

The report Crocker referred to was actually a letter six pages in length that he wrote to Sheriff Hewett as a case update. In reality, the sheriff called the media and set up a press conference for the next morning. Then he handed the decision to the District Attorney to find an explanation of support, whether it fit or not. The sheriff had other fish to fry before the night was done.

With David Crocker and Chief Deputy Larry Jones once again in tow, Hewett made his last visit to the Buffs. Their daughter Tanya was with them when he told them about the decision that would be announced the next morning. They began to ask questions. How could Dee shoot herself and not cause bruises on her body, they asked Hewett.

48

"Well, she stood up and she put the gun behind her head and she shot it." Tanya argued that her sister had not had a mark on her face. The family reminded him that Dee didn't have any sand, scratches, anything like that on her face from falling.

"Well, she went down on her right knee and shot herself."

Harriet said that she still would have hit the pavement hard enough for there to have been some marks of some kind.

"Well, then she must have laid down and done it."

- *Buff v. Bureau of Justice Assistance Public Safety Officers' Benefits.* (1-18-03). P. 57.

Prior to releasing the information concerning her death, Gore's office faxed the official statement to the Bald Head Police Department telling them it is the last opportunity to make changes. The first sentence was changed to include "died by self inflicted wound as stated by Sheriff's Office and DA's office." Gore's office changed the line to read "died by self inflicted wound."

- Gore, Rex. (12-09-99). *Fax* to David Cox.

The next morning Karen Grasty contacted SBI Agent Tony Cummings who told her as far as he was concerned, the case "was still under investigation." She asked Wade Horne to say that Bald Head Island would not accept the decision and would still investigate. Horne informed her that they would accept the DA's ruling. He told Grasty "No. Let sleeping dogs lie. As long as you are an employee of the Village of Bald Head Island you will not to talk to the press."

- *Buff v. Bureau of Justice Assistance Public Safety Officers' Benefits.* (1-18-03). P. 17.
- Calhoun, Terry. (7-13-05). Former BHI chief: 'I know she was murdered.' *The State Port Pilot.* P. 6A.

So Rex Gore stood up and told the world, "I am satisfied that Miss Jones was killed by her own gun and by her own hand." And he continues to say so to this day. In one of his last statements, he added, "I always thought that law enforcement had done a thorough job ,,, We're moving on."

- DA's statement. (12-15-99). *The State Port Pilot*. P. 9.
- Little, Ken. (6-03-06). SBI reinforces suicide ruling in officer death. *Morning-Star*. Pp. 1B.

Brunswick County District Attorney Rex Gore ruled the death of Officer Davina Buff Jones as a suicide based on findings from the police investigation as provided to him through David Crocker's report. Each on will be examined here.

1. The gun was found on the scene at the body. This is true. If Dee had shot herself, it may not have been as close as it was. However, it also could have been placed where it was found.

2. Her Glock was covered with blood. True. It has been used to kill her. It had been located near her head at the time of the shot. The weapon was less than two inches from her head when her body was found. Her head was turned so that the blood ran from the wound in her head to the ground where the gun was found.

3. The weapon was seen in the victim's right hand. False. Fire Chief Kent Brown said the gun fell from her hand but he never left the opposite side of the back of Dee's truck from where her body lay. In the dark, he could not clearly see. EMS personnel said it fell. Gore cited Cain's second interview where he said the gun was in Dee's hand, yet Cain went to great pains to explain to Monty Clark (Cain's *third* interview) that her hand rested *on* the gun and showed with his hand that she was *not* holding the gun. Nevertheless, let's address the question head on: does the position of the weapon found in the hand of Davina Buff Jones indicate a suicide? Martinez responded

that it did not. "In the study *Weapon Location Following Suicidal Gunshot Wounds* by J. C. Garavalia, M.C. et. al., it was determined that in 498 suicide studies, the gun remained in the hand only 24 per cent of the time. In the case of handguns (365 cases), the gun was found in the hand 25.7 per cent of the time. There was no correlation between the frequency of the gun remaining in the hand and such factors as gender or caliber. Conclusion: it does *not* determine predictability.

- Martinez, Michael. (2-20-01). *Report.*

4. There was only one large pool of blood that indicated that Jones fell immediately where she was shot. False. The drag marks indicated that she had been brought from the direction of her truck. There is the problem of the bloody palm print on the back of her truck that she certainly would not have been able to make. Plus there is blood spatter in a totally different place that was never mentioned by Crocker in his report.

5. There was blood only on the right side of the victim's head. True. That was not because she was shot behind her right ear as police

continued to insist to ridiculous limits. There was even an incorrect and hilarious (if it were not for the circumstances) diagram at the SBI lab of a head wound. The caption says the projectile was still in head but there was a 2nd hole here. Then it shows an entrance wound. This is satisfactory police work????? The entrance wound in her head was between where these two x's are drawn. Neither Crocker nor Gore ever saw the autopsy pictures yet they continued to insist that Garrett had drawn the injury incorrectly. Marion Warren disagreed with Monty Clark about where Dee's head wound was. Clark told him. Warren replied, "I guess I stand to be corrected."

> ▪ *Buff v. Bureau of Justice Assistance Public Safety Officers' Benefits.* (1-18-03). Pp. 102-103.

6.   Dee's flashlight was left in her truck. True. But, it is not clear whether it was *left* in the truck or *put back in* the truck. Due to the kind of radio she was using with the type of shirt she was wearing that night, she had to hold the mike in her hand to talk into it. It would be hard to carry a flashlight, hold and talk into your mike and pull your gun if needed.

7.   Jones' vehicle was backed in to the cul-de-sac with the park lights on. True. That is the way the vehicle was supposedly discovered. There is no indication that is the way the officer herself left it. If she were going to kill herself, what statement would she have been making by leaving park lights on or by backing the truck into the cul-de-sac? Chief Grasty had said that officers on night duty liked to sit at that place and do paperwork or smoke or watch the traffic from the last ferry. It would not have been unusual for Jones to be there with her park lights burning.

8.   Furthermore, assailants could have either turned them all off or on or just left parking lights burning.

9. There was nothing stolen from Dee's truck. True. The agenda here was elimination – murder – not theft of time sheets or police flashlights. Dee was killed as a hit – not as a robbery victim.

10. There were no prints found on the scene. True/false. Dee's prints were not even on the Glock that killed her – her own gun. The crime scene was in chaos from the beginning. Fire Chief Brown had the island's fire truck on the scene in the wee hours of Saturday morning, along with his volunteer firemen, some of whom were village council members who had filed less-than accurate complaints about Dee because they didn't like her. As eager as Brown always was to please management, who knows what could have been done. There were prints found, there were prints identified, there were prints unidentifiable, there were prints ignored.

11. There were no signs of struggle or altercation at the scene. True. Dee weighed 90 pounds soaking wet and stood 4'10" in cowboy boots. She was being confronted by at least three people, with at least one gun trained on her. How much struggle could there have been? Did the police expect to find her truck turned onto its side? Furthermore, some experienced murder/suicide detectives who have studied the case concluded that Dee was killed quickly and had no time for struggle. "We know from the timeline that there was between 7 – 15 minutes before Cain arrived on the scene."

- Grasty, Karen. (3-18-04). *Letter* to Loy and Harriet Buff.

12. Keith Cain's second interview put Dee's weapon at the head area. True/false. Cain's testimony changed each time as to how the gun was in reference to Dee's head. It was always in the area near her head. It also could have been *placed* near her head.

13. Gore said the GSR proved positive on her right glove. False. The test results for her gloves were the same as for the three men in the boat and Keith Cain. More on this later.

14. The FBI trace metal analysis proved positive with the ammunition in Dee's clip and spare clip. True. That was never in dispute. All of the Bald Head Island policemen had ammunition from the same batch. Who pulled the trigger on the gun is what is in dispute.

15. The cartridge distance tests consistent with range casting was found. True/false. If the cartridge was tossed where it was found, what difference does the test make?

16. Major case print analysis was another point still pending at the time of the decision. Undeterminable. Actually most of the prints found on Dee's truck belong to people on the Bald Head Police Force. The bloody palm print on the back of her truck that needed to be analyzed was dismissed by Tony Cummings as being hers. How she was supposed to have been able to leave it and then get yards away to the place where they found her body was never explained by Mr. Cummings.

17. There were no latent [suspect] prints found on the duty weapon. Indeterminate. This is curious. There were unidentifiable prints, but not Dee's. Her prints were not found on her own gun. Martinez wrote: "The action by Officer Cain in mishandling the weapon could have smudged any recognizable prints from the weapon." He also pointed out the "… contradictory statements on the handling of the weapons by Cain and Brown."

- Martinez, Michael. (2-20-01). *Report. P. 6.*

18. The audio tape analysis for identification of any background or voices. Indeterminate. The analysis was never conducted at Quantico. Bald Head Island police had Signalscope, a company in the area, do so and they discovered two places they identified as Dee talking.

19. The body suffered an extreme hard contact wound. True. "The gunshot wound was dead center in the back of Dee's head with an *equal fracture.* That would be as a result of placing that weapon directly in the back of her head and pulling the trigger with *no waiver.*"

- *Buff v. Bureau of Justice Assistance Public Safety Officers' Benefits.* (1-18-03). Pp. 31-32.

There was an interesting exchange between Warren and Hardee concerning Dee's wound. Warren told Hardee, "I understand that you think that the entry wound is at a different place than what I told you." Hardee answered, "No, I just happen to know that the entry wound is in a different place than what you told me according to the medical examiner's report."

Later Hardee would ask Monty Clark why Gore would make a ruling based on the wrong information about the gunshot wound. Clark replied, "Because somebody who didn't know told him."

- Hardee, Gene. (2-11-00). *Interview* by Monty Clark. P. 27.

20. There was no stripping outside. There was soot and powder within. There were gasses within. True. All of these arguments come from a person being shot from a gun pressed execution style against the back of the head. The degree of the gun to the head was 30°. It is an impossible angle to do to one's self, much less produce a wound that is an equal fracture, meaning the crack in the skull broke equally to the right as it did to the left. "When the muzzle of a firearm

touches ... the target, hot gasses escaping the muzzle typically rip, tear, shred and/or melt the material of the target."

- Doyle, Jeffrey Scott. Gunshot Residue. Retrieved 10-14-07 from http://www.firearmsid.com/A_distanceGSR.htm

21. The angle was consistent. False. There were government 'experts' who claimed such a shot was possible, even Crocker, who refused the opportunity to demonstrate it in court. Most of the women used to reconstruct the feat were larger than Dee. As Skoler noted in his decision, the gunshot reconstructions were faulty. Those who were trying to reconstruct suicide were not approximately the same height and weight. One was one inch taller, the other two significantly taller with longer arm length. The firing angles were *inconsistent* with an 'upward and slightly to the right trajectory.' The reenactment report using a 4 o'clock midline entry and angle conflicts with 'upwards and slightly to the left.'

- Skoler, Daniel. (1-18-03). *Hearing officer claim determination. PSOB Case Number 2000-48.* P. 9.

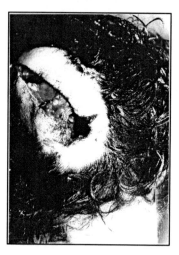

A review of the photograph of the entry wound to the back of Officer Jones' head shows a mark slightly to the right of the bottom of the wound. The gun itself caused this – the recoil spring. It is more at the 5 o'clock 30 degree position. "This creates a critical difference in the position of the weapon when fired and critically makes it much more difficult for a person to shoot themselves."

- *Buff v. Bureau of Justice Assistance Public Safety Officers' Benefits.* (1-18-03). P. 3.

On the same subject Lattimore wrote, "To self-inflict a gunshot wound to the posterior mid-line of her head and accomplish a slight upwards trajectory, she would have had to have aimed the gun at the front of her face with her thumb on the trigger, then raised her arms over her head so that the gun would be in the mid-line and upside down. In this position the Glock would have ejected the casing to the left. The casing was found to the right of her body. Moreover Decedent's arms would have to be long enough to accomplish this sufficient to have her hands below the barrel of the gun in order to get an upwards trajectory of the bullet."

While under study the commission tried to reconstruct such a shooting position as described in the paragraph above and was unable to do so. They concluded, "A mid-line entry wound with an ascending pathway does not appear to have been physically possible for a woman of Decedent's size and arm length to accomplish with her service weapon."

- LATTIMORE, BUCK, Chairman, N.C. Industrial Commission. OPINION AND AWARD for the Full Commission. (Filed 27 June 2005). I.C. NOS. 980154 & LH-0286, LOY BUFF, Father of DAVINA BUFF JONES, Deceased Employee, Plaintiff v. N.C. LAW ENFORCEMENT OFFICES AND RESCUE WORKERS DEATH BENEFITS ACT and STATE OF NORTH CAROLINA CONTINGENCY AND EMERGENCY FUND, Defendants. P. 17.

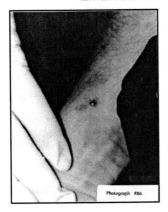

Photograph #86

22. There was a fresh bruise on Dee's right arm in the wrist area. The state's own attorney Dahr Tanoury elicited this testy response from Pathologist Garrett. Tanoury asked, "Did you find any bruises or lacerations on the face; did you notice anything remarkable?"

Garrett answered, "One more time. Absolutely no evidence of an injury to the external surfaces of the body except the   gunshot wound."

- Garrett, C. L. (11-25-03). *Deposition*. P. 26.

The position is located in the place where a reflexive movement would have brought Dee's hand up if someone had just shoved a gun to the back of her head. The hot casing coming out of the chamber, ejecting to right could have burned her, nicked her on its trajectory. A small piece of her own skull exploding out could also have nicked her arm. Garrett could not use the excuse that it was so early in the morning or that he was working in the dark, small confining area that where Hiltz had been. Remember, too, that there had been an SBI agent with both men. SBI agent Miller had time to call from Garrett's autopsy to get word back to Bald Head Island that it was a suicide even before the Indigo press conference, but he couldn't notice this injury on Dee's arm.

23. No defensive wounds. There were no fingernail residues. True/false. Monty Clark brought up the theory of the above injury being a sign of defense to Crocker. Crocker's hands went up and he said, "I don't want to go there. I don't want to hear this!"

- *Buff v. Bureau of Justice Assistance Public Safety Officers' Benefits.* (1-18-03). P. 106.

24. Her demeanor on the 911 tape was too calm. There were no background noises on the tape. There is, perhaps, the most insulting statement ever made, not only concerning this case, but any call made by police personnel anywhere. A calm demeanor in the center of grave danger is paramount in successful crisis management, yet they fault this woman for doing so where she is literally facing death. Police academies the world over may need to change their teaching tenets if this point holds water. Any citizen calling for help should

apparently expect the arriving police officer to arrive in pieces, screaming and crying hysterically before attempting to aid the victim or catch a bank robber. Needless to say, we know more now about what was really transpiring concerning the tape transmission than we did, so we will cover this in detail further in the book. Dee was actually trying to use her radio transmission to get help.

25. Dee was diagnosed as depressive suidical. False. This is absolute manipulation of detail. Dee was taking medication for depression, more specifically for anxiety attacks. She was taking Effexor XR. There are many people in this country taking this medication and they are not considered depressive suicidal. Dee was diagnosed as being suicidal by her ex-friend Will Hewett who is not a doctor.

26. Three subjects on a golf cart just before she was killed heard her say "stand by" on her radio as she was leaving them. True/false. These three said they did. The police have tried to say that these were three to whom Jones was referring on her radio and that there were no others who approached her with a gun. As soon as she saw these three she decided to go kill herself.

27. Dee was under a doctor's care. True. Does this imply that everyone who is under a doctor's care is going to go kill themselves? Suddenly a doctor's waiting room seems to be a much scarier place.

28. She told the doctor of wishes to drive her car into a tree. True. As the doctor explained, the two of them had discussed thoughts Dee had when she was frustrated and angry over the situation at her job. People do make such comments when they are frustrated, but Dee never made any attempts to carry out such thoughts. Actually

she had told him that she would not take her own life "because she did not have anyone to take care of her dogs."

29. Dr. Reschley had made an appointment for Dee to begin working with a psychiatrist in Wilmington beginning on October 27, 1999. "She had plans for her life ... she had applied to other police departments. ... She had her dogs to take care of .... was not an impulsive person ... had hope and could see the light at the end of the tunnel."

- Reschley, Keith. (10-24-99). *Interview* by G. W. Johnson. P. 2.

30. Conversations with Laura Atkins in Texas, spoke suicidal twice that day. Laura complained later that she even agreed to talk to SBI Agent Janet Storms, saying that the SBI agent only wanted to talk about suicide. Laura was sick the day Dee died and Dee was very concerned about her friend. They talked several times that day before and after Laura's appointment with a doctor.

31. Dee called her ex-boyfriend just before she died. True. During the short conversation with Scott Monzon, Dee said she wanted to be friends with both he and his wife. It was not a 'good-bye' call.

- Monzon, Scott. (2-10-00). *Interview* by Monty Clark.

32. Dee recently told her ex-boyfriend the "world was crumbling around her." Will Hewett relayed this comment that was made during the hurricane that had come through the area shortly before she died. She was feeling pressure from her job; Scott Monzon had moved out and gone back to his ex-wife. She probably did feel like it was not her best time. Everyone has been down at one time or another but it doesn't mean they are going to shoot themselves.

33. She had used alcohol excessively recently. True. On the Wednesday night before she died, Dee drank more than she characteristically did. She had just discovered that Scott Monzon had come back to her long enough to go back to bed with her and then tell her he had moved back in with his ex-wife. Her reaction was similar to what many women in that position would feel: betrayed and angry.

34. The Oak Island Police Department was called for a welfare check. True. That same Wednesday night while she was under the influence, she had driven to Scott's house, talked to him and then gone home. Scott, a police officer for the town, called in and asked for the on-duty patrol to check on her and make sure she was at home and safe.

35. Dee threatened suicide two days before, according to a male friend. True/false. First of all, we have only Will Hewett's word. Second, this was during the time she had discovered the truth about Scott Monzon. Third, she had two dogs she repeatedly referred to as her 'babies' that would have prevented her from doing anything to herself.

36. The location of the shot is consistent with female suicide (vanity.) While vanity may be involved in some female suicides, the location of this wound was ruled by experts to be a strange, unusual and albeit, impossible task for her.

37. The victim was observed that day, possibly upset. True/false. Steve Diggs, a worker for Bell-South was named in Gore's argument as having seen her that day. No other information, testimony, affidavit or photograph has been forthcoming concerning this man.

Keith Cain, ferry passengers and crew have all testified that Dee was in a very good mood, so it is even harder to determine when Mr. Griggs could have seen her. Bell-South employees are not usually at work on the island after 6:30 pm when her shift began. If Mr. Diggs did see her upset, perhaps police should have questioned the man further about other things because she must have been alone at the time he saw her.

38. Jones had filed a sexual harassment charge on a Bald Head Island employee. True. Dee was determined to see the case through to its end. If anything, this was one of the reasons she was killed.

39. The victim destroyed a negative evaluation the same day of the incident. False. There has not been any evidence introduced to show that a negative evaluation on that date existed.

40. The victim tore up her personnel record and threw it into the trashcan in the police office. False. Absolutely false. She was completing a self-evaluation and tore up her work notes. The personnel files were under lock and key. This will be discussed later in more detail.

41. She broke directives (separated from partner of own accord). We will address later.

42. DA Gore added, "Am I positive Miss Jones committed suicide? The evidence convinces me to a certainty beyond a reasonable doubt but only God and Miss Jones know what truly happened."

- Gore, Rex. (12-09-99). *Press Release*. Pp 1-2.
- Crocker, David. (nd). *Letter* to Ronald Hewett (Case update).
- Officer's death termed a suicide. (12-10-99). *The Charlotte Observer*. P. 4C.

Seeking Support

The death of Davina Buff Jones had been ruled on before all of the evidence tests had been returned and the case had been closed by the county's district attorney. The Buff family was left in the position of having lost a daughter and having her branded as a suicide as well.

At first they were stymied by exactly what avenues were available to try and clear their dead child's name. The new mayor of Bald Head Island Billy Berne said that a judgment had been made and "We moved on." The editor of the *Island Gazette* rejoiced and thanked Gore for doing a great job. Tourists and residents could again roam Bald Head Island without fear. Dee Jones had shot and killed herself. But the Buffs didn't believe it of their daughter, Harriet's 'little butterball.'

- Page, Reid. A. Jr. (12-10-99). *Letter* to Rex Gore.
- Bald Head officials accept DA ruling on officer's death. (12-12-99). *Morning-Star.* P. 1B.

It's not that the family was not aware of Dee's problems. They were and they would have been able to accept a ruling of suicide had it been proven to them. However, there were a lot of unanswered questions.

> "We, as a family realize that if she was killed and murdered, that because of the contamination we might not have the ability to ever prosecute someone based on the evidence we have. And we can live with that. What we cannot and refuse to live with is the assertion and the assumption that the District Attorney came to about Davina. We believe that she was never given the benefit of the doubt from the very system she was serving. ... We cannot live with the fact that the District Attorney used his personal opinion as representative of the truth."

- Buff family statement. (12-15-99). *The State Port Pilot.* P. 9.

At this point, neither side made much headway in swaying the other side to change their opinion. Rumors were rampant that there was a police cover-up. Other stories from the island whispered that the officer had been killed when she interrupted a drug deal. That was what her physician had been told by his secretary that Saturday morning when he had come to his office. Later in the morning, he was working in Dosher Hospital when a policeman told him that she had killed herself. Suicide never crossed his mind until that conversation.

- MacLeod, Norman. (2-10-00). *Interview* by Monty Clark.
- Reschley, Keith. (10-24-99). *Interview* by G. W. Johnson.

The Buffs, Dee's friends, and others who believed Dee's death to be a murder began a long effort to garner support to overturn the DA's decision. Loy Buff wrote then Attorney General Mike Easley who grew up in the area and knew District Attorney Gore and Sheriff Ronald Hewett. Easley also was well acquainted with the environment on Bald Head Island, owning property there himself. In his position as Attorney General, Easley had direct control over the State Bureau of Investigation whose officers had worked on Dee's case. "What I want to emphasize to you is that my confidence in the investigation and the professionals involved has been shattered," Loy wrote.

- Buff, Loy. (5-28-00). *Letter* to Attorney General Mike Easley.

Easley responded with a sentence of condolence followed by a paragraph extolling the SBI as one of the best investigating units in the nation, putting the death of a police officer as a top priority on which they spend many hours. "While no one may ever know exactly what occurred on the night she died, I understand that the evidence has been found to be more consistent that Officer Jones took her own life."

Easley also took issue with Buff's assertion that the suicide ruling had been rushed to appease due to pressure from the Bald Head Island community. "I cannot speak for the local district attorney, but I can assure you that the investigators at the SBI do not go about their work concerned about how their conclusions might play locally." As to the matter of getting the case reopened since Gore had closed it, the Attorney General offered this comment. "You are correct that the decision of whether and how to proceed in this matter rests solely with the local district attorney. Under the laws and constitution of the state, it is his jurisdiction, and my office has no power over him." He ended his letter by telling the dead officer's father if he uncovered new information the SBI agent Tony Cummings would be glad to investigate any new lead.

- Easley, Mike. (8-14-00). *Letter* to Loy Buff.

A mutual friend also contacted the Attorney General and other political friends in Raleigh. He wrote his friend Loy.

"I was told it was a closed case and to leave it alone. I am sorry I could not do more."

- Doe, John*. (7-23-01). *Letter* to Loy Buff.

The Buffs were not the only ones trying to solicit help on behalf of the dead officer. Others who had considered Dee a friend tried to get help from influential people. They wrote letters, they made phone calls. Several other people tried to contact William Bennett, home owner and vocal newspaper source of outrage quotes when the death occurred. Loy sent Bennett a request himself. A friend of Dee's from the island contacted him, going into great detail in his email about the murder and the effect of the friendship between Easley and Hewett. "It is NO WONDER that Dee's father has hit roadblock after roadblock." Neither man received an answer to their communications.

- Buff, Loy. (nd). *Letter* to William Bennett.
- Doe, John II* (nd) *Email* to William Bennett

Senators John Edwards and Jesse Helms, Representatives Mike McIntyre, David Vinroot and other politicians were contacted without success. Even local support and friends vanished across time. One family friend who, as a police officer had gone to Bald Head that night, swore that he would repeat in testimony what he had told Loy he had seen and heard. Yet when it came time to do so, he told Loy to have the hearing officer stop by his office. It grew harder to live around people the Buffs knew were withholding information about their dead daughter.

- Buff, Loy. (nd). *Letter* to Senator Jesse Helms.
- Buff, Loy. (nd). *Letter* to David Vinroot.
- Buff, Loy. (2-02-01). *Letter* to Senator John Edwards.
- Buff, Loy. (7-11-05). *Letter* to Mike McIntyre.
- Buff, Loy. (8-24-07). *Interview* by Elaine Buff.

By this time, they never talked to District Attorney Rex Gore. They never would. Sheriff Ronald Hewett had talked to them two times. Once he had come to their home with his assistant and Lt. Crocker. His assistant was Larry Jones, a friend and golfing buddy of Loy Buff. The trio had come to tell the Buffs that a portion of the 911 tape would be played on the local television stations within a few hours. Hewett said he was going to release it because if he didn't do so, the reporters would just go get a court order and he did not want the police to appear to be uncooperative about it. The family had just learned of its existence when he told them of it, but he did not play the tape for them at that time. He described it. They would hear it for the first time along with all the stations' other viewers. The other time they talked to him was when he came to tell them that Gore had made a decision that would be announced the next morning.

- Buff, Harriet. (5-20-06). *Interview* by Elaine Buff.
- Hart, Tanya. (8-27-07). *Interview* by Elaine Buff.
- Hart, Tanya. (11-27-07). *Interview* by Elaine Buff.

The next morning, the Buffs felt completely blindsided by what they heard. Suicide! How could such a decision be made before all of the evidence had been tested? All of the suspects had not been exonerated? They felt that hardly any time had been spent really investigating what had happened to their daughter. Now she had been branded as a suicide when they felt in every fiber of their being that that was not the case.

Through the fog of loss and the bitterness of white hot anger, they realized they had one avenue left to them. The case was closed as far as Brunswick County was concerned. As long as Gore refused to re-visit the case, that was the end of the line.

However, they could pursue trying to get death benefits through the avenues open to them since Dee had been a member of the Fraternal Order of Police and other organizations for police personnel. If they could pursue court hearings for those procedures, they could have evidence and investigation materials subpoenaed. Lawyers and court officials could have a chance to question and cross exam those who had been at the helm of the case.

If, during these hearings, the family could prove that their daughter had not committed suicide, they could get her death certificate changed from suicide. It was never a question of gaining money: it was clearing Davina's name.

The Buff family gathered around the dining room table one night and discussed the option and what it might ultimately require. They all unanimously agreed. They must do whatever it took to clear Davina's name.

This is what drove them forward down a path they never picked and never wanted. There was no turning back now.

Chapter Eight

North Carolina Industrial Commission Hearing

Loy and Harriet Buff began their sojourn for justice by appealing Dee's denial of Workmen's Compensation benefits. The local unit settled and changed her death to 'undetermined' in April, 2001.

This hearing would pit the family against the law enforcement of the county and the state. A little family of father, mother and two sisters would go up against a state's attorney general, a county sheriff, a district attorney and wealthy landowners on an exclusive island. Each side had a lot to lose. One side felt they had already lost too much – a daughter. No matter the cost, they had to go on. On Halloween after Dee's death, the Buffs' car had been taken out into the street in the middle of the night and vandalized, a substance resembling blood poured all over the steering wheel and driver's side window. Police refused to write up the incident, calling it a prank. The sisters felt like it was a threat but the parents didn't care. They were not backing down.

On October 23rd of 2003, almost four years to the date of Dee's death, Deputy Adrian A. Phillips presided over a hearing of the Buffs versus the Village of Bald Head Island, North Carolina League of Municipalities, and North Carolina Rescue Workers CAP Death Benefits Acts. The witnesses included Loy Buff, police officers from Bald head Island, State Bureau of Investigation agents, Brunswick County Sheriff's Department officers, the Buffs' private investigator, firearms experts and two of Dee's former boyfriends. Henry Foy was the attorney of record for the Buff family. Dahr Tanoury appeared for the North Carolina Department of Justice.

Once the hearing began, the Buffs learned that the state would be contentious from the beginning. They realized that any victory would be wrung from the jaws of justice. "In the absence of even the semblance of a proper homicide investigation, it must be concluded that the Industrial Commission's investigation is the best work to date done on the case." But it would come at a price.

- Calhoun, Terry. (7-06-05). Officer's death wasn't suicide. *The State Port Pilot*. Pp. 1A, 10A.

During the proceedings both sides presented opposing opinions; one firearms expert said Dee could have committed suicide using a Glock with an overall length of 6.97 inches; another said Dee could not have. Detective David Crocker declared Dee did, but he declined the opportunity to demonstrate in court how she did it using her Glock, which had been brought to the hearing.

Dee's service weapon was a Glock Model 23 using .40 caliber shot. It's overall length was 6.97 inches with a barrel four inches long. She kept thirteen rounds with one in the chamber. The gun weighed between three to four pounds. The trigger could only be pulled from the center. Because of a safety mechanism, the Glock's outer trigger can only be activated when the inner trigger has first been depressed. It takes around seven pounds of pressure to pull the trigger.

- *Buff v. North Carolina Law Enforcement Officers and Rescue Workers Death Benefit Act and North Carolina Contingency and Emergency Fund. P. 274-275.*
- Bissette, Brenda. (11-01-99). *SBI Investigative Report* File No.: 992665(ALA).
- Kokalis, Peter G. *Polymer perfection*. Retrieved 3-29-06 from http://www.remtek.com/arms/glock/model/40/23/index.htm

Psychological specialists had prepared psychiatric autopsies, some saying she was likely to, others saying she was not likely to have committed suicide. Opinion seemed tied to in some cases to who was paying for their services.

For example, the Bald Head Island insurance company's representative said she committed suicide. One psychologist had used an instrument he had seen in a magazine he was currently reading. The categories helped him make his decision. He admitted he had never used the instrument before – he had used it this time incorrectly. He also testified he would not use it again. This was welcome news in the Buff family camp.

Dr. Alan Berman, in his psychological autopsy, ruled Dee's death 'undetermined' and listed ten reasons why he believed that the officer had not committed suicide.

1. Dee "... had suffered similar losses and stressors throughout her adult life. Although they affected her, she was able to cope with each and every one before."
2. Although she had multiple instances of prior suicidal ideation, almost all were expressed without serious intent and in an off-handed way. Most importantly, she had no prior suicidal behavior, particularly in situations similar to those occurring in her final weeks of life.
3. She allegedly kept an active journal of writings. None have been produced to indicate that she was seriously contemplating or planning her suicide. If this were a planned suicide, it is very likely that her writings would substantiate that plan.
4. She was intensely devoted and attached to her dogs. She would not have readily abandoned them
5. There is no evidence for advance planning of her suicide.
6. All observers who saw or spoke with her that day (10-22-99) told that her mood was upbeat and that her behavior and demeanor exhibited nothing out of the ordinary.
7. She was actively looking for a new job.
8. At the site of her death, the truck was left running and the flashlight was still in the truck.
9. Her body had no bruises, so she would have had to kill herself while lying down.

10. She left no note.
- Berman, Alan L. Ph. D. (5-28-02). *Psychological Autopsy.* np.

SBI laboratory reports showed that the blood on the Glock matched Davina Buff Jones' DNA profile. Trace debris from the Glock, pubic hair combings, pubic hair and head hair of Jones had been sent for analysis. The hair analysis exam resulted in finding one animal hair.

- Gregory, James. (03-01-00). *SBI Investigative Report: Trace evidence* File No.: 992665(ALA)

The pants of Officer Jones had been sent to the SBI lab because of a scuff on the right knee. "The right knee area of pants revealed the presence of scuff marks. Microscopic examination of the scuff marks show the presence of mineral materials embedded in the fabric of the pants as well as abrasions on the fabric itself.

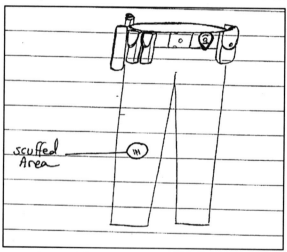

- Luper, Tim. (11-01-99). *SBI Laboratory Report: Pants.* Agency File No.: 992665(ALA

This scuffed area was evidence to the Buffs that at some point Davina had been forced to her knees. From the stand, David Crocker testified that Jones' pants were not torn or damaged in any way.

- Crocker, David. (10-23/24-03). *Buff v. Village of Bald Head Island Police Department, North Carolina League of Municipalities and North Carolina Rescue Workers Cap Death Benefits Act.* North Carolina Industrial Commission. P. 281.

The following guns and ammunition had been sent to the lab for firearms examination and identification request.

1. Glock – serial number AEB231 (Keith Cain's weapon) K-1
2. One (1) caliber .40/10mm fired jacketed bullet Q1
3. One (1) Speer caliber .40 S&W fired cartridge case Q2
4. One (1) blue pullover shirt R-1 received separate
5. One (1) Glock AEB224 (Dee Jones' weapon) K-2
6. One (1) Speer caliber .40 S&W cartridge
7. Twelve (12) Speer caliber .40 S&W cartridges

The Q-1 bullet taken by Pathologist Garrett from the brain of Davina Jones during the autopsy in Jacksonville had similar rifling characteristics as the test fired from the K-1 and K-2 pistols and some similar microscopic markings as the tests fired from the K-2 pistol, however, the Q-1 bullet and test lack sufficient microscopic agreement whether or not K-1 or K-2 fired Q-1. The Q-2 cartridge case was fired from the K-2 pistol."

- Bishop, E. E. (10-25-99). *SBI Investigative Report: Firearms and ballistics.* File   No.: 992665(ALA).

No latent noted or developed handprints were found on Jones' gun, a fault some attributed to the handle of the Glock. Six latent prints had been lifted from the front left panel and side of Dee's truck. Later these would be identified as belonging to John B. Jones and David Lee Cox of the Bald Head Island Police Department.

- Luper, Tim. (10-28-99). *SBI Laboratory Report: Latent prints* Agency File No.: 992665(ALA).

- *Buff v. Village of Bald Head Island Police Department, North Carolina League of Municipalities and North Carolina Rescue Workers Cap Death Benefits Act.* North Carolina Industrial Commission. (10-23/24-03). Exhibitions Part I, p. 272.

Police Chief Karen Grasty and Interim Police Chief Lt. Gene Hardee of the Bald Head Island Police Department had actually been outside of most of the inner workings of the investigation. It had been handled by the SBI and the Brunswick County Sheriff's Department. They did not lack experience. Hardee had been a policeman for twenty-six years. The chief had been a police woman in the state, serving in Claremont, Hickory, and Newton and being wounded in the line of duty before coming to Bald Head. Moreover, she had not had the easiest time working with island management herself.

A great amount of testimony centered around the location of the spent casing found at the scene. As testimony unfolded, not only was it apparent that the crime scene had been compromised when the body was removed and the murder weapon moved twice before investigators arrived, it became apparent that the casing had also been moved. In the crime scene pictures there appears little doubt that either the casing was picked up when first discovered and then replaced or it repositioned itself.

The casing is pictured here where it is purported to have fallen after it was expelled from Jones' gun. It is almost horizontal and aligned with the picket fence itself.

Yet in this picture, the casing is clearly seen perpendicular to the fence and lying beyond the fence, not almost beneath it.

- Davis, Sam. (10-23-99) *Davina Buff Jones Crime Scene Photographs.*

The importance of the spent casing was paramount to proving or disproving where the officer was if and when she shot herself. According to the pictures, that location was contaminated during the recording of photographs. This is not an indictment of Sam Davis. This is merely a statement of fact. Somehow, that casing was moved. If Jones did not kill herself and the whole scene had been staged, the position of the casing did not matter. It could have been placed there as well as the gun being placed under her hand.

Another source of contention was the results of the Gunshot Residue (GSR) Tests conducted on Dee, Keith Cain, and three fishermen found near Bald Head Island in the early hours of October 23rd. The GSR stands for Gunshot Residue and is composed of soot, lead, barium, and antimony from the cartridge primer compound that has been discharged when a gun is fired. If a shooter is holding a weapon, the residue is on the back of the shooter's hand since they are holding the gun. If they have handled a recently fired weapon, GSR will be on the palm of their hand. However, it should be remembered that the presence of GSR in and of itself does not prove shooting a gun. "If the victim of a close range shooting attempts to grab the gun or instinctively shields the head, significant deposits can be left on the hands."

- Aaron, Robert. (nc). *Gunshot primer residue: The invisible clue.* FBI Laboratory: Washington, DC. Retrieved 11-20-06 from http://www. hackcanada.com/blackcraw/survive/gunshot.txt

Investigator David Crocker explained why Keith Cain had been given a GSR test. "As part of an investigation, anybody who's there, it's part of our policy to take gunshot residue from them."

- Crocker, David. (10-23/24-03). *Buff v. Village of Bald Head Island Police Department, North Carolina League of Municipalities and North Carolina Rescue Workers Cap Death Benefits Act.* North Carolina Industrial Commission. P. 256-257.

The GSR test was performed on Cain two hours and eight minutes after the shooting and Jones' GSR was done two hours and forty-eight minutes after her death.

At 1:25 am on Saturday, October 23rd, 1999, three men had been stopped by authorities near Fort Fisher, running without lights coming from the direction of Bald Head Island. The trio claimed to be fishing and said they knew nothing about the murdered officer until they were notified when the police had stopped them. They had GSR taken three hours, two minutes, three hours, seven minutes, and three hours, thirty-two minutes elapsed time after the event.

- *Buff v. Village of Bald Head Island Police Department, North Carolina League of Municipalities and North Carolina Rescue Workers Cap Death Benefits Act.* North Carolina Industrial Commission. (10-23/24-03). Exhibits Part I, P. 325.

Brunswick County officer Norman MacCloud submitted the GSR kits on these three men on October 28, 1999 to Gene Caison who sent them to the SBI Lab on November 1, 1999. For each man, there was a sealed kit containing five (5) vials with hand wipings and four (4) vials containing SEM lifts.

Items belonging to Jones tested for GSR included the gloves she had been wearing and her portable police radio. The black gloves were bicycle gloves with cut-off fingers. The general results of the GSR test for her were word-for-word the *same* as the results for Keith Cain and each of the three fishermen in the boat stopped off of Fort Fisher. "Barium, antimony and lead, indicative of gunshot residue, were not present in significant concentration on the hand wiping submitted. It is note (sic) however that this does not eliminate the possibility of the subject could have fired a gun."

- Luper, Tim. (10-27-99). *SBI Laboratory Report.* Agency File No.: 992665(ALA
- Luper, Tim. (11-01-99). *SBI Laboratory Report: GSR on 3 in boat.* Agency File No.: 992665(ALA

Dee's police radio had no GSR, neither did her left glove. There were three minute particles on the back of her right glove. That could have been there from previous training and it could have been there for months. There was also GRS found on Cain.

- *Buff v. Village of Bald Head Island Police Department, North Carolina League of Municipalities and North Carolina Rescue Workers Cap Death Benefits Act. North Carolina Industrial Commission. (10-23/24-03). Exhibits Part I, p. 123.*

Dee was right-handed. "Characteristic particles could have originated from discharging a firearm, handling a firearm, or being in close proximity of a firearm when it discharged."

- Luper, Tim. (11-01-99). *SBI Laboratory Report: GSR. Agency File No .: 992665(ALA)*

As Michael Martinez, a forensic scientist questioned in 2001, "Would it really be unusual to find GSR on the glove of a police officer?" Apparently this expert thought that a lot of time was spent on a question that was really not pertinent to this situation.

- Martinez, Michael. (2-20-01). *Report.*

Although Chief Grasty had requested, as is customary in the death of a police officer, for the SBI take charge of Dee's case, David Crocker testified that Sheriff Hewett instructed him to take charge of processing and securing evidence on the island. Upon Crocker's arrival at Bald Head, Captain Charlie Miller told him that the crime scene tape was up and the scene was secure so Crocker had Jones' body moved to the depot from the dock. There he examined her body, took the GSR, and photographs. According to his statements, he checked her portable radio and mike, reporting that "… it was still working and it was still operating on channel 1." Once finished there he inspected the ambulance that Fire Chief Kent Brown had already cleaned out in order to transport arriving officers to the crime scene a quarter of a mile away from the dock. He found nothing of significance.

- *Crocker Testimony. (10-23/24-03).Buff v. Village of Bald Head Island Police Department, North Carolina League of Municipalities and North Carolina Rescue Workers Cap Death Benefits Act.* North Carolina Industrial Commission.

The mysterious drag marks found at the scene were another source of disagreement. They were included in the crime scene diagram done by SBI Agent Daly, but were not always evident in the drawings made by others at the crime scene. They are of special interest and importance because of the questions they raise concerning other people there with Dee at the time of her murder and the whereabouts of certain parts of her clothing that have disappeared while in the protective care of the police on Bald Head Island.

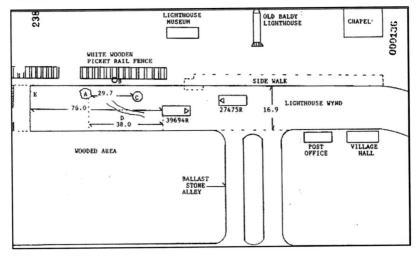

The vehicle slightly to the left of Old Baldy is the Blazer driven by Keith Cain. It is in the last position where he left his vehicle. There is a triangle, its point to the left, showing the direction in which it is facing. Dee's truck is shown sitting to the Blazer's left, slightly down, the triangle on top pointing to the right. Her truck was facing out of the cul-de-sac.

A rickety, rustic fence opens at the far left to allow golf carts to enter here from the marina. The picket fence is shown running at the far edge of the road. A tiny circle shows where the bullet casing was found. The first circle to the upper left behind Dee's truck is the trash pile from the museum construction site. 29.7 feet behind that is a second circle, the site where Keith Cain testified he found Jones' body.

The curving double lines running from the back of Dee's vehicle to where her body was found are the drag lines or marks in question. They are visible in the picture above.

According to Karen Grasty there were "deep marks … from the back of the pickup truck that led to where her body was lying …. There was blood spatters in that area, leading up through there." Grasty further explained, "Blood spatter marks to – in the same area coming from the drag marks, before you get to the pool of blood, which – the large pool of blood which would have come out of her head after she had been laid down." In other words, it appeared that Dee had been dragged from the direction of her truck with her feet leaving two lines in the dirt where either her toes or heels had been pulled.

Additionally, drops of blood had fallen as she had been

dragged, leaving a trail of blood droplets. As any hunter can attest, a wounded animal leaves a trail of blood that can be used to track the animal to where it falls when it dies. These blood droppings or trail were visible along the lines or drag marks made from the back of Dee's truck to the place where her body was face down on the ground.

The wound Dee suffered was fatal, but the heart still continued to beat for a while, pumping more faintly, blood continuing to issue forth until it had emptied out onto the sandy soil. Her heart finally stopped by the time she was at the marina and was hooked to an EKG machine. The EKG readings were still showing an erratic but still beating heart for a few moments until it finally ceased to beat.

So at the time that Dee's body was put down on the ground near the lighthouse, all the blood issuing from the massive hole in her skull poured out onto the ground then, leaving a large pool of blood that finally snaked its way down the path, due to the slope away from the lighthouse. The drag marks and blood spatter prove that she could not have been killed where the body was found. According to his testimony, Crocker was not aware of drag marks at the scene.

- *Buff v. Village of Bald Head Island Police Department, North Carolina League of Municipalities and North Carolina Rescue Workers Cap Death Benefits Act.* North Carolina Industrial Commission. (10-23/24-03). Pp. 106-107, 276.

The 911 tape was supposed to have been sent away to be analyzed but that had been cancelled by Gore's suicide decision. Police Chief Grasty sent a copy to Signalscape. Their analysis showed no evidence of other persons talking, however, this could have been because Dee had been using a lapel mike. "…it could probably not have picked it up because it was so close to her mouth and it was so low and he (the analyst) didn't pick up signals from it because it's based on signals." The interesting thing about the analysis is that there were two sections, the second and third PS2 sections that are "utterances that contain human audio made by the officer." In other words, Dee talked two other times after the squelch that were not picked up clearly by C-COM. Had Hewett sent the tape to Quantico or closed down C-COM that night, more information may have been gained. "...if Sheriff Hewett would have allowed his communication center to shut down while the original was analyzed we may have learned something from it."

- Jane Doe*. (7-24-07). *Telephone interview* by Elaine Buff.
- Grasty, Karen. (7-28-00). *Email* to Martha Lee.
- Ross, Robert. (07-07-00). Bald Head Island tape analysis.

On July 19, 2004 Deputy Commissioner Adrian A. Phillips faxed her fifteen page ruling on the case. There were three decisions.

1. At the time of her death Dee was an employee of Bald Head Island Police Department.
2. The disturbance of the site where Decedent's body was found and the disturbance and contamination of the crime scene made it impossible to make a definite showing that the manner of death was suicide. The location and pathway of the gunshot wound are not consistent with suicide. The determination of suicide is very unlikely and the Commission finds that Plaintiff has proven by sufficient evidence that her manner of death was not suicide but rather by homicide.
3. Since she left behind no spouse or children, her estate would receive $25,000,00.

- Phillips, Adrian A. (7-19-04). *Judgment of Industrial Commission.*

The Buff family was ecstatic. They had won!

The Commission had found that there was enough evidence to prove that Dee did not commit suicide. But the happiness was short-lived.

The North Carolina Department of Justice, headed now by the Attorney General Roy Cooper, appealed this decision. Attorney General Mike Easley, with his Bald Head Island ties, had become governor of the state. Nothing about this case was going to be simple. This time, the family had to face the Justice Department in court before the full Industrial Commission. The case was headed toward another showdown.

Chapter Nine

Industrial Commission Appeal 2005

Henry Foy declined to serve as the attorney for the Buffs as they faced the appeal. Foy was a good friend of Rex Gore and did not give the Buffs any choice but to search for another attorney in this high-profile, politically-charged case. Attorneys were afraid to be seen talking to Loy Buff. They still had to work in the county and they couldn't afford enemies in high places. So the Buffs had to work at finding someone up to the task.

This time they were represented by H. Edward Geddings, Jr. of Oak Island. The full board addressed the case on January 25, 2005. They went back over the findings of the original board. They questioned, they studied.

Ultimately, the full board upheld the finding of Adrian Phillips. Not only did they support the finding, they ruled that the state had not shown reason to reconsider the evidence, receive further evidence or rehear parties. The appeal would seem to be an attempt to thwart the Buffs at every turn and/or force them to give up. But the Commission did not comply. They supported the family.

The commission also declined to support Gore's suicide decision and police investigation methods. "While defendant asserts that the decedent's death was a suicide, the Full Commission is unable to make that conclusion as the investigation into a possible homicide was not conducted to its fullest potential." They noted that the body had been left uncovered and the head and feet were not bagged or

otherwise protected, trace evidence was unable to be
examined. "The commission listed forty-six stipulations for
their ruling, including these:

44. The Full Commission finds as fact that although
    decedent had prior suicidal thoughts, the greater
    weight of the evidence shows that decedent was not
    suicidal at the time of her death.
45. The greater weight of the evidence shows that it is
    highly unlikely that decedent would be able to
    position her pistol in a manner to achieve the
    trajectory of the bullet which caused her death.
46. Based upon the greater weight of the evidence,
    decedent was a law enforcement officer killed in the
    line of duty. Her death resulted from bodily injuries
    sustained while in discharge of her official duties.

The decision, signed by Commission Chairman Buck Lattimore,
Commissioner Bernadine S. Balance, and Commissioner Thomas J.
Bolch awarded the Buff family $50,000.00.

> - I.C. NOS. 980154 & LH-0286, LOY BUFF, Father of
>   DAVINA BUFF JONES, Deceased Employee,
>   Plaintiff v. N.C. LAW ENFORCEMENT OFFICES
>   AND RESCUE WORKERS DEATH BENEFITS ACT
>   and STATE OF NORTH CAROLINA
>   CONTINGENCY AND EMERGENCY FUND,
>   Defendants. OPINION AND AWARD for the Full
>   Commission by BUCK LATTIMORE, Chairman, N.C.
>   Industrial Commission. Filed 27 June 2005.

Once again, the little family went up against the giant and
won against overwhelmingly tall odds. Not only that, but they won big
with an award double what was awarded the first time. Plus, the
commission scolded the state in process.

It would seem the book and story of Davina Buff Jones
would end here on a triumphant note, but, sadly, it doesn't. The
family was able to get someone outside of Brunswick County to
notice the woefully inadequate and shabby way their daughter's
death had been handled. They had received some vindication in the.

press. There were people who did believe that there was more to the story. They had received some remuneration although they had spent far more and it would never take the place of their daughter.

But it doesn't stop here. It whimpers and falters on, unable to put itself out of its misery. It would be at the end of 2006 and into 2007 before all of the hearings would end. Every time there was a decision, the papers would scream headlines. Gore would promise to revisit the case. The SBI and he would declare they were satisfied with their findings and nothing really would change. But they would be glad to look at any new evidence. If there were any, they would find some way to dispute it.

Three different times a group of people had gathered, heard the details of the case, summoned their own experts, considered evidence. Three different rulings overturned the suicide decision, yet the results were always the same. Gore saw no reason to change his mind. "It's pretty clear that it's a suicide." Clear to him, maybe. Yet not clear to all of the other hearing members.

- Family hires investigator to probe officer's death. (5-23-00). *The Charlotte Observer.* Np.

Davina's death still lurked in the minds of those on the island who had considered her their friend and felt that she would never have committed this act. Some of them actually worked for the village but couldn't say anything in her favor for fear of losing their jobs or retirement.

Davina's death still troubled her parents who could not believe they had struggled so much through the halls of justice that they had not had time to begin to mourn the bouncy, petite middle child now gone from their lives.

Davina's death still festered beneath the skin of siblings and parents and the two dogs that bounded out to Dee's truck every time they could escape from the Buffs' house. They sat out in the cab of Dee's silver Nissan waiting for her until they were dragged back into the house, a practice they continued until Dee's sister took the truck home with her to Charlotte.

Chapter Ten

The Public Safety Officers' Benefits Program Hearing

The Public Safety Officers' Benefits Program "provides death benefits in the form of a one-time financial payment to the eligible survivors of public safety officers whose deaths are the direct and proximate result of a traumatic injury sustained in the line of duty or certain eligible heart attacks or strokes."

- Public Safety Officers Benefits Program retrieved 10-05-07 from http://www.ojp.usdoj.gov/BJA/grant/psob/psob_main.html

The Buffs completed the paperwork to begin the application process and sent it but the process required information from the North Carolina State Bureau of Investigation. "Difficulties in obtaining … the full investigation report and file relating to the officer's death … delayed issuance of the agency determination until June of 2002." This was an example of the kind of stonewalling the family would find when it needed any kind of help from state or local authorities in trying to settle Dee's estate matters. Even once the hearings had been completed.

The Bureau of Justice Assistance ruled against the Buffs, mistakenly under the impression that the SBI had earlier ruled Davina's death a suicide. That erroneous decision was appealed by the Buff family in mid-July, 2002. The Bureau of Justice Assistance (BJA), the administering agency for the PSOB program, designated a new hearing be set for January 18, 2003, in Southport, NC. Daniel Skoler, officer for the new hearing, noted that the determination of suicide in Davina's death had been made by District Attorney Rex Gore, not the SBI. The SBI had only referred to it as a 'death investigation.' That difference in the origin of the designation would prove to be of great significance.

- Skoler, Daniel. (1-18-03). *Hearing officer claim determination. PSOB Case Number 2000-48.* Pp. 6, 12.
- Calhoun, Terry. (3-08-06). Federal ruling says Jones died in 'line of duty.' *The State Port Pilot.* Pp. 1A, 6A, 7A.

The claimants represented themselves, Loy Buff being assisted by his daughter Beverly Buff Sadler of Charlotte, NC. Witnesses were again called and questioned. Skoler requested expert forensic review from the Armed Forces Institute of Pathology (AFIP) and psychiatric/psychological review from Dr. Thomas Valk.

This hearing officer was the gentleman who was supposed to leave his hearing room and go see the former Buff friend to find out what he saw on Bald Head Island the night Dee died. The man would not come to the hearing.

When giving his decision, Skoler listed his reasons for believing that Davina had not taken her own life. Her "at risk" level for suicidal behavior had been posited by behavioral experts at being no greater than "moderately elevated."

1. a lack of Jones' fingerprints on her gun
2. unexplained drag marks from truck to body location
3. no signs of strain or anxiety during work hours
4. leaving "to do" list
5. no suicide note
6. no previous concrete suicide attempts
7. 911 call "out with 3" 3 Hispanics not mentioned in SBI files
8. lack of scrapes or bruises from shooting herself

Skoler also spent time discussing the great physical difficulty and unlikelihood that Jones shot herself to obtain the trajectory and angle that killed her. The "posterior midline" back-of-the-head wound is extremely rare and unlikely by suicide (close to .6%) eliminating a wound consistent with an "almost straight up and back" trajectory as in Jones' case.

The investigation or lack thereof came under fire again. There were some prime suspect leads "which appear not to have been pursued in the SBI-led investigation." Skoler mentioned the one eyewitness, who saw a golf cart with three men leaving the street where Dee had been murdered.

Skoler and the Department of Justice, then, ruled in the family's favor. "Officer Jones' surviving parents are entitled to payment of death benefits as provided by the public Safety Officers Benefits Act for officers where death is the proximate result of personal injury sustained in the line of duty."

- Skoler, Daniel. (1-18-03). *Hearing officer claim determination. PSOB Case Number 2000-48.* Pp. 1-24.

The SBI had tried to slow down, if not stop the family from filing, much less winning this case. But the family had persevered. They had eked out a little more justice for Davina.

During all of these hearings and invitations on the part of District Attorney Rex Gore for Loy Buff to turn over any evidence he may have found, Gore never did relate to the reporters that he himself had never talked to the Buff family. As a matter of fact, when he was asked by someone about another case, he said that he was not there in a capacity to help the family.

He said it was his job to represent the big thing called the 'state.' During the same interview process, an assistant district attorney Lee Bollinger made the comment that he did not represent the family, either. He was there also to represent the state. Neither man explained who was to represent the victims' family. Perhaps someone should do so.

Just as sure as Dee had wanted in the darkness near the lighthouse for someone to come to her aid, her family and apparently, other families in the district wait in vain for someone to aid them when they are huddled against the system who 'protects' the state.

Chapter Eleven

Perry Mason Cried Here

The judges residing at the various hearings could not believe what the Buffs were having to face in addition to the loss of their daughter and they were vocal in expressing their thoughts. "The claimants in this matter have endured a woefully inadequate police investigation, and sloppy forensic investigation." Skoler discussed the nature of the Public Safety Officers' Benefits Program's function. "This hearing officer believes that the PSOB Act requires the legislation's administering apparatus (including appeal decision makers) to resolve doubts in favor of benefit eligibility." He further pointed out, "Unlike virtually all PSOB hearings, the claimant's contentions before the State Industrial Commission were opposed at all major junctures with opportunities for evidence presentation, witnesses, and argument, by state agency proponents of a suicidal scenario (in this case represented by the State Department of Justice). ... They ... presented several adverse witnesses and experts on the suicide issue, and conducted an active program of cross examination and challenge of claimant evidence and contentions."

> - Skoler, Daniel. (1-18-03). *Hearing officer claim determination. PSOB Case Number 2000-48.* Pp. 6, 19, 22.

Tanoury's grilling of Monty Clark about the two separate locations of the bullet casing showcases how far and how ridiculous the state's contentious position was during the hearings. The following exchanges took place during Tanoury's cross-examination of Mr. Clark. The two had been discussing the fact that the bullet casing had been moved and Clark had observed that that fact had contributed to tainting the crime scene evidence. Tanoury continued to press the former policeman now detective that moving the bullet

casing had not tainted the collection of evidence at the crime scene.

Q. Okay. You would agree that the shell casing, though it may have been removed prior to being photographed – it wasn't moved more than a couple of inches. Right?

A. Makes no difference whether it's a couple of inches or a mile.

Q. Would – that's a yes or ---

A. It makes no difference.

Q. That's a yes or no question.

A. Yes, it made a difference. It made a difference.

Q. How did it – how did it contaminate the ballistics test in this case?

A. I didn't say it contaminated the ballistics test.

Q. Okay. How did it contaminate the findings – how did it alter the findings, if that shell casing had not been moved more than a couple of inches, prior to being photographed?

A. I'm going to try to answer your question the best I can. I can only say that what happened with that shell casing would have made everything else in line with it questionable. I don't think there would have been a problem there. I don't have any question with that. But, the fact of it is I have no doubt that the shell didn't come out of Davina' gun. Okay? I have – I have no problem with that. I have no problem with the report that it did. But, the fact of it is, once the contamination starts, it starts affecting everything else down the line, as you go into the purposes of entering this information as evidence.

Q. Okay. How did the moving of the shell casing, say a couple of inches, affect the latent print analysis?

    MR. FOY: Objection.

A. It has nothing to do with latent prints.

    The COURT: Overruled.

Q. Well, you just said moving the shell casing affected everything else. So now, it didn't affect the latent print analysis, did it?

A. It's not going to affect the analysis of it. Absolutely not.

Q. Well, how did it affect the outcome of the analysis of the latent prints on the gun?

A. Do you want me to answer that question?

Q. Yeah.

A. If you brought a suspect in that door today and tried to convict him on the evidence that's collected in this case, you'd not convict the man.

    MR. TANOURY: Objection. Non-responsive

A. You would not convict the person.

Q. How did – how did – how did it affect – moving that shell casing a little bit –

how did that affect the collection of GSR on Officer Jones' body at Indigo Plantation? How did it affect all the other elements of this case?

A. It didn't.

Q. Thank you. That's --- I was looking for a yes or no on that.

A. Okay. I'm sorry.

- *Buff v. Village of Bald Head Island Police Department, North Carolina League of Municipalities and North Carolina Rescue Workers Cap Death Benefits Act.* North Carolina Industrial Commission. (10-23/24-03). Pp. 360-363

In his remarks, Martinez noted, "The standard operating procedure of most trained forensic pathologists is to assume every gunshot case a homicide unless proven otherwise." That would seem to be far removed from the attitude struck by the exchange between Tanoury and private investigator on the ropes for trying to point out what any investigator and attorney worth their salt ought to already know.

- Martinez, Michael. (2-20-01). *Report. P. 3.*

After all the hearings had ended, the family even had trouble filing the necessary paperwork to get the money they had been awarded by the courts. Information was needed from the office from the District Attorney. Someone helping to file workman's compensation could not get verifications needed from the District Attorney. That fight was still going on as late as March 8, 2004.

- Buff, Loy. (2-19-04). *Notes: Davina's Benefits*
- Buff, Loy. (3-08-04). *Notes: Davina's Workman's Comp.*

"Why? That's the real question, isn't it? – Why? – the how is just scenery for the suckers. ... it keeps people guessing like a parlor game, but it prevents them from asking the most important question – Why?

- Stone, Oliver and Zachery Sklar. (1992). *JFK: The book of the film: The documented screenplay.* Applause Books: New York. P. 110

Why was Jones killed?

Who benefited?

Who had the power to cover it up?

Benefits and Power

"I am not vested in this being a suicide. I'm vested in doing the best I can to make the right decision, and if there is additional evidence, I would like to see it."

> - Little, Ken. (7-03-05). DA willing to re-examine officer's death. *Morning-Star*. P. 6A.

One wonders: what else, Rex Gore, do you need to see?

As a local reporter observed, "Particularly telling was commission testimony from a suicide expert who pointed to research based upon the scientific method which showed only 2 back-of-the-head gunshot wound suicides reviewed. All 261 of the compared suicides were cases of self-inflicted gunshot wounds to the head or neck. That fact alone should have been enough to prevent the District Attorney from arbitrarily ruling suicide in the light of very little evidence, and almost no review of evidence which might have reached the more likely conclusion of murder. ... That's exactly what Gore did. In ruling suicide, he ignored the probable to choose the possible."

> - Calhoun, Terry. (7-06-05). Officer's death wasn't suicide. *The State Port Pilot*. P. 10A.

Another hearing won by the family, another refusal by Gore to change his decision caused this same reporter to write what many were thinking:

"If District Attorney Rex Gore's position on the
Davina Buff Jones case is correct, and the US
Department of Justice and the NC Industrial
Commission are both wrong, our District Attorney
is wasting his talents by continuing to
serve the 13th Judicial District of North Carolina.
His brilliance and wisdom are needed elsewhere

to better serve even more people."

- Calhoun, Terry. (2-01-06). Federal ruling: Officer was killed. *The State Port Pilot.* P. 1A.

No matter how resolute Gore presented himself to the public, in private he admitted to Gene Hardee, "I've got a lot of questions." Hardee's response? "I came that close to saying, 'If you've got damn questions, why did you make this decision?'"

Hardee, Gene. (2-11-00). *Interview* by Monty Clark. P. 26.

Of course, people from Bald Head fell in step behind Gore. Morris Rogar, a village councilman said, "I think people will accept what they say, and we'll just have to go on from there." The mayor Freeman Berne added, "Dee was a part of our community and we always will remember her and the incident, but we have to bring some closure and go on from here."

- von Kolnitz, Cece. (12-10-99). Family, friends doubt suicide conclusion. *Morning-Star.* Pp. 1A, 8A.

Chapter Twelve

The Drug Trade and Bald Head Island

Southeastern North Carolina has a history of hurricanes and stained justice such as Hurricane Hazel and the judge who announced in court, "There's two kinds of law in my court: One is North Carolina's, the other is mine." His income was widely known to be padded by illegal slot machine proceeds. Other members of his prominent and powerful family have their own pet funding methods.

There are district shameful stories of the murder victim who lay yards from his own backdoor but went without being found by law enforcement for months. Twins sitting in a truck in front of many witnesses were attacked and one was killed. The other was even injured to the point of losing a finger while fending off his attacker before he was able to get a hunting gun from the back window of his truck and shoot and kill his attacker. Even with witness testimony to support him, the surviving twin was sentenced to ten years in jail. He had killed the relative of a legislator. Justice in North Carolina is sometimes skewed.

Drugs also infest the area. Years ago the district found itself with a new District Attorney named Bubba Lee Geer who served before Mike Easley took his turn in the office. Greer intended to clean up the drug corruption. His plan was derailed when he had an automobile wreck on US 17 and was killed. Word was that his steering had probably been tampered with in similar fashion to what may have happened to the car of Sheriff Buford Pusser of McNairy County, Tennessee

Today, drug houses and other places of distribution are well-known throughout the area, both in poverty-stricken and wealthy areas. In one predominantly black area of the county, school busses are pressed to pick and deliver children on one street because the adults there try to tip over the bus. One newspaper carrier quit a delivery route due to the "terrifying things" going on at a marina in the early hours of the morning in one of the most prestigious gated towns in Brunswick County.

Old Baldy, the lighthouse on Bald Head Island, has a light that does not rotate. Its beam shoots straight up into the night sky. That beam is an easy navigation source for a pilot to use in coming in for a low drop of drugs into the water for pick-up. Then the pilot can fly directly on out into the ocean without lights. The operation can be done almost undetected unless someone happens to be outside. The operations are usually done in the fall and winter while the island has less than 200 permanent residents.

At least one Brunswick County resident has witnessed a plane flying at tree-top level height, without lights flying toward Bald Head and called 911. They were told, "Forget it."

That particular flight happened during a cook-out with more than one person seeing the plane. The police at Oak Island have witnessed such flights. These are not crazy, alarmist people seeing the flights. Even though the authorities and dignitaries may deny reports, drugs do exist and were being transported, being dropped, and being used around Bald Head Island in the late 1990's.

The day after Hurricane Earl in 1998, five men left Southport to go fishing. Off Bald Head Island near Fort Fisher, the men came across nineteen kilos of cocaine. They decided not to report their special catch to the authorities, but to keep it for themselves. However, their story did not have a happy ending. Only one is still alive today. One died mysteriously. Two of them drowned on a subsequent fishing trip in the same boat they were in when they discovered the drugs. One committed suicide. The fifth man was caught driving erratically on I-40 in Virginia. When he was pulled over by the state highway patrol, cocaine was found in the car. The man was imprisoned and will be released in 2008.

- Buff, Loy and Harriet. (11-13-06) *Interview* by Elaine Buff.

Jones was not the only officer to know of drugs on Bald Head Island. One narcotics officer from the sheriff's department "took a job over there to do something about it, too. He didn't last over there very long." The problem existed before Dee Jones ever became a police officer. "... there are other officers ... that worked over there that saw what was going on and knew it was going on and were told, 'You didn't see nothing.'" The drug activity continues. "Anybody, any law enforcement officer who works over there, or anybody who lives over there, if they tell you it doesn't go on there, they're lying through their teeth."

- Doe, Jane*. (7-24-07). *Telephone interview* by Elaine Buff.

Trucks and businesses delivering supplies to the island by barge do so every day without being inspected. Any thing can be transported daily without discovery.

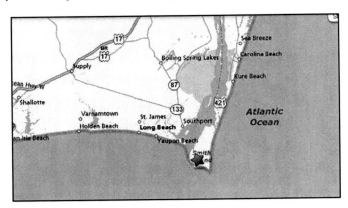

Map Quest shows the location of Bald Head Island is located off the North Carolina coast in the Atlantic Ocean. It is reachable by ferry from Southport or by private water craft. The island has an elevation of 5 feet and boasts a land area of 4.29 square miles. The island in 2000 had 173 full-time residents. The established median household income was $62,083 with a median house/condo value of $525,000. The population was 95.4% White non-Hispanic, 2.9 % Black, 1.2% American Indian, and 1.2 % two or more races. The people who live there twenty years or older are for the most part, highly educated with 100% being high school graduates, 68.7% having a bachelor's degree or higher, 26% with a graduate or professional degree. Only 5.9% are unemployed. According to research in 2007, there were no sex offenders living there. In 2000, the average property tax was $4,950. In 1999 70 buildings were constructed at an average cost of 255,000.

The wildlife on Bald Head is outstanding with an abundance of sea creatures, crocodiles, and even deer such as this one standing along side on of the golf trails on the island on a sunny summer morning.

What do the people do who can afford to live in such idyllic surroundings? For men in industry at the top of the list at 23% are real estate, rental and leasing, professional, scientific and technical services followed by public administration at 14%. Men in construction comprise 9%, 7% are professional and commercial equipment and supplies merchant wholesalers. Another 10% are listed as working in metal and metal products, transportation, support activities, and couriers.

The following are listed as the most common occupations for men. Fire fighting and prevention workers including supervisors (14%), top executives (12%) other management occupations except farmers and farm managers (12%) other sales and related workers including supervisors (12%) business operations specialists (9%) architects, surveyors, and cartographers (9%) advertising, marketing, promotions, public relations, and sales managers (5%)

For females, the most common occupations are: other sales and related workers including supervisors (24%), other management occupations except farmers and farm managers (16%), other financial specialists (16%), transportation, tourism, and lodging attendants (14%), top executives (5%), business operations specialists (5%), librarians, curators, and archivists (5%).

- Bald Head Island. http://www.city-data.com/city/Bald-Head-Island-North-Carolina.html

The picture of the harbor shows that Bald Head Island is a rental haven for those wanting to get away from it all for a few days or weeks into a cocoon of fun and frolic available to those with expensive tastes and a wallet worthy of the price of that retreat. Unless terribly wealthy, someone wanting to retreat must save for a long time or pool money with others to arrange for this getaway and that gives one the feeling of total freedom to do whatever they desire during those hours they are on the island.

Chapter Thirteen

Bald Head Island Police Department

Bald Head Island has a different kind of reputation, one that does not include drugs or danger of any kind. It is portrayed as a retreat where is no worry or harm in a enchanting seaside setting. George Mitchell, a Fortune 500 member, bought the island but it is run by his two sons, Kent who has an office on the island, and Mark who lives on Wrightsville Beach. In 1999 Woody Fulton was "in charge" and his wife Joy (Joyce) was director of public relations.

- Hewett, William L. (2-08-00) *Interview* by Monty Clark. P. 52.

There is an image projected and protected for the tourism and real estate revenue to be attained at all costs; everyone who works there must remember that. The clientele served on this island are moneyed, privileged, and pampered; powerful and dangerous. "That's an unforgiving place over there."
- Hewett, William L. (2-08-00) *Interview* by Monty Clark. P. 10.

At one time there were only three police officers when there were not as many residents or tourist on Bald Head Island, when it hadn't yet been 'discovered',. As the bottom line grew, so did the number of police staff. During that time, not all of the police officers seemed to be particularly dedicated to police work during their shift. Some engaged in sex while on duty. While on duty other officers actually skinny dipped in the club pool. By 1998 the employees on the police force had a substantial amount of law enforcement training and emergency training; they were far more professional in their approach to their duties. That improvement had happened in spite of less than stellar police facilities counting cramped conditions with nowhere for holding interviews or storage.

- Grasty, Karen. (11-17-98). *Memo: Police Department Turnover* to Wade Horne

It seems an improved and more professional police presence was not valued on the island. In a place where a week's rental can cost $7,000.00 in July, the police station was still a single wide trailer at the corner of Muscadine and Stede Bonnet. The ten police officers had to bring their own paper towels and toilet paper to work. It was a volatile situation. According to Grasty, "We were scum .... They wanted guards, not police."

- Griffin, Anna. (6-02-02). Murder or suicide. *The Charlotte Observer.* P 12A.

Some would have the public believe that Dee Jones was a square peg of discontent trying to fit into a well-running, highly professional police department on an idyllic island but that was not the case. As far as needing police protection, many businesses there appeared to operate on the premise that they needed no protection. In a 1998 memo concerning building security, Lt. Gene Hardee documented officers finding unlocked doors at island businesses twenty-eight times from September 23rd to November 14th. He was concerned because alarms once activated couldn't be reset until employees arrived on the island the following morning. Of even more concern to him, officers get lax if they keep encountering open doors and could unknowingly put themselves in harm's way thinking alarms to be of no concern if there actually was an intruder. One of the businesses found unsecured was supposed to be closed for the season.

- Hardee, Gene. (11-15-98). *Memo Re: Building Security Check* to Chief Karen Grasty

What really seemed to upset the islanders was how they perceived themselves to be treated by police. In April, 1998, Chief Grasty sent out a memo to all of her officers containing directions with a script on how to correctly answer the telephone at the police station. In bold capital letters she explained:

> "I HAVE RECEIVED TWO COMPLAINTS OF AN OFFICER BEING RUDE ON THE PHONE. I DO NOT WANT TO RECEIVE ANY MORE COMPLAINTS ON THIS."

- Grasty, Karen. (4-07-98). *Memo: Telephone* to all officers.

Equipment furnished for police duty was also not the best. Radios in the vehicles were old and not always in proper working order. Both Wade Horne and Lt. Gene Hardee were aware of the problem. Even C-COM knew about their bad condition. At one point Chief Grasty prevailed upon a company to reduce the prices of two mobile radio units, but Village Manager Wade Horne denied her purchase request.

- Grasty, Karen. (4-08098). *Memo: Radio Purchase* to Wade Horne.

The relationships between the Village Manager, the Police and Fire Department Chiefs were not the best and caused problems. The relationship between the Village Manager Wade Horne and Police Chief Karen Grasty appears to have been a tenuous one almost on a daily basis. Horne and Grasty carried on communication in the form of memos by her and yellow sticky notes from him.

One exchange sets the tone between the two. Horne sent Grasty a note asking how much money had been used and was hence available for the next year's spending for grant officers. She answered that the records were in the accounting office at town hall. One May 11, 1999, he returned a sticky note: "I know where the records are kept for finance. I would like you to get a copy of all grant info for a discussion with me."

- Horne, Wade. (5-11-99). *Note re: grant money* to Karen Grasty.

The chief apparently felt that she herself suffered sexual harassment from a Council member, who would later file an important complaint against Officer Dee Jones about her speeding and then had to apologize. He made "Monica Lewinsky jokes" to Grasty after he was warned. Nothing came of the complaint because Village Manager Wade Horne mishandled the documentation.

- Grasty, Karen. (nd). *Personal writing*

Grasty further felt that her job was contributory to the trouble with her back that eventually forced her to apply for disability. She noted, "I was made to carry and haul water bottles, ammo boxes, EMS stretchers, and equipment after I made it known I could not do so. I was then ordered to do it."

- Grasty, Karen. (nd). *Personal writing.*

Horne made Grasty cancel doctor appointments. She checked calendars for time conflicts before making appointments, and he would still force her to break them. "Wade told me I would need to be at work and would have to skip doctor's appointment. I worked Monday – Saturday, 8 am – 6 pm."

- Grasty, Karen. (5-04-99). *Memo* to Wade Horne.

Grasty's job performance evaluation on March 18, 1999 by Horne included some statements concerning areas in which he felt she needed improvement. She took exception and wrote a letter to him giving her reasons. He responded with a yellow sticky note on March 19 which included the following remark: "However, those items are issues that I see needing attention/improvement during the next review period."

- Grasty, Karen. (3-18-99). *Memo: Performance Evaluation* to Wade Horne.

The relationship between Horne and Fire Chief Brown was strained, both in a competition for favor with the Bald Head management. In the middle was the police department. It was for a bad situation waiting for a tragedy to happen.

Chapter Fourteen

Working on Bald Head Island

Davina Jones was not the only police officer to find it hard to serve on Bald Head Island. It was and is a special place. It demanded a special kind of police officer. "...they wanted somebody for protection. But as far as actually arresting anybody, or carrying side arms, or carrying any type of chemical spray, or actually carting somebody off in handcuffs, they did not want that. ... They want to put up a mask and say that nothing ever goes on here. And it does. Drugs, illegal consumption of alcohol, you name it."

- Hewett, William L. (2-08-00) *Interview* by Monty Clark. P. 53.

The island movers and shakers didn't want improved police personnel that would hassle them about locking their business doors at night, locking up their alcoholic cabinets and coolers, about selling alcohol and cigarettes to minors at the store. They wanted to drive their golf carts while drunk or high on drugs, even if that meant allowing their children drive them around. Business owners liked those police members on the squad who would call and tip them off when the ALE officers called from the mainland to say they were on the way to the island. Somebody like Dee wasn't even allowed to go purchase cigarettes at the store while they were there, afraid she would spill the beans about her training officer tipping off the owners that they had been coming.

- Jones, Davina B. (1999). *Bald Head Island Restaurants.*

"I know for a fact that there are people who come to that island, because I've seen them, and they are scary individuals. You don't know who's lurking around over there. That place is dark. It's grown up, little thin walkways and everything. It's easy to do something over there and get away with it."

- Hewett, William L. (2-08-00) *Interview* by Monty Clark. P. 61.

Homeowners and agencies rent houses. So at any given time, there is no way to know exactly who is on the island or what they may have brought with them or what they are there to do. Tram drivers who pick up people at the ferry and deliver them to their rentals and vice versa when they are leaving know. They can tell you they have seen just about anything brought onto the island.

When Dee was hired In January, 1999, she was the only female officer besides Chief Grasty. By October, 1999, another female and two males had been hired. They all were walking that thin Bald Head line between keeping things peaceful and keeping the pretty people happy. Each had their own special assignments.

Karen Grasty – Chief; Gene Hardee – Investigations/Routine Patrol; Robert Willis – Routine Patrol; Dexter Ludlum – Crime Prevention; Officer/Routine Patrol/Juvenile; Keith Cain – Routine Patrol/*Crime Scene Security*/Background Investigation; Brad Stone – Property/Evidence Control/Bike Patrol Leader/Routine Patrol/Field Training Officer; Travis Snead – Records Assistant/Internal Affairs/Routine Patrol; Aaron Muscle – Bike patrol Technician/Bike Patrol Leader Assistant/Routine patrol; Dee Jones – Routine Patrol/Sexual Assaults/Child Abuse; Robin Wallace – Routine Patrol.

After Dee's memorial service, they gathered for a picture.

None of them are employed on the island now.

Davina Buff Jones

She grew tired of having to explain that Davina came from her father's name David, so she gave herself the nickname "Dee." Her father called her "Vanny." Her sisters called her "Beany." Her two dogs knew her as "Momma." By choice, she became Officer Jones.

Some of the police painted a picture of a troubled and depressed, suicidal young woman who had had trouble working with and handling the public. Others working on Bald Head had trouble working there as well, especially if you were female or had trouble looking the other way while a law was broken.

The thirty-three year old woman who supposedly knelt on a whim in the dark on an elitist playground off the coast of North Carolina and took her own life was the middle child born to Loy and Harriet Buff in Charlotte, North Carolina on July 29, 1966.

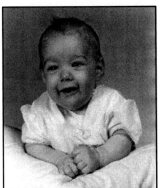

When old enough, each of the Buff girls had gotten to fly on a plane with their dad, then a salesman for the Colgate Company. It was on one such airline trip that Dee's hearing loss became apparent.

She had been sick weeks earlier, but seemed to have recovered as children do, yet as the plane was landing in Cincinnati, she began to hold that side of her head and wail to her father "Daddy, Daddy! I'm never going to hear again!" Not knowing what was wrong, he got the best help for her he could once at the hotel and she seemed to recover by the next morning. They drove back home at the end of the week end, so there was no repeat happening on a return flight. They discovered her hearing loss in that right ear when her mother took her to the doctor on the following Monday. Because of the residual infection from

the earlier illness weeks before, Vanny had lost the hearing in her right ear.

- Buff, Loy. (9-12-07). *Interview* by Elaine Buff.

To compensate for the loss of hearing in that one ear, Dee learned to read people's lips. The loss made her talk too loud at times, unable to judge the volume herself. It accounted for the bray of a laugh her sister Tanya keeps home movies to help remind her children of the aunt she doesn't want them to forget.

- Hart, Tanya. (8-27-07). *Interview* by Elaine Buff.

All three of the Buff daughters were raised as equally loved as possible, yet sometimes the girls did not always get along so well, particularly Tanya and Dee. Their fights sometimes were Herculean. When Beverly was little, Dee did consider her little sister her own and helped look after her.

- Sadler, Beverly Buff. (October, 1999). *Davina "Dee" Elaine Buff Jones: Reflections on her life and death.*
- Buff, Loy. (9-12-07). *Interview* by Elaine Buff.

As a young child Dee struggled with colds and illnesses including asthma for which she needed shots. Harriet had been taught by a friend how to administer the shots. They had used an orange to practice on as blonde curly-haired Davina watched it all with intense blue eyes. Later on, her mother stood, dreading to give her young child still another shot, knowing the pain it would also inflict. Looking brave and wise beyond her years, Dee looked up at her and said, "Just give it to me, Momma." Thankfully, Dee outgrew the asthmatic condition by the 6th grade.

Her bouncy attitude radiated and reflected through her two

sisters, her home, and the neighborhood. Pre-teen years found her feeling gangly and saddled with braces. But once the braces and baby fat disappeared, a beautiful young lady emerged. Her sisters Tanya and Beverly laughingly recall that they depended on Davina to attract the boys. By the ninth grade, she had blossomed and posed happily with her date at the prom that year. As

she grew older Dee and her mother shared that same tenuous relationship shared by many teenagers and youth as the young one spreads wings and searches for their own identifies. Many times

parents struggle wanting to intervene, yet not knowing when or how to give advice. If Harriet went to pick up a list for Dee at Dee's house, she might find herself searching a mound of empty mail envelopes to find it because Dee never seemed to throw anything away. She would receive a bill, take the

enclosed envelope, use it to enclose the check and the bill and mail it, and then keep the envelope it had come it – for years. Maybe she would write a poem on its back or re-write a particular country song she liked. Daddies don't seem to notice or worry about such, but it always jumps out at a mother. Otherwise, Dee was a neat house keeper. What was a momma to do?

The choice in males was also a topic of discussion. As is so often, Dee's choices didn't meet Harriet's approval or Loy's either. But Dee was over twenty-one, so they did the best they could, as parents do. They loved their daughter.

Dee tried to keep a lot of problems to herself. She, in spite of her beauty and personality, wanted and lacked just what most

women desire from the time they are little. She wanted a man who would love and cherish her and children she could love. Dee loved being an aunt, but she longed to be a mother. She had been raised in love and now she had love she wanted to share in addition to what she lavished on Adam and Precious. She wanted to feel good about herself, she wanted to feel needed. She wanted to be loved. Just like almost everybody else does.

Eventually, Loy quit traveling for Colgate and opened the Peddler Steak House in Charlotte. All three girls and Harriet worked there with him. Dee took over the job as hostess and did the job, according to Harriet, better than she herself could have

done it. During this period of her life, Dee was convivial, observant, and hard-working. NASCAR drivers, golfers such as Gary Player and Arnold Palmer were regulars and policemen were always there enjoying discounted meals. Bobbie and Judy Allison, their sons Davy and Clifford and their families and their pit crews ate there. Michael

Jordan and the UNC basketball players came to the restaurant. Even the Shriners from Brunswick County would eat there when they came to Charlotte for the Shrine Bowl each year. Davina was used to dealing with the rich and famous long before she arrived on Bald Head Island.

At the age of twenty-four, Dee married for the first time in October, 1990. Her husband Harry Adams had previously been married and had a son. The couple lived in Lancaster, South Carolina where they had horses and trained people to ride them. The couple had financial problems, ending in a declared bankruptcy. They were divorced after four years.

Davina's second marriage was to Jeff Jones of Goldsboro, North Carolina. He, too, had previously been married and had a daughter. He was mentally and verbally abusive. The marriage lasted two years. During this time, Dee discovered that he was taking a medication that prevented her from becoming pregnant. She discovered the medication, called the pharmacy and discovered that the medication was used to treat herpes. This discovery led to the downward spiral of the marriage. Davina argued a lot with the mother about her step-daughter. It was during an altercation with the mother that Dee spat on the woman, was charged and found guilty of simple assault in 1994. She disclosed this incident without comment on her job application at Bald Head Island. The men she chose to allow into her life were each controlling and abusive, unable to return the love she so readily gave. In fighting for the step-daughter, she was trying to do what she thought was best for her. She finally decided she was better off on her own.

- Sadler, Beverly Buff. (October, 1999). *Davina "Dee" Elaine Buff Jones: Reflections on her life and death.*
- Atkins, Laura. (10-27-07). *Telephone interview* by Elaine Buff.
- *Buff v. Village of Bald Head Island Police Department, North Carolina League of Municipalities and North Carolina Rescue Workers Cap Death Benefits Act.* North Carolina Industrial Commission. (10-23/24-03). P. 21.

Dee came home to Oak Island where her parents were living. After some reflection and urging from some friends, she decided to enroll in Basic Law Enforcement Training (BLET) at Brunswick Community College. However, she got into a shoving match with a fellow student who made a desultory remark about Dee being unable to be a police officer due to her diminutive size. She quit the program and re-enrolled at Cape Fear Community College in Wilmington, graduating on December 8, 1998.

While the family was not exactly thrilled with Dee's choice of career, she was ecstatic. She felt she had found her place. Once she had been hired and had her uniform, she put it on and got her mother to take her picture in the front yard of their home on Oak Island. She felt classy in her size 6 Reeboks that cost $69.99, the x-small pants at $53.70 a pair. She didn't have them on but the heavy weather polo shirt costing $57.00 and her x-small jacket for $186.50 would come in handy because she was cold natured. Her smile that day, posing for her mother was worth a million dollars.

In Dee's work life prior to Bald Head Island, she had been usually described as a good worker. She was a young teller at a Charlotte branch of Security Bank in 1985 when she and fellow teller worked together to foil a customer's attempt to defraud the bank out of a large sum of money. The two were commended for their quick-thinking actions by their branch manager and the main office.

- Carter, Steve. (10-24-85). *Security Bank Memo* to Carl Dean.

Davina loved animals and worked for a veterinarian who said of her, "Because of her personable nature, she got along with her fellow employees. She maintained a friendly attitude throughout her employment. Making the customers happy was one of her best assets." She had wanted to become a veterinarian for big animals, but the injury she received from a horse damaged her back and put an end to those aspirations. Though a horse caused her serious injury, she never lost her love for them.

- Inglesby, Henry. (11-16-95). *Recommendation.*
- Atkins, Laura. (10-27-07). *Telephone interview* by Elaine Buff.

Deborah Hewett, manager of the Brunswick Community College Book Store described her as "... a dedicated, smart, dependable and very hard-working person. ... She gets along well with co-workers and people in general. .... She doesn't hesitate when it comes to getting the job done."

- Hewett, Deborah. (1-22-99). *Recommendation.*

Finally, James Walton Jr., Director of Basic Law Enforcement Training at Brunswick Community College recommended Dee for the Bald Head Island police position writing that "Ms. Jones is a very responsible person, who is serious about her education. She is also very serious about becoming a law enforcement officer. I feel Ms. Jones will make some department a very good officer."

In her graduation picture, she was by far the tiniest of the graduates, but her heart was as big as anyone else's where police dedication was concerned.

Her baby sister agreed. "She was honest and full of integrity. ... She did things by the book. She was strong in her conviction that no one is above the law – if you do something against the law and get caught, you have to pay the penalty. We were raised that way by our parents. It was central to who [sic] she was and she chose a career that she felt stood for those values." Time and time again, she did what she had been trained to do – treat everyone the same way – fairly and by the rules and the book she had taken an oath to uphold. Unfortunately, those values would get her into trouble on Bald Head Island.

118

- Walton, James L. (10-16-98). *Recommendation for Bald Head Island Police Position.*
- Sadler, Beverly Buff. (October, 1999). *Davina "Dee" Elaine Buff Jones: Reflections on her life and death.*

Anyone who could afford a few nights stay in a cottage by the ocean felt they had the right to do as they pleased during their time on the island.

They ran headlong into Officer Jones who tried to operate under the concept that the law was for everyone. So she made waves when she refused to tear up citations once she had written them. She tired of giving warnings over and over to the same people.

Residents and council members especially took delight in finding new reasons to run, not to her superior officer, either Chief Grasty when she was on the island or Interim Chief Hardee, but straight to Village Manager Wade Horne to voice their disapproval of the way Officer 4206 did business. Then the news of her latest infraction would trickle down from the head honcho to the police department.

The complaints began to add up and, gradually, somehow within several short months, this same Davina, the hard worker, the people-pleaser, the one with the friendly attitude in all her other jobs, would be painted as a suicidal, depressed, inept, abrasive, headstrong liar.

Chapter Sixteen

Doing Her Duty

Professionally things seemed to be turning a corner for Dee Jones. She had landed a job on Bald Head Island as a patrol officer. Friends and family felt relief; nothing ever happened on Bald Head. Although they were uneasy with her choice of a career, they felt it was a safe place for her to begin.

On a personal level, Dee had not been as successful. That prince charming she chased in heart had tarnished over time. Both sisters had successful marriages and children. That fulfillment still eluded her; she was the sister who had failed in that respect. She had failed her father and mother; she felt like the black sheep of the family. Dee was close to all of her family, but there was no one closer to her than her daddy and she had failed him. She saw herself as the family's black sheep and that hurt. She had failed herself. She was no Cinderella yet.

She took both of her doomed marriages as a reflection of a shortcoming within herself. She saw each failed relationship as her own fault, not that of anyone else even when one of her husbands had had a venereal disease which he had not told her about at first. As further testimony to her relationships with her past husbands, both of them came for her funeral, though one of them was too distraught to attend the memorial service. One of them lost his job due to the fact that he took time off to attend.

She grew more and more worried about not being able to have the children she wanted so much. Her shortcomings sometimes threatened to overwhelm her, dogging her as if she had a cement block chained to an ankle. She had begun to take anti-depressants.

"To deal with what she had had to deal with in the last few years, and what was going on with her job, anybody would have had a hard time with that," said Laura Atkins. And Laura should know. She was Dee's best friend, the one Dee called when Dee was down, when Dee started off the phone conversation with, "I need a Laura-fix." In fact, on the day she died, Davina talked to Laura three times, telling her during their last conversation, "Call me tonight if you want to." Laura is adamant that Dee would not have killed herself without saying good-bye. It seems that Dee was her own worst enemy when judging her herself and her own faults.

- Atkins, Laura. (10-27-07). *Telephone interview* by Elaine Buff.

Dee sought solace through writing. She had put her thoughts on paper from the time she was in high school Her journal recording of a school trip through the West showed that her writing was always brutally honest. Taking notes or describing observations, rewriting favorite song lyrics, Dee wrote prolifically. She made lists of what to do on a daily basis. She re-wrote the lyrics of her favorite country songs. Horoscopes were a passion and she copied hers down on a daily basis. Sometimes she added drawings to go along with what she wrote, such as house plans. And even in the darkest times, her humor still bubbled through. Here is a poem she wrote several years before her death, apparently after seeing the movie "Forrest Gump" and reflecting on his philosophy of life.

Life is <u>not</u> like a
box of chocolates …
Life <u>is</u> like a can of
jalapenos
You never know which one
is gonna
burn your
ass.

She kept calendar cartoons of the Far Side, of sayings that took her fancy. She observed life and wrote it down.

Much was made of the fact that Dee made 170 visits to the mental health clinic in Wayne County. This was something that she did not disclose on her job application at Bald Head. This would have eliminated her as a candidate for the job. Having depression would do that.

Dee herself may not have realized at the time that she was depressed. She was in an abusive marriage, a second attempt to find that elusive happiness with a man too much patterned after the first failed groom. Away from home, she had found someone to whom she could talk. Harriet Buff, thinking to help her daughter, encouraged her to keep seeing the counselor, not dreaming the trips would come back later to paint her daughter in such a negative light.

During the same period, Dee spent time in the doctor's office being treated for vaginal infections and bouts of colds she couldn't shake. Depression does lower the body's ability to fight off illnesses. There was much tension over the step-daughter. It is not hard to realize why there would have been a need to find someone in which to confide. Depression in and of itself does not constitute, is not interchangeable with mental illness. In fact, Laura Atkins characterized her as "A very strong person. She had that 'little person complex' and she kept her weak side hidden except to her friends."

- Atkins, Laura. (10-27-07). *Telephone interview* by Elaine Buff.

Family members were aware of her struggle and tried to lift her spirits, especially Mama Sue, with whom Dee had a special bond, one that even drove Mama Sue up on a horse for the first time in her life to celebrate Dee's wedding in 1991. "I love you (10) that's TEN bushels <u>see</u> and that means a lot you know." Mama Sue wrote more of the family news and then closed her letter: "I have always had a pet poem I have always said to myself when I was down and it has always helped me. It goes like this:

> Be still sad heart and cease repining
> Behind those clouds the sun is still shining
> Thy fate is the common fate of all:
> Into each life some rain must fall.

He (God) never fails us if we trust Him.

- Mama Sue. (8-22-86). *Letter* to Dee.

Any single person probably can understand those times when Dee was happy and satisfied with her life as well as those times when aloneness and loneliness loomed so large. "Look at the big picture, Dee! It says, 'the future' – there is plenty of time. But what about savoring the time – now?" If Dee had a big problem, it was to find happiness within herself and not depend on a man for it. Unfortunately, she never appreciated what others saw in her. She was striking. When she entered a room, her personality shouted, "Here I am!" She laughed a lot and cared about people. Dee had a fire about her, as her uncle would remind mourners at the memorial. Her life did burn out all too quickly.

- Buff, Davina. (1997). *Personal writing.*
- Atkins, Laura. (10-27-07). *Telephone interview* by Elaine Buff.

She had times when she despaired of ever being happy but she would rebound with the help of Adam and Precious and especially Laura Atkins, her best friend, who had moved to Texas. "My personal life has gone to hell, it seems. ... What next? Run, Dee, run. You were told that you have an advantage being female, singe/divorced and no children. Search for that job and go to it. Fill out those apps. and leave all behind. ... You talked to Laura yesterday. Listen to her! Quit evolving yourself around these men – it brings you down. Be your own and get on with it! 'There is no normal life – there's just life ... you get on with it.' Do what you have to do and that's taking care of you and those two wonderful, life saving dogs. Do it."

- Buff, Davina. (11-22-98). *Personal writing.*

Precious Queen and Lord Adam, two Australian Shepherds were the anchors of Davina's life. She referred to them as her 'babies' and went to great pains to take care of them. She showered the dogs with the love and affection dedicated to the family she didn't have.

When Dee had started school to become a police officer in January of 1998, she became friends with a fellow student named Scott Monzon. He was almost ten years younger, but they first became good friends and then became romantically involved around October or November of that same year. He was divorced with a child and Dee knew the ex-wife. Like in her other past relationships, she fell hard for the man whose treatment of her was less than stellar; Monzon could be abusive and possessive. Around the same time, she became acquainted with Will Hewett when he worked on the island. They had a friendship, innocent on her side, but Hewett fell hard for Dee, a fact that did not sit well with Monzon.

Monzon and Dee had a rocky relationship. He was a police officer on Oak Island where the couple shared a house. He left the house, then came back, made love to her one last time and then announced that he had actually moved back in with his ex-wife. They were going to try to make things work for the sake of their child. Dee was devastated. Upset and distraught on October 20, 1999 she drank too much, drove to the place where Monzon was with his wife, then drove back home. Monzon called and asked the police on duty that night to check on Dee at her house to make sure she had arrived safely and to get her to stop driving until she had sobered.

While Monzon had lived with her, the two police officers compared the way his job and hers was done on a daily basis. He was quite aware of her growing frustration. Dee saw Dr. Keith Reschley, the Buff family's doctor, who prescribed medication for her condition he would later describe as "dysphoria" or "sad and blue".

- Reschley, Keith. (11-14-03). *Disposition.*

Monzon tried to talk Dee into becoming an EMS; she was a better EMS. Additionally, he worried because of her size but also because she was deaf and her holster was not a secure one. To prove his point, he would come up behind her at home and sneak her gun out of its holster before she knew what was happening.

- *Buff v. Village of Bald Head Island Police Department, North Carolina League of Municipalities and North Carolina Rescue Workers Cap Death Benefits Act. North Carolina Industrial Commission.* (10-23/24-03). P. 483.

Chapter Seventeen

Bald Head Island Police Officer 4206

In a psychological autopsy, Dr. Alan Berman characterized Jones as being

> "suspicious and distrustful of others. She was irritable, resentful, readily frustrated. She was verbally aggressive and angry often explosively, after which she would feel guilt."

- Berman, Alan L. Ph. D. (5-28-02). *Psychological Autopsy.* Pp. 1-12.

Davina Buff Jones was initially employed as a police officer for Bald Head Island on January 18, 1999. Prior to that, she, as standard practice, had undergone a medical exam and a psychological evaluation. She was "found to be in good health, physically and mentally."

- LATTIMORE, BUCK, Chairman, N.C. Industrial Commission. OPINION AND AWARD for the Full Commission. (Filed 27 June 2005). I.C. NOS. 980154 & LH-0286, LOY BUFF, Father of DAVINA BUFF JONES, Deceased Employee, Plaintiff v. N.C. LAW ENFORCEMENT OFFICES AND RESCUE WORKERS DEATH BENEFITS ACT and STATE OF NORTH CAROLINA CONTINGENCY AND EMERGENCY FUND, Defendants. P. 4.

Dr. Tonn's psychological exam revealed nothing that "would indicate that she cannot perform the duties of a police officer." Ricky Simpson, a former instructor of Jones at Cape Fear Community College during her BLET classes, said that Dee had been concerned about her size. But in exercise classes she could carry a 150 pound student 50 feet across the floor. Simpson said her size was never a problem. Dee wanted to be a police officer and she was not going to let her size stand in her way.

- Tonn, Henry. F. (12-30-98). *Psychological evaluation of Davina B. Jones.*
- von Kolnitz, Cece and Victoria Cherrie. (11-05-99). Evidence builds case for suicide. *Morning-Star.* Pp 1A, 8A.

In the beginning of her employment, Dee's badge number was 4208. 4206 at that time belonged to Keith Cain. Her badge number was changed to 4206 on January 14th. It remained hers until the night of her death.

In her January work notebook, Dee listed learning notes. "Mikes in vehicles: red – village, blue – C-COM." She listed instructions on how to use the grid book to locate houses. Sheriff Hewett was holding a Drug Task Force Meeting at Kirby's Steakhouse. She was off duty that day and sought Chief Grasty's permission to be attend. This was the first indication of her early interest in working the drug scene. She wanted to be an under cover police officer almost from the very beginning of her career.

During the first month on the job she noted two adults and two children in a golf cart with a boy approximate eight-years old driving. She also recorded reports of a peeping tom on the island and the possibility of it being a policeman and she jotted down a name to go with it.

- Buff, Davina. (1999). *January Duty Notebook.*

In February Jones was asked by Chief Grasty to complete a self evaluation. This would be the first of many self evaluations she would be asked to complete during her tenure of less than a year as a police officer on the little island. She then met with the chief to discuss the evaluation instrument. At that time Grasty and Jones agreed that Dee needed to learn to "take constructive criticism" and learn all she could to be a good police officer. The future looked very bright.

- *Buff v. Village of Bald Head Island Police
  Department, North Carolina League of Municipalities
  and North Carolina Rescue Workers Cap Death
  Benefits Act.* North Carolina Industrial Commission.
  (10-23/24-03). Exhibits Part II. P. 1005.

By March Dee was gathering information for reports and completing reports very accurately and "handled herself very professionally." However, she "needs to work on voice commands. She has trouble making people follow her commands. She needs to speak up and show she cannot be tested."

- *Buff v. Village of Bald Head Island Police
  Department, North Carolina League of Municipalities
  and North Carolina Rescue Workers Cap Death
  Benefits Act.* North Carolina Industrial Commission.
  (10-23/24-03). Exhibits Part II. P. 1005.

These will be extraordinary words when scant months later the very same people will brand her as aggressive and abrasive. Verbal timbre alone can sometimes fail to convince a drunk that you will not be intimidated, especially if you are a scarcely five feet tall female and your partner has left you alone in charge of five or six youth who believe that they have been entitled since birth to do as they please.

According to evaluations also from the month of March, Jones got more positive words from her superiors. "She's getting better with talking with people and handling situations." On March 17th, she completed another report. "She done [sic] a good job on it and getting information from the victim. She's handling herself very professionally and uses her time very well." A later entry states, "Dee is a good officer, she does good work and is willing to learn." At this point it would appear that Dee was living up to the potential described by Walton in his recommendation. It is funny how much difference a few months make when the wrong people decide that Davina has seen too much of what they consider their own private business.

- *Buff v. Village of Bald Head Island Police Department, North Carolina League of Municipalities and North Carolina Rescue Workers Cap Death Benefits Act.* North Carolina Industrial Commission. (10-23/24-03). Exhibits Part II. Pp. 1006-1007.

On the 18th of March Officer Jones was stopped by two gentlemen on foot around 0830 (8:30 am) on North Bald Head Wynd at Timbercreek. They wanted to report three subjects who had passed them in a golf cart traveling toward Marina Wynd. The witnesses had smelled a strong odor and saw that the cart's interior was fogged with smoke. They told the officer, "The odor was not that of cigarettes." One of the gentlemen stated, "It was dope."

Jones and her training officer were called to a house that should have been unoccupied on March 29, 1999, where there was a loud party in progress with several males and two females. There were numerous beer cans in view when the officers arrived. The females had not been drinking and were over eighteen years of age. They were asked to leave and did so. The males were asked to produce identification and did so except for one. He gave the male officer a hard time at first. Subsequently he blew .18 on the alco-sensor and received a ticket.

- *Bald Head Island Incident/Investigative Report.* (3-29-99).

Although that event seems to have proceeded without incident, Robert Willis, Dee's training officer, verbally disciplined Dee as a rule in front of her fellow officers or people. Dee didn't like his choice of language or comments when they were alone either. As a rule, Dee was very conscious of things said to her that were said to embarrass or discredit her. "She said she was uncomfortable working with him. As far as the comments, I can't remember if it was toward or around her when they were alone. There wasn't anybody else around but the two of them and it just didn't make her feel comfortable."

130

- Hewett, William L. (2-08-00) *Interview* by Monty Clark. P. 57-58.

At the beginning of July, Dee attended a Public Relations Committee Meeting at the Village Hall where she made the following notes:

> Improve ☺ attitude
> Community relations
> Stop talking too much – keep opinions to self
> Job performance
> Commitment
> Time management log – account for location and what you were doing

- Buff, Davina. (July, 1999). *July Duty Notebook.*

Upon their island holiday check-in Bald Head Island visitors received the following information from the police chief during 1999.

Island Guest Rules concerning golf carts include:

1. You must possess a valid driver's license to operate a golf cart on the island (G.S. 20-7A).
2. If you have a learner's permit, you must have a licensed driver accompany you. (G.S. 20-11B).
3. Drivers must observe all traffic signs. The island's speed limit is 18 m.p.h.
4. Golf carts should not be operated by anyone who is or has been consuming alcohol.

- Grasty, Karen. (1999). *Bald Head Island Guest Rules.*

This order would prove to be a special frustration for Dee. Monzon, a police officer for Oak Island, would naturally discuss job situations with her. "They wouldn't let her do her job the way she felt it needed to be done. The way I did it over here."

- Monzon, Scott. (2-10-00). *Interview* by Monty Clark. P. 11.

The problem was that some residents didn't feel that rules should apply to them and others paying hefty rental fees felt that money freed them from rules as well. It was financially important that residents and renters stay happy. One stays put; the other returns.

That meant that either rules must be obeyed or they would have to be 'bent.' Dee did not believe in bending rules.

On July 14, 1999, officers received a directive to stop underage drivers. They were told to notate if they had a license, call complainant and advise. July 10th brought another self-analysis task. This is Dee's list from that assignment:

1 Taller image – order placed 15 years ago and still on back order
2 Ability to be tactful
3 Community relations
4 Ability to overlook things and know what not to overlook
5 Lower tone of voice at all times – self control techniques
6 Stop trying too hard
7 Public relations
8 Attitude and appearance
9 Be seen but not heard
10 Enforce only when necessary – prevent mistakes on my part
11 Stop talking so much, learn by listening
12 Be more careful on the job. Safety.

On the 25th Dee jotted down the number of a Brunswick County drug agent. She issued a citation for failure to carry an annual permit sticker. At 1950 (7:50 pm) hours she chronicled, "Lt. Hardee stated I haven't done nothing all day. Should be well rested." Another line down she added, "Dee, shut your hole (mouth)."
  ▪ Buff, Davina. (July, 1999). *July Duty Notebook.*

July melted into August as Dee continued to do her job. For August 17th, she recorded the following events: four medical calls, one fire alarm, one violation with unlicensed operation, one civil citation unlicensed operation, one escort (police), one check on female assaulted on 8-16-99.

  ▪ Buff, Davina. (August, 1999). *August Duty Notebook.*

Tucked into her book was the August, 1999 Police Monthly Report.

Special Investigations	22	Grills Violations	6
Impounded/towed Carts	4	Larceny Reports	8
Disturbances (other)	8	Lost Children	2
Arrests	2	Medical Calls	20
State Citations Issued	3	Narcotics	--
Stop Sign Violations	7	Noise Disturbances	3
Speeding	2	Police Vehicle Escorts	4
Alarms Residential/Business	37	Property Damage to Vandalism	6
Business/Residential Keepchecks	1118	Property Found/Returned	10
Citizen Assistance	32	Registrations Bicycle	10
Fire calls/Alarms	13	Registrations Gas Vehicle	2
Golf Carts Abandoned	11	Registrations Golf Cart	60
Golf Carts Found	15	Suspicious Persons	8
Golf Carts Missing, Stolen	18	Traffic Accidents	5
Illegal Parking	7	Unlicensed Drivers	4

- Buff, Davina. (August, 1999). *August Duty Notebook.*

With drugs so apparently prevalent on Bald Head by witnesses who worked there and lived there, it is curious to find not one citation issued for narcotics during the height of the season. Jones wrote at least thirty (30) tickets that are in evidence, perhaps more. The sort of offense throughout her citations were failure to wear a seat belt, for underage drinking, running a stop sign, parking where not allowed and exceeding safe speed. These seem hardly reasons for bringing her into the crosshairs of people wanting to eliminate her. Gene Hardee repeatedly told Jones to overlook the drinking and driving on the island.

- Jones, Davina Buff. (10-04-99). *Letter.*

Other superior officers told her she tended to write tickets rather than either give repeated warnings or simply look the other way. Keith Cain told her she didn't have to hand out a ticket. "Every time we catch somebody you don't have to ... pound their heads down."

- Cain, Keith. (1-25-00). *Interview* by Monty Clark. P. 12.

She incurred the wrath of one tourist on September 14th when she stopped the woman's inebriated husband who was letting one of his children drive his golf cart while still other smaller children were with him. The man was in the back seat, apparently without glasses he was supposed to be wearing to drive. Jones took possession of the bottle of hard liquor he was drinking and poured it out. While she was writing the ticket, the man's wife, who was following behind in another golf cart began to berate Jones because there were alligators on the golf course. Jones advised the woman to call animal control if the alligator was a problem. The woman said she didn't appreciate living on an island with the animal.

- Jones, Davina Buff. (9-14-99). *Operations Report.*

Davina did excel in one particular area. She was a good investigative officer. She worked hard at solving the cases assigned to her. The current open cases were displayed on the chief's white board in the police trailer. Dee's open cases were always the shortest list on the chief's board. Dee always worked her cases until they were finished. That was one aspect of her job she really exceeded in doing well. Sometimes she even helped work  on cases of other officers, which was not always appreciated. She brought home this Polaroid picture to show off her talents to her parents.

But Dee was not perfect. She couldn't look the other way but so many times. There are notes where she did warn people about

134

infractions and how many times she had already warned them and they had continued to do the same thing over and over. So she cited them; and they didn't like it.

Sometimes her choices were not the best ones, either. She should have realized that some things were not acceptable and should not be done where a public was ever on guard to find her at fault. She wouldn't harm anybody; she never learned it did not work the other way around. And no matter how many times she warned herself, she did continue to have trouble holding her tongue.

During her career on the island, there were seven complaints lodged against her. The first on occurred on March 3rd when Gene Hardee questioned her about calling home during duty. He told her only one employee lived in the particular area coming up on the phone bill and had the same last four digits as her phone number. He said former employees had used *69 and Chief Grasty had not known or caught on about it. Jones told him she had not charged any calls and had call waiting. Such a charge by her superior bothered her.

- Jones, Davina Buff. (3-11-99). *Journal.*

Six days later she and her superior officer Brad Stone forgot to unlock the Village Hall for a committee meeting. A complaint was made to Village Manager Wade Horner, who complained to Chief Grasty by sending a sticky note stuck to the meeting's minutes. The note said: "K--- Door was not opened again. Next time will <u>require</u> formal documentation for files. Handle it. Thanks." After talking to Stone and Jones, (who were not the only officers who forgot to unlock the door – it was a continuing problem at the department), Chief Grasty made Jones and Stone go to the home of the Council liaison and apologize in person for failing to unlock the door prior to the meeting.

- Grasty, Karen. (3-17-99). *Memo* to Wade Horne.

At the end of April there was a fire on Ft. Holmes Trail. A fire scene tape surrounded the area to keep unauthorized people from the area once the fire had been extinguished. Dee was on duty when a volunteer fire fighter arrived back at the scene intending to cross over the tape with his wife to show her the scene and where he had worked to help put out the fire. Dee denied him access to cross. He complained to Wade Horne, adding that she not only had denied him access to the fire scene, she had embarrassed him in front of his wife.

Fire Chief Kent Brown was consulted and said that April 29th he had explained to his volunteers that they were not allowed to cross the tape lines unless they were needed to fight a fire. Word was that no other volunteers complained.

- Grasty, Karen. (4-27-99). *Letter* to Kent Brown.

However, council member Gayle Sanders told Wade Horne at least seven volunteers had complained to them about Dee's attitude. The complaints went, once again, not to the police chief, but to the Village Manager. Chief Grasty told Dee she had to conduct herself in a friendlier manner when dealing with the public. Grasty wrote to Town Manage Wade Horne and Fire Chief Kent Brown expressing apologies for the episode, even though Dee Jones was lawfully correct in keeping out sightseers from a fire scene while it was still surrounded by the yellow tape.

- Grasty, Karen. (5-03-99). *Memo* to Wade Horne and Fire Chief Kent Brown.

Nine days later while working with Dexter Ludlum, Dee faced the most dangerous situation before the night of her death. The two had received a call from the River Pilot Café where a loud and unruly group of young customers were causing havoc.

Seven males and one female were exiting the restaurant, seen in the picture above on the far right, one breaking a bottle on the way out of the door. Ludlum told the one who had broken the bottle to clean it up and the rest to go to the ferry. They approached the officer, refusing to do as he asked. Ludlum repeated the order and told Jones to escort them to the ferry on foot and remain with them until the ferry arrived.

Out of sight of Ludlum, three of the males came back towards Jones, telling her she wasn't so bad, she couldn't make them do anything. She pulled out her ASP baton, flipped it out in a downward motion and held it by her right side and told them to start walking.

As they passed the sales office, they saw an elderly couple sitting at a nearby table. The male subjects started to shout and scream at the couple. Jones told the group to hush and keep walking. Two of the males turned back on her again. She raised the ASP to the ready position and advised them to keep walking. They did so, but kept turning to tell her what she was in 4-letter terms. Once at the ferry landing, several of the males refused to sit down as directed.

Officer Ludlum called her on the radio and told Jones to get everyone's ID. They had been caught earlier in the day with beer in a golf cart and had produced ID at that time. One refused to produce ID now. Jones told him to or she'd take it. She used profanity during the statement. She knew better, but this was one of her lapses in judgment. No matter how frustrated, she did not have the luxury of ever letting it out of her system. One of the other inebriated youths immediately demanded her name and badge number, saying that it was probably fake and she didn't have the right to harass them or ask for ID.

At that point one of them began to verbally threaten four Bald Head Island tram employees who were standing at the back of the depot office. One of the intoxicated youths tried to jump over the ferry bench to reach the four employees. Dee pulled her ASP to get him to sit back down.

When her superior officer arrived on the scene, one of the males was showing Dee his chest and a scar on his torso. Ludlum took two of the males off to talk. Meanwhile another of the males pulled his pants and underwear down to his knees to show her his privates. Jones told him to fix his attire or go to jail. Ludlum came back and said that they all understood now that they could go to jail. He returned to the River Pilot Café, leaving her to handle the situation until the ferry came.

When the ferry arrived, Jones explained the situation to the captain. Ludlum contacted Dee for help in transporting one of the youths who had passed out on the deck area of the River Pilot to the county complex. They held the boat for five minutes while she went to get the male to the ferry.

EMS, Chief Brown, and Ludlum were using an ammonia stick under the subject's nose when Dee arrived back at the restaurant. He had urinated on himself. Jones put the subject's North Carolina driver's license in her pocket and handcuffed him. The EMS helped her get the subject to the ferry. Ludlum advised her that the magistrate would hold him until sober at the complex in Bolivia.

The males from the earlier trouble blocked Jones from leaving the boat once it docked at Southport. A police officer waiting with a vehicle for Dee to use told her he had them from there. She took the transport car to Bolivia, delivering the male to jail. Then she returned to Indigo and returned by ferry to the island to complete paperwork.

On May 12th, Andy Scott, manager of the River Pilot Café, wrote to Chief Grasty thanking Jones and Ludlum for their assistance with the difficult patrons on May 8, 1999. The group had gotten so out of hand before he called for the police that Scott decided to and did close the restaurant for the night.

- Scott, Andy. (5-18-99). *Letter of thanks* to Police Chief Karen Grasty.

But Jones was called onto the carpet. It seems that the youth who was inebriated was not so drunk as to forget his dignity had been insulted. He had held onto Jones' name and badge number. It didn't matter what the group had done to the officer; she had used profanity towards them and unsheathed that baton on innocent victims. Somebody had complained. Big time.

Jones got a written reprimand placed in her personnel file. Grasty informed Jones that young man taken to Bolivia should have been charged with consumption of alcohol under age. Dee was not to draw her ASP baton, OC spray or weapon unless there was "a threat of danger." Officer Jones had written that she had felt danger each time the males had turned and approached her, trying to surround her, on the way to the ferry.

The chief said that Dee had not used proper force escalation procedures. She was not to use foul language. She could not demand an ID. "I am not tolerant of the display of your actions regarding this incident. You were out of line. Instead of defusing a situation it appears that your actions created escalation. ... I do not expect to see a repeat of this type of behavior on your part. You may come in to discuss the situation with me at my convenience." Grasty signed the summary, as did Robert Willis and Dee.

Did Ludlum come under scrutiny since she was following his orders throughout the incident? She did tend to use profanity; that was wrong. In this case, she appeared to be put in a dangerous, volatile situation where Ludlum could more appropriately have handled the males while she did whatever needed to be done at the restaurant.

A parent could have been more concerned about a son's overindulgent drinking and arrogant behavior in a public restaurant than in embarrassing an officer. His actions had forced a restaurant to close. The restaurant manager's satisfaction and the officer's concern for her own safety were not of concern when a customer's displeasure was in the balance. Dee ended up apologizing once again.

- Grasty, Karen. (5-12-99). *Memorandum Improper Procedure* to Officer Dee Jones.

Dr. Berman's description of Dee makes more sense. She was caught up in a work atmosphere, Bald-Head style.

Chapter Eighteen

The Crime Scene Re-visited

Processing a crime scene has three simple steps:
1. scene recognition,
2. scene documentation,
3. evidence collection.

Mike Byrd of the Miami-Dade Police Department stressed that "The entire investigation hinges on that first person being able to properly identify, isolate, and secure the scene."

- Byrd, Mike. *Duty Description for the Crime Scene Investigator.* Retrieved on 10-05-07 from http://www.crime-scene-investigator.net/dutydescription.html

Keith Cain was the first officer on the scene but he went into shock upon finding his partner dead. Fire Chief Kent Brown arrived shortly thereafter. He was the only one on the island with a fire arm for police back up during police night duty.

For whatever reason, Brown considered the area a "hot zone" (testimonies varied) and once EMS Danny Kiser and EMS Mike Tripp arrived on the scene in an ambulance, Brown had them remove Jones immediately from the crime scene. Testimonies here varied, too, as to Jones' condition and who said what about it when.

Then, Jones' gun was moved to a point between the truck of Brown and police department Blazer of Cain and placed on the ground between them before ending up in the floorboard of Cain's Blazer. Some testimony attributed that action to Cain's decision, some to Brown's instruction, some to a suggestion by an EMT on the scene.

So it is not clear who moved Jones' gun the first time. Grasty said that EMS Danny Kiser moved it while in a letter she later said that Fire Chief Brown directed Keith Cain to move the gun to the pavement. In Cain's first interview, he told the officer that he picked up the gun and "put it in the passenger side floor of his police Blazer without securing or examining it."

When interviewed by Lt. Gene Hardee a month later, Cain said he went and brought the gun from the dark because he feared someone might still be out there who could pick it up and use it. By January, 2000, Cain testified that he, with Brown accompanying him, went back down to recover the gun and "brought it back to where our vehicles were." There was never any controversial testimony as to how the victim's gun was moved the second time.

After Brown left the scene, Cain moved the gun to the floorboard of his Blazer.

- Cain, Keith. (11-15-99). *Interview* by Gene Hardee.
- Cain, Keith. (1-25-00). *Interview* by Monty Clark.
- Grasty, Karen. (8-29-01). *Interview* by Henry Foy.

When Brown left the area to go to the marina, Cain was once again in control of the crime scene. He was left with an unarmed Danny Kiser and they both huddled in the scant protection of his Blazer door until help from the mainland could arrive. Once Cain was relieved, he was given a GSR test, put on the ferry where he received first aid and oxygen, observed at an area hospital and then taken home. The rest of the work at the crime scene was done without the benefit of the presence and input of the first officer on the scene.

As Byrd explained, "In a scene recognition, the plan is to decide what evidence may be present, what evidence may be fragile and need to be collected as soon as possible." The scene should be secured by establishing a perimeter in order to restrict entry and protect destruction of evidence. It is usually defined by a yellow tape with black lettering. Its point is to include all primary and secondary locations while excluding non-essential personnel.

There is usually an inner perimeter where the crime actually occurred; an outer perimeter which includes the surrounding area where there are exit and entry points; and an extended perimeter where any evidence might have been thrown by the suspect(s) while fleeing the scene.

- Byrd, Mike. *Duty Description for the Crime Scene Investigator.* Retrieved on 10-05-07 from http://www.crime-scene-investigator.net/dutydescription.html
- O'Connor, Tom. *An Introduction to crime scene analysis.* Retrieved on 10/05/07 from http://faculty.ncwc.edu/TOConnor/315/315lect04.htm

The Bald Head Island crime scene tape covered the area where the two police cars sat. Daly indicated it as "an open area located at the dead end of Lighthouse Wynd, approximately 115', 2" south of the intersection of Lighthouse Wynd and Ballistic [sic] Stone Alley, 40', 6" east of the U.S. Army Survey Post-BH-2." He gave the GSP coordinates as 33.5225 north and 78.0002 west." Brunswick County Sheriff's Detective David Crocker was satisfied with the tight crime scene. He said it had given the person running the log a clear view of who went in and out, completing what task while on the scene. "Crime scene tape is for – keep people out and for – able to keep, on a log, who does make entry."

- *SBI report: crime scene on Bald Head Island.* (10-23-99). Pp. 2.
- *Buff v. Village of Bald Head Island Police Department, North Carolina League of Municipalities and North Carolina Rescue Workers Cap Death Benefits Act.* North Carolina Industrial Commission. (10-23/24-03). P. 258.

Chief Karen Grasty argued that it was too small and should cover all the area that went all the way back through the golf cart path to the marina, down both roads, and past the point where the ambulance was parked and beyond Village hall because of the alternative ways of escape.

Even though Grasty's opinion appears to be backed by a more widespread professional police procedural opinion, her words were ignored by the sheriff's department and SBI agents. The crime scene area was not expanded.

- *Buff v. Village of Bald Head Island Police Department, North Carolina League of Municipalities and North Carolina Rescue Workers Cap Death Benefits Act.* North Carolina Industrial Commission. (10-23/24-03). P. 104-105.

All things considered, it would seem obvious that the scene recognition stage was crippled from the removal of the body, the moving of the victim's gun several times and the small size of the crime scene. The following picture, taken from satellite, shows the golf cart path leading from the lighthouse at the ten o'clock position, running through woods and entering the undergrowth going towards the marina. To the right, the remnants of the pier can still be seen where a boat could have easily been tied for a quick getaway. Lighthouse Wynd runs past the chapel in a four o'clock position. Ballast Stone Alley runs away from the lighthouse in a seven o'clock position to the main road.

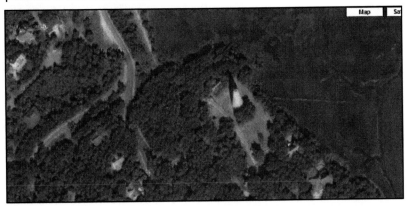

- Aerial map of Old Baldy. Retrieved 10-20-07 from http://maps.google.com/maps?ll=33.861876,-77.990138&spn=0.11,0.18&t=h

Good scene documentation allows others to take the finished work and reconstruct the events that occurred at the scene in a court room presentation. To properly document a crime scene, an investigator will take notes and reports in chronological order without opinions, analysis or conclusions. Photographs of clear overall, mid-range and close-ups will be taken. Finally, sketches will be done to document the scene. These are not done to scale but have the advantage of covering large areas and leave out clutter found in photographs. Diagrams can be drawn by eye-witnesses as well as investigators.

- Byrd, Mike. *Duty Description for the Crime Scene Investigator.* Retrieved on 10-05-07 from http://www.crime-scene-investigator.net/dutydescription.html
- Baldwin, Hayden B. *Crime Scene Processing Protocol.* Retrieved 10/05/07 from http://www.feinc.net/cs-proc.htm

Some diagrams from the scene have already been used here to help illustrate the action taking place on Bald Head Island that night.

There are two kinds of evidence; one is testimonial, the other is physical – or any other material items that are at a crime scene. Evidence may prove that a crime has been committed, help establish important elements in a crime, link a suspect with a crime or a suspect, identify a victim or a suspect, corroborate verbal testimony, or exonerate the innocent.

- Byrd, Mike. *Duty Description for the Crime Scene Investigator.* Retrieved on 10-05-07 from http://www.crime-scene-investigator.net/dutydescription.html

Evidence may be impressions such as fingerprints, tool marks, footwear, fabric impressions, tire marks, and bite marks. Forensic biology includes blood, semen, body fluids, hair, nail scraping and blood stain patterns. Trace evidence can be gunshot residue, arson, accelerant, paint, glass, and fibers. Firearms encompass weapons, gun powder patterns, casings, projectiles, fragments, pellets, waddings and cartridges.

- Byrd, Mike. *Duty Description for the Crime Scene Investigator.* Retrieved on 10-05-07 from http://www.crime-scene-investigator.net/dutydescription.html

On October 23, 1999, in the earliest minutes of the morning, the body of Officer Davina Buff Jones had been removed to the ferry landing by ambulance. According to EMS Kiser's report, he had covered Jones' body with a sheet.

- Kiser, Danny. (10-23-99). *Interview* by recording officer.

Later eyewitness accounts described her body on a gurney dockside uncovered, no sheet in sight. Perhaps there was no one guarding the officer's body. What else may have changed during that time?

Employees from Eb and Flo's were able to clearly view her body when they were ordered to gather and wait for the ferry to take them off the island due to the murder. It is not clear who gave that order although it is known that Kent Brown had gone to the ferry landing where he told the ferry captain to report any unusual activity or anyone trying to leave the marina. Then he opened up the Village Hall to be used as a headquarters, so he seems to be the one in charge until mainland officers arrived.

When the first ones did reach the island, they told him they were taking over. Brown refused to step aside and said he would assist them. He contacted C-COM and advised them they had a 10-44 (DOA). C-COM was not aware that the body had been moved from the crime scene until later on in the morning when they overheard traffic concerning the body being loaded onto the ferry.

Brown ordered the island's fire engine to the crime scene to utilize the light on the back of the truck and portable lighting to illuminate the scene. That included bringing in volunteer fire department members, some of whom had had tenacious dealings with Jones.

Police Chief Karen Grasty had been out on medical leave for months prior to Dee's death. She had been summoned to the island. Lt. Gene Hardee had been serving as the interim Chief in Grasty's absence. He had been away and just returned to his home late that afternoon when he got the call. When he arrived at Bald Head, Sheriff Hewett and his S.W.A.T. team had just landed. When Hardee and Hewett arrived at the crime scene, Hardee ordered Brown to get his firefighters and fire truck off the crime scene. Brown's actions over these two days would cause Town Manager Wade Horne to relieve Brown of his duties with the Police Auxiliary. The rift between Brown and Horne would grow wider.

- Brown, Kent. (2-11-00). *Interview* by Monty Clark.

Contrary to published reports, it was a less than coordinated landing of professionals onto the island when police did arrive from the mainland. One city police chief on the scene described it later. "It was the most chaotic thing I've ever seen in my life! There were guns everywhere. If someone had yelled, 'There he is!' there would have been bullets flying everywhere!"

- Buff, Loy and Harriett. (8-24-07). *Interview* by Elaine Buff.

Kent Brown said that after the body was moved there was no investigation done. Around 3:00 am he observed 15 deputies sitting around on the front porch of the Chandler restaurant and six or eight standing around at the lighthouse. They were drinking coffee, smoking cigarettes or spitting tobacco juice. In his personal and professional opinion, their actions showed a lack of attention to the incident and depicted an opinion that the cause of death had been decided.

- Brown, Kent. (2-11-00). *Interview* by Monty Clark.

Some officers went to the island in the honest desire to find the killer of a fellow police officer. Their devotion will always be appreciated. Their honest efforts were wasted alongside those among them who had a different agenda.

Police Chief Karen Grasty arrived at Indigo Plantation for transport to the island. Grasty requested that the State Bureau of Investigation (SBI) handle the case because that is standard procedure in the death of a police officer. SBI Special Agent Janet Storms told her that she herself was not going to the island yet, she would wait for her crime scene team to arrive.

Towboat USA, a personal towboat service, took Grasty and other officers to Bald Head. Sheriff Ronald Hewett and his S.W.A.T. team arrived shortly before her. When she met Hewett, she asked to go to the crime scene.

> "Well, don't you want to see the body first?"
> "Well, I assumed it would be at the crime scene."
> "No. It's been moved to the ferry dock."
> She said, "Why is it at the ferry dock?"
> He said, "The whole crime scene's been moved."
> "What do you mean 'moved'?"
> Hewett told Grasty when he and S.W.A.T. team had arrived, Dee's body was on the dock landing on a gurney, uncovered. They had secured her in the office, put a guard on the door and notated who came in or out.

- *Buff v. Village of Bald Head Island Police Department, North Carolina League of Municipalities and North Carolina Rescue Workers Cap Death Benefits Act.* North Carolina Industrial Commission. (10-23/24-03). P. 78.

Grasty was surprised to find Brunswick County Detective David Crocker processing Jones' hands and body. She told him not to touch Jones, the SBI would do that. He answered that he had been requested to process the body for gunshot residue by Janet Storms. Storms had authorized him to do so. Storms would later tell Grasty that "David was fully qualified and that she had authorized that because the Brunswick County detectives were so good that they (the SBI) let them do SBI investigations in Brunswick County." Furthermore, Crocker told Grasty "that Brunswick County would do the investigation and process evidence."

- Grasty, Karen. (nd). *Letter* to Caddell. P. 4.
- Grasty, Karen. (8-29-01). *Interview* by Henry Foy. P. 2.

Crocker himself testified that due to the weather causing such high seas, he wanted to take the GSR test on the island because he was concerned about losing evidence from the body during the crossing.

He apparently wasn't so worried about the other evidence on the body when he later was intending to send it uncovered on the high deck of the ferry for the twenty minute trip to Southport. Nor, apparently, did the steady stream of visitors into the 'secured' area where Davina's body lay bother him.

From 1:15 am until 2:18 am eighteen people found their way into the tiny ferry landing office to look at her. Sylvia Timmons (a Village Council member and EMS), Shipmate McKellar from the ferry, Shallotte Police Chief Rodney Gause, Brunswick County Sheriff's Department Sergeant Randy Robinson, Lt. John Ingram, EMS John Johnson, EMS Brian Johnson, EMS Trish Brown, ferry Captain Rodney Melton and finally, at 1:24 am, Lt. Gene Hardee were all listed as 'with the body.'. Trish Brown had been at the scene. Except for Hardee, none of the rest of these 'visitors' had any police expertise or reason to be with in the vicinity of Jones' body.

　　While the Brunswick County Sheriff's Department went about doing their work, inquiry teams of David Grasty, David Cox, Robin Wallace and other Bald Head Island Officers checked all persons leaving and entering the island until the next morning. Gene Hardee and Bald Head Island Police sat up checkpoints at different intersections from and to ferry access later in the evening of Saturday and for several days.

- Grasty, Karen. (8-29-01). *Interview* by Henry Foy.

The official police 'canvass' was actually a questionnaire filled out by those leaving the island the next day and a 'search' that was effectively ended around 3:00 am Saturday morning when the decision of suicide had already been made. The fact is, SBI agents did not arrive on Bald Head Island until around 4:35 am on October 23rd. Bald Head Island Police officers and Brunswick County Sheriff's Department Investigators were in charge prior to that.

- Clark testimony. *Buff v. Village of Bald Head Island Police Department, North Carolina League of Municipalities and North Carolina Rescue Workers Cap Death Benefits Act.* North Carolina Industrial Commission. (10-23/24-03).
- U.S.Department Of Justice Office Of Justice Programs Bureau Of Justice Assistance Public Safety Officers' Benefits In The Matter OF: Police Officer Davina Buff-Jones Appeal Hearing PSOB Claim #00-48. January 18, 2003. P. 40.

At 1:40 am Detective Crocker and Detective Sam Davis, Sheriff Hewett, EMS Michael Tripp, EMS Danny Kiser and Fire Chief Kent Brown were with the body. This audience is understandable, given that these people are the vanguard of the police on the island who would work with the SBI once they got to the island. At 2:08 am Chief Grasty again returned to the body and Lt. Gene Hardee returned at 2:18 before the body was transported at 2:21 am.

It is interesting to note that while all of this activity was taking place, no one had notified C-COM of any activity concerning the moving of the body or its imminent transfer to the mainland, not to mention the visitation taking place on the island.

Detective Sam Davis took pictures of Dee's body on the gurney in the ticket office. SBI Special Agent Daly arrived with other

SBI agents and documented the crime scene location by GSP coordinates, noted the crime scene tape, noted that a crime scene log was being maintained, documented the weather conditions as clear with a temperature of approximately 55° Fahrenheit.

Daly noted two vehicles within the crime scene tape. One was a 1995 Ford Ranger pickup truck, white in color, NC permanent registration 39694-R, VIN1FTDR15UOSTA31470, NC inspection sticker 54,776,186 esp. 6/2000 registered to Village of Bald Head Island said to have been operated by Jones of the night of Friday, October 22, 1999. It is the truck in the distance in this crime scene photograph. The second vehicle, shown in the foreground, was a 1996 Chevrolet Blazer, white in color, NC permanent registration 27475-R, VINIGNDT13W9T2270925, registered to the Village of Bald Head Island, said to have been operated by Officer Keith Cain of the Bald Head Island police Department at the time Jones' body was found.

Daly noted the large pool of blood and listed its center approximately 40'6" east of the United States Army Survey Marker BH2 behind the picket fence in the marsh area and approximately

115'2" south of the intersection of Lighthouse Wynd and Ballast Stone Alley.

At 5:40 am Daly observed Detective Sam Davis of the Brunswick County Sheriff's Department photographing the crime scene. Less than an hour later, Daly seized from the floorboard of Cain's Blazer, a Glock brand, model #23 semi-automatic, .40 caliber handgun, serial #AEB224, which had been issued to and was in the possession of Officer Jones at the time of her death. He removed the magazine and counted 12 live bullets with one in the chamber.

Davis was listed as being the locator of the shell casing between the sixth and seventh rung of the picket fence. Davis sketched the crime scene and also processed both the left driver's door and left front quarter panel of Jones' vehicle. Further, the report states that Davis 'lifted numerous latent prints, which were collected and bagged.'

According to the report, by 12:35 pm, Davis departed by ferry for his return to Southport. The crime scene no longer existed, it had been washed down by the fire department. At 1:10 pm Daly transferred items of evidence seized by Davis over to Detective Marlow of the Brunswick County Sheriff's Department, via an SBI 69-B.

The items were the following:

1. A yellow post-it note from the victim's book bag
2. A note from the victim's book bag
3. A planner calendar from the victim's book bag
4. A paper towel with a telephone number from the victim's book bag
5. A Glock, model 23 .40 semi-automatic handgun serial #AEB224 and a Glock magazine
6. 12 Smith & Wesson Speer .40 caliber bullets from the victim's gun
7. 1 .40 caliber spent shell casing from the ground near the pool of blood
8. Eight latent lifts from the driver's side door and the left front quarter panel of the victim's vehicle along with a set of victim's fingerprints provided by the Bald Head Island Police Department.

- *SBI report: crime scene on Bald Head Island.* (10-23-99). Pp. 1-5.

Although Crocker testified he was concerned about losing evidence on the crossover due to the turbulent weather, Brunswick County detectives were intending to send Dee's body across the river uncovered, Grasty, with the help of her husband, sandwiched the body between sheets and pinned them together. Further, she provided the escort to accompany the body on the crossing. Once the body arrived at the morgue, the following items were listed as being seized by SBI Special Agent Storms at Dosher Hospital.

1. One set of keys (3 keys)
2. One black leather ID containing operator's license & $4
3. One tube of cherry chap stick
4. One Glock. 40-caliber magazine with 13 live rounds

- Storms, Janet. (10-23-99). *Transportation of Jones' body/Observation of coroner report.* Pp. 1-2.

Storms observed and searched Jones' personal vehicle parked in the northeast end of the lot "A" space "2". The 1994 gray/silver Nissan extended cab pickup truck was searched on Saturday morning, October 23, 1999, beginning at 9:12 am. The search ended at 9:41 am with no items being seized.

- Storms, Janet. (10-23-99). *Report: Search of Davina Buff Jones' Nissan truck.*

This is parking lot A where Dee's truck was parked when it was searched by SBI Agent Storms.

Chapter Nineteen

The Sexual Harassment Suit

Soon after Dee was hired, her training officer Robert Willis told her that Mike Ilvento had been asking about her marital status and such. Ilvento was an EMS based at the island fire station next door to the police station. He was of Italian descent with a scar on one side of his face, short in stature and known by some on the island as "the Troll."

- Hewett, William L. (2-08-00) *Interview* by Monty Clark.

Willis told Jones if Ilvento asked about Dee again, Ilvento would be "very sorry." In late February or early March, Jones answered a call at Eb and Flo's.

The manager there was having a cardiac event. Dee was too short to hold the saline bag and someone else taller had to take the bag from her. When the patient was all right, Ilvento took his right hand and rubbed it across her shoulders once or twice and down the outside part of Jones' left arm and uttered, "Thank you, Dee." She could not understand why he was thanking her because she felt she had been unable to help in the situation. She did not like the manner in which he had touched her. She reported the incident to Chief Grasty when she got back to the police station. Grasty told Dee she would speak to Fire Chief Brown about the matter. A few days later, Brown asked Dee is she had had any more trouble with Ilvento. She told him no.

There was a money-raising event on the island for the Special Olympics. Dee was serving food when Ilvento came through the line. He received a plate of food from her, winked, and took a seat across a space from her. When she looked up, he winked at her again. At this time there was no verbal communication and Dee did not report the incident.

On August 7th police and EMS responded to a call concerning a child at the Chandler Building. He had fallen off a golf cart earlier in the day but was now unresponsive. According to Dee's written account, when she arrived on the scene, the child was seated on his mother's lap, straddling the woman's waist and leaning against her torso. Robert Willis and Mike Ilvento arrived almost immediately. Dee stood before the mother with the child's weight remaining supported by the mother's lap with the child's back being leaned against Jones' torso. Dee immobilized his head through the use of her two hands, the boy's head approximately at her waistline.

Ilvento proceeded to fit the child's neck with a cervical collar but it was the wrong size and had to be removed. When he was fitting the second collar, Ilvento's hand moved down from Jones' waist area, slipped in the area of her vagina and moved around for several seconds. Then he came back up, finished attaching the collar. When he was finished, Jones and Willis got ready to move the gurney with the child on it to the ambulance. Thinking that Ilvento was following the gurney, Dee pushed the gurney so quickly when leaving, Willis, who was guiding from the front, admonished her to slow down.

The officers were driving separate vehicles, but as soon as they had returned to the station, Dee immediately reported to Willis what Ilvento had done. Willis was not only her immediate supervisor but also her corporal. She added that if he ever did it again, she was going to arrest him. Willis' response was that it was obviously a mistake and he urged her to "let it go." Jones said nothing else to others thinking that Willis would follow through with the appropriate channels and reports.

Later Jones attended a "feel-good" committee meeting around August 8th with Ilvento, Josann Campanello, Heather Hardee and two other women. During the meeting Ilvento was taciturn and called away on an emergency call. After he had gone, Dee expressed the wish that he wasn't on the committee. Josann lectured her about the bad relations between the police and fire departments. Though she didn't give details, Jones talked about her trouble with Ilvento. The women urged her to report the problem. Dee then reported the matter to Gene Hardee who told her to write it up. She did so in a letter dated September 8, 1999. After her death, the letter and all copies disappeared. Dee's copy was in a bag taken by SBI Agent Janet Storms from Loy Buff. Putting the matter into print was not one Dee welcomed, but it was one that Hardee demanded that she do.

- Jones, Davina Buff. (10-18-99). *Interview* by William Fairley.

Her boyfriend Scott knew that the ordeal had created a great pressure on her. "I do remember that she made the comment – she came home very upset at one point and was telling me that they didn't take her serious [sic] and she didn't think anything was going to happen and that she felt like she was being railroaded into – just brushing this under the carpet. She felt the village management, not the police was trying to stonewall and try to get her fired."

- *Buff v. Village of Bald Head Island Police Department, North Carolina League of Municipalities and North Carolina Rescue Workers Cap Death Benefits Act.* North Carolina Industrial Commission. (10-23/24-03). P. 450.

According to her friend Will Hewett, Dee was anxious to get the matter resolved. She felt it was necessary because she didn't want it to happen to anyone else.

- *Buff v. Village of Bald Head Island Police Department, North Carolina League of Municipalities and North Carolina Rescue Workers Cap Death Benefits Act.* North Carolina Industrial Commission. (10-23/24-03). P. 493.

She talked to Grasty, who was home on sick leave, to Gene Hardee, Heather Hardee, Kent Brown and then filed a formal complaint. Dee told her sister Beverly that she wanted to do the right thing in seeing that this guy was held accountable for his actions, especially given the position he held. She was not interested in a lawsuit, just in making sure he was disciplined. According to Dee, the situation at work started to decline from that point.

- Sadler, Beverly Buff. (October, 1999). *Davina "Dee" Elaine Buff Jones: Reflections on her life and death.*

Dee discussed the situation with her mother several days before Dee died. "She was determined that she was going to protect anybody that came into contact with him since he was an EMS. And she was to the point that she thought that was more important than worrying about getting fired. She was adamant about that because she could have easily thrown up her hands and protected her job and everything like that, but that wasn't Davina."

- *Buff v. Bureau of Justice Assistance Public Safety Officers' Benefits.* (1-18-03). P. 51.

Gene Hardee and Kent Brown talked by telephone with Karen Grasty concerning Dee's charge. They decided to have the island's attorney William Fairley investigate her accusations. At the time of the 2003 hearing, there was no information in Jones' personnel file concerning the case but Hardee denied knowing anything about expungement of information from Jones' personnel file. The hand written account that Dee had provided had a copy in the materials confiscated by SBI Agent Storms, but she denied having it. When Loy Buff tried to get it from William Fairley, the Village attorney, Fairley told Buff he would never get it or any other material concerning the case.

- *Buff v. Village of Bald Head Island Police Department, North Carolina League of Municipalities and North Carolina Rescue Workers Cap Death Benefits Act.* North Carolina Industrial Commission. (10-23/24-03). P. 34-38.

Jones' desk calendar for September showed on September 12th she started "nights with Keith on 6 pm boat." The 14th she had to catch the 7:00 am boat for a meeting with Wade Horne and Gene Hardee. On the 26th she had an appointment at Bill Fairley's office.

- Jones, Davina Buff. (1999). *Work calendar.*

Dee was upset by the interview with Fairley. She felt that he unduly forced her to go over embarrassing details and had a stenographer there who recorded every move she made. It was after this ordeal that she contacted the Fraternal Order of Police (F.O.P.) attorney to represent her. The Bald Head Island police and management hit the ceiling when they found out she had contacted them. They railed about her not going through proper channels.

At the end of the month Jones again had a complaint lodged against her. This one was brought about by her own lack of judgment. One of her buddies who was a Bald Head Island transportation employer who engaged in horseplay with her frequently. It included verbally insulting and sparring with each other.

During this particular time, she used profanity and unsnapped her holster, placing her hand on her weapon. Unbeknownst to them, the whole incident was caught on tape by a tourist who lodged a complaint about what they had seen. It had taken place on a ramp at the dock. The complaint took Dee totally by surprise. She could not believe it had been blown so totally out of proportion. By this time, the situation in which she found herself was dissipating rapidly and any opportunity would be seized to bring her before the powers that be as being incompetent.

- *Buff v. Village of Bald Head Island Police Department, North Carolina League of Municipalities and North Carolina Rescue Workers Cap Death Benefits Act.* North Carolina Industrial Commission. (10-23/24-03). P. 454.

The doctor had put Dee on Zoloft and then changed that Effexor to help her handle the increasing stress in her life, mainly from her job. Her aunt gave her advice from California. "As far as the job goes, welcome to the real world. It is so hard to find out how much people talk about doing the right thing and how quickly money and position make some people above the rules. ... And try not to join them but to be the example of doing the right thing." Further on in the letter, her aunt urged her to persevere as she had so many times before in her life. "As long as you continue to know what is really right and when you are doing as told, you will be able to make it."

- Hale, Pat. (10-06-99). *Letter* to Dee.

On October 9th Jones helped some adults get their golf cart unstuck in an area near the South's then new construction site. The two had been shell hunting. Dee advised them to use the beach access or use Middle Island to hunt shells. Later she received a call from C-COM. They told her that the sea-shell lady had called in to thank the officer that got her cart out of the sand and to say that she was the nicest officer/person she'd ever met.

On the same day, the officer gave an island resident a verbal warning for running a stop sign. He became verbally abusive because "12-year olds are driving around!" She suggested that they should try to set an example for the tourists. The gentleman grew highly upset. A member of the Bald Head Island transportation group observed the stop and warned Dee later that the man would complain. He did.

Eventually Dee found out that Kent Brown never did talk to Mike Ilvento. In fact, Ilvento knew nothing of her complaint. She contacted Norman MacCloud, her local Fraternal Order of Police (FOP) representative for help, telling him that she didn't want to sue, she just wanted advice. The fire department, shown in a 2007 picture, has been located right beside the police department site from the time Dee and Ilvento worked on the island. He was always right next door to her. The situation made her feel uncomfortable.

During a cookout at the home of Karen Grasty, Dee told the chief she needed to talk to her in private. Then she told Grasty about speaking to MacCloud. Grasty was not happy. She told Dee that Robert Willis had been written up because of the way he had (or had not) handled her complaint in the beginning. She added that Dee's notifying FOP or anyone else outside the department was an offense for which Dee could be fired. That served to immediately frighten Dee. But once Dee had gotten upset, Grasty told Dee that she wouldn't fire her.

Grasty informed Dee that MacCloud had been incorrect in telling Dee that she could sue Grasty and the village. Grasty said he was only telling Dee that because he wanted to 'get into her pants.' The only one Dee could sue, Grasty explained, was Robert Willis.

Additionally, Grasty warned that it was Dee's word against Mike's and that two other witnesses, one of them a village council member and EMS, Sylvia Timmons, had been questioned and said she had seen nothing.

All of this was a shock to Dee. She had not been told that any of this had occurred; she had been kept in the dark about the questioning. Actually, the lawyer investigating the problem for the county listed the date of his interview with Timmons as occurring on October 22, so how Grasty knew what Timmons would say is unknown; however, the incident and Grasty's veiled threat really upset Jones.

As if she didn't have enough trouble already, on October 8th Dee wrote a citation at 11:30 am for a driver consuming a malt beverage. When she got to the police station, Lt. Gene Hardee called her into his office, locked the outside door and started a recorder. He began questioning her about the horseplay incident on the dock. Dee wrote, "I was taken aback by the complaint. The

164

incident was 'horseplay' and exploded into unreal information being reported."

Later in the day, the gentleman who had received the ticket for consumption that morning called complaining. He wanted the citation voided because he had been told he could drink and drive a golf cart. He didn't say by whom.

Lt. Hardee talked to Dee about voiding the ticket, but she said no. "I wasn't going to void another ALE citation. ... He, being disappointed in me, advised I call the man and tell him how to pay the citation." Hardee told her that if the man decided to protest the citation, the attorney would embarrass her in court. "I told Lt. Hardee that it didn't matter. I'd call the man. I did."

Hardee was "quite cold" to her all day yet requested that she take him by golf cart to the landing so he could catch the 5:30 pm boat. On the way to the ferry he told her that the Village Manager had asked him to notify her that William Fairley, the Village attorney, would be coming to ask her questions about Ilvento. He said that the earlier taped conversation was to stay between her, him and the chief. Actually, Dee ended up having to present herself in Fairley's office where she endured a rather contentious grilling under the watchful scrutiny of a stenographer.

Before her shift ended, she was waylaid by an island restaurant waitress who spoke to Dee in private about problems she was having with Kent Brown. She confided, "He touches and hugs me and makes comments about sexuality when his wife is not around." No wonder he had such a problem talking to Ilvento about such matters.

Once Dee got home, she called Norman MacCloud and requested the number of the F.O.P. attorney. She really had not wanted the incident to get this far but felt she now had little choice..

"Though I wanted to keep things to a minimum, I couldn't. It would be unfair for me to be questioned without someone to advise <u>me</u>."

- Jones, Davina Buff. (10-04-99). *Journal entry.*
- Jones, Davina Buff. (10-08099). *Journal entry.*

She felt she had been backed into a corner. She had been.

Chapter Twenty

No Riding Alone

On October 13, 1999, Keith Cain and Dee were on duty when Corporal Willis delivered an envelope and two additional memos to them. The envelope contained a short notice concerning shift responsibilities. It was addressed to both officers from Gene Hardee with a copy to Wade Horne.

> EFFECTIVE THIS AM, OFFICER JONES WILL RIDE WITH OFFICER CAIN AT ALL TIMES. OFFICER JONES WILL COMPLETE ALL THE REQUIRED PAPERWORK DURING THE TOUR OF DUTY. OFFICER CAIN WILL SUPERVISE AT ALL TIMES AND WILL CORRECT ANY INAPPROPRIATE ACTIONS IN A CONSTRUCTIVE AND PROFESSIONAL MANNER.

- Hardee, Gene. (10-13-99). *Memo: Shift responsibilities.*

This is in direct opposition to the memo Grasty had sent out on January 14, 1999. "When there are two officers working, I want you in separate vehicles."

- Grasty, Karen. (1-14-99). *Direct order.*

This is the order that in effect demoted Dee back to being an officer in training. The October 13th order is the one that so many people had trouble remembering after Dee was killed. There were many explanations for it according to whom you asked: it didn't mean that she couldn't go off by herself to take a break or a ride or a smoke; it was taken out of context; it was lifted. Dee never, ever told anyone it had been lifted. It was quite to the contrary, as far as she was concerned. If it was lifted, it was lifted after she had been killed.

The Wednesday it was delivered, Dee felt as if Willis tried to get a rise out of her, hanging around for a few minutes after the two partners had read the memo, asking if they had any questions although he had already said he did not know the reason for the envelope. About 7:08 the phone rang and Willis answered. He kept saying, "Sir," "Not as of yet," "Seems fine," and "Yes, sir."

Dee worked in the office while Cain took Willis to catch the 7:30 am boat. Then Cain had to attend a Public Safety meeting at the Village Hall at 8:30 am. It was nearly 10:00 am when inactive Chief Grasty called from home. She asked how things were going that morning. Dee replied, "Your typical Wednesday morning." After a pause Grasty asked if Lt. Hardee had talked to the partners that morning. Dee answered no, but Corporal Willis had.

Grasty said she had called to explain her decision because she knew Dee would be upset. The decision was not to be viewed as a reflection on Dee but Grasty was putting all new officers back into training. They had been told different things and led in wrong directions. She assured Dee it was for her benefit and not to be upset. She said Dee needed more training, that things hadn't gone as well as she had hoped because Grasty had been out on sick leave. She asked if Dee had any questions.

"My response was a change in subject concerning Sunday's medical call." Grasty answered that she didn't believe the complaint (about Dee's speeding in the truck), calling it "bullshit." Dee then asked if a particular drug agent had called. He had paged her earlier in the week about doing some work with him. The police chief answered that she had declined the request. The negative answer cut across Davina's grain but she held her tongue as Grasty explained to Dee that Dee needed more experience first, that Grasty did not trust the Brunswick County Sheriff Department drug units and therefore, Grasty had turned down their request that Dee work with them.

"I then brought up that if she wanted me to get more experience, this would be perfect and that I trusted the agents." Grasty hesitated and again said no. Dee fell silent. Desultory comments went back and forth about the health of each other and then more silence. Grasty again told Jones not to be upset and to call if she had any questions. Then the call ended.

- Hardee, Gene. (10-13-99). *Memo: Shift responsibilities.*
- Jones, Davina Buff. (10-13-99). *Journal entry.*

Dee's doctor knew what effect this order had had on her. "Jones was very upset that she could not write any tickets without getting permission form another officer." Jones told him that she had to have that officer riding with her at all times.

- Reschley, Keith. (11-14-03). *Disposition.* P. 3.

She had discussed the situation with her friend Laura in Texas. Laura related that Dee's partner Keith Cain had warned Dee that "they were trying to get rid of her, that she should be careful." Laura believed that this directive and its effect of returning her to rookie status hurt Dee more than anything else that was done to her on the job to this point.

- Atkins, Laura. (10-27-07). *Telephone interview* by Elaine Buff.

When Skoler questioned Grasty about the directive, her response was:

> I think maybe that was taken out of context. There had been some discussion prior to, you know about some things that she thought she needed to improve in some areas based on, you know, who she as a training officer. Not based on her performance, but based on what she felt uncomfortable doing and some things that she didn't feel right about. I think a lot of the problem came in as far as who they had as a supervisor at the time on the island during my absence. Now I don't know in what context it was taken

between her, her doctor and whomever, but that was the reason for it on my understanding.

- *Buff v. Bureau of Justice Assistance Public Safety Officers' Benefits.* (1-18-03). Pp. 24-25.

During the 2003 hearing, Grasty was asked if the move had had anything to do with the fire tape, Ilvento, or Taussig incidents.

No, actually, the way it was relayed that she was still in training ... and she and Gene Hardee had sat down and talked and I had talked with the three of them on the phone that it would probably be to her benefit to have another officer with her on any kind of calls or anything – for her benefit, to stop this kind of thing and for her to have a witness on her behalf, so to speak, so that she wouldn't have this sort of thing of he-said, she-said, going back and forth, because the island was the world's worst for it."

- *Buff v. Village of Bald Head Island Police Department, North Carolina League of Municipalities and North Carolina Rescue Workers Cap Death Benefits Act.* North Carolina Industrial Commission. (10-23/24-03). P. 153.

For it not to have had anything to do with the complaints that had been levied against Jones, she certainly seemed to refer to those situations a lot. Grasty added, "She could drive alone, you know, if she drove the pick-up. ... So you know, it wasn't under command that she had to ride with someone all the time."

- *Buff v. Village of Bald Head Island Police Department, North Carolina League of Municipalities and North Carolina Rescue Workers Cap Death Benefits Act.* North Carolina Industrial Commission. (10-23/24-03). P. 154.

This would seem directly opposed to what Scott Monzon described as Dee's reaction. During the 2003 hearing, Tanoury asked Monzon if he knew Dee had been told she was not allowed to drive alone. Monzon answered in the affirmative. Tanoury asked him what she had said about it.

SM: Just that she was told not to answer calls – if I

remember it right, she was told not to answer calls by herself – not to drive to a call by herself.

DT: Did she tell you why that restriction was placed on her?

SM: No. And from what I understand, she didn't understand why.

- *Buff v. Village of Bald Head Island Police Department, North Carolina League of Municipalities and North Carolina Rescue Workers Cap Death Benefits Act.* North Carolina Industrial Commission. (10-23/24-03). P. 479.

Dee never understood why she was placed under this order, much less said anything about Gene Hardee and she sitting down talking about anything she needed to improve. She wrote about the times Hardee and she talked, but she never discussed this. The directive was a total shock to her.

Dee kept saying she had to have someone with her at all times. There was never any written indication that the order was lifted before she died. The only problem occurred when her partner let her leave the station on the night she died. If it hadn't been lifted, why did he allow her to leave? Also, on October 13th Grasty sent Horne an email that addressed the directive. "I think the decision to put Officer Jones back under another officer for additional training was a very good one. We'll discuss this further during my visit next week."

- Grasty, Karen. (10-13-99). *Email* to Wade Horne.

It is almost as if, once Davina was dead, no one wanted to admit that this order had ever existed. Of course, if it had existed, then someone had some explaining to do concerning why Dee was allowed to leave by herself halfway through her shift. Perhaps that was why everyone's memory got so cloudy.

Keith Cain had an even harder time with his memory. When Monty Clark, the Buff's private investigator questioned him, they had the following conversation.

MC: Did you have any knowledge or recollection of Dee being advised not to drive by herself?

KC: She had ridden with me for a while then, but the last I heard, she was allowed to ride on her own if she wanted to.

MC: Do you remember any directives or any orders from Chief Grasty or Lt. Hardee at that time about Dee not riding by herself in a vehicle because of an incident involving her going to [sic] fast or something like that?

KC: All I know is that we had been riding together for a while. *I don't know why.* (My emphasis).

MC: Did Dee ever make any remarks about having to go back and have a training officer, of having to ride with somebody? Did she ever say anything to you or talk to you about that?

KC: Ummm ... I know sometimes she liked to be able to just do what she wanted to. I wasn't her training officer either.

MC: But nobody had given you any direct orders that she is not to be riding by herself?

KC: No.

MC: Nothing like that at all?

KC: Just kind of keep my eye on her and make sure everything is all right.

MC: So to the best of your knowledge, it was okay for her to drive alone?

KC: Yes

MC: You made a statement a few minutes ago that you were told to look after her or something like that.

KC: I mean ... everybody ...

MC: Everybody looks after everybody, yeah ... Had you been given specific orders or requests to sort of take care of her?

KC: I told her myself ... just settle down a little bit ... don't relax but ... every time we catch somebody you don't have to ...

MC: Pound their heads down ... (both laughing) ... I understand.

- Cain, Keith. (1-25-00). *Interview* by Monty Clark. Pp. 11-12.

When Cain testified in 2003, he said of Jones, "I was told to keep an eye on her." He thought he clarified the situation with this comment. "Just try and watch over her, help her out on calls."

- *Buff v. Village of Bald Head Island Police Department, North Carolina League of Municipalities and North Carolina Rescue Workers Cap Death Benefits Act.* North Carolina Industrial Commission. (10-23/24-03). P. 230.

Jones herself had clearly reacted to the order and written about it. Her ex-boyfriend Scott Monzon had not forgotten either. Two days after the shooting he told Lt. Gene Caison of BCSD about the directive. "One of the memos to Dee was that she was to ride with Keith Cain at all times and she would not be allowed to issue any citations to anyone without her senior officer first approving the citation."

- Monzon, Scott. (10-24-99). *Interview* by Gene Caison. P. 3.

When being interviewed by Monty Clark, Monzon wanted to know, "Why was she by herself? She showed me a memo where she wasn't supposed to be by herself."

- Monzon, Scott. (2-10-00). *Interview* by Monty Clark. P. 22.

Monzon did reiterate that Dee had had trouble with the village management. "They wanted her just to be a security guard, just someone to be there and respond to calls, but not be an outgoing officer and try to find violations – criminal violations – and write citations and make arrests."

- *Buff v. Village of Bald Head Island Police Department, North Carolina League of Municipalities and North Carolina Rescue Workers Cap Death Benefits Act.* North Carolina Industrial Commission. (10-23/24-03). P. 451.

There certainly was an order telling Jones she could not write tickets without approval. She could not ride alone any more. She was to complete all the paperwork during the shift. How could Keith Cain conveniently forget all of those details?

And how could everyone else?

From beyond the grave, Davina has produced the proof by leaving her copy of the hated directive behind, so we know now that it did without doubt exist.

It does pose an interesting question.

Why *was* Jones by herself?

Chapter Twenty One

Sun-Drenched Drugs and Moonlit Money

The federal Drug Enforcement Agency (DEA) had asked for Bald Head Island Police cooperation in a drug suspect surveillance operation. Chief Grasty said she had been told by Village Manager Wade Horne "not to speak of it further." She thinks protecting the island's reputation was the concern. Dee had done two undercover training sessions with the Carolina Beach Police Department in March and April of 1999.

- *Buff v. North Carolina Law Enforcement Officers and Rescue Workers Death Benefit Act and North Carolina Contingency and Emergency Fund.*

During her regular work hours, Dee had observed and noted some activity she thought centered around bona fide drug activity; some were large enough to involve suitcases of money being exchanged for drug deliveries at the lighthouse after dark. "She told me several months before she was killed, she got information that they were making big drug deals down by the lighthouse. not quarter bags, kilos, big suitcases of money were being transferred. She told me, 'I'm gonna make me a good drug bust.'"

- Monzon, Scott. (2-10-00). *Interview* by Monty Clark. P. 23.

In the waning weeks of September, Dee had saved two children from drowning and had accompanied them to Dosher Hospital to make sure they were going to be all right. But such acts of heroism were not going to save her job. She had antagonized too many people by refusing to void lawfully written (and earned) citations, she had embarrassed village council members by not letting them have their own way, and now she was stepping on important and dangerous toes concerning drug traffic.

Dee and her sister Tanya had a long day together in early October. At one point they discussed Dee's job in detail. Dee was unhappy with being told to look the other way a lot by her superiors. She also told her sister that there were certain people that she had been told she needed to stay away from but she didn't give any names."

- *Buff v. North Carolina Law Enforcement Officers and Rescue Workers Death Benefit Act and North Carolina Contingency and Emergency Fund.*

On the morning of her death, her younger sister Beverly talked to Dee on the telephone from Charlotte. Dee called Beverly around 11:30 am. During the conversation, Dee talked to both of her nieces and about her other sister's pregnancy. They both believed it was going to be a boy. Dee and Tanya were working together to train a horse named Apache that Dee had bought from Tanya and Dee was pleased with how that was going.

Beverly asked how things were going on the job. At first, Dee merely said things were okay, but under pressure from Beverly, Dee began to talk about her disappointment in the complaints about her job performance and that she felt it had started because of her complaint about the sexual harassment. But Beverly pressed harder about how Dee really felt. "Do you feel hopeless, or do you see a better day ahead?"

Dee said she did. "Yes, I know things will get better eventually – maybe not here. I'm putting in applications in other places like Asheville and Greensboro." Dee told Beverly that she had kicked Scott out. He wanted her to wait for him until he could tell if things were going to work out with his ex-wife. She had laughed at that. She told about him wanting to bring their laundry to her house to use her washer and dryer. She had told him to forget it!

Then Dee talked about Adam and Precious. She described in detail to Beverly how she had rigged a cover for the back door so they could go out and in while she was on night duty. Beverly suggested they stay outside, to which Dee defensively said, "No!" They were getting on in age; Adam was ten and Precious was nine. Both had arthritis and Dee wanted them where they could be warm. The conversation between the sisters lasted between thirty and forty-five minutes.

- Sadler, Beverly Buff. (October, 1999). *Davina "Dee" Elaine Buff Jones: Reflections on her life and death.*

It certainly would appear that there had been rising pressure on Dee to quit her job. There had certainly been an effort to paint her as a bad or ineffective police officer, especially after she had pursued the problem with Ilvento. There was one final trump to play against Dee. She was placed on night shift.

From Gene Hardee's perspective, it was done because the complaints had come in the daytime and she was under a lot of pressure and being out in public more in the day might be contributing to her problems. "Maybe you would want to go on night shift for a while to get out form under some of this pressure. And then … just lay low for awhile."

- *Buff v. Village of Bald Head Island Police Department, North Carolina League of Municipalities and North Carolina Rescue Workers Cap Death Benefits Act. North Carolina Industrial Commission.* (10-23/24-03). P. 154.

Her October time sheet showed the original night shift was to be from October 8th through October 19th but apparently this decision elongated her night duty hours.

- Jones, Davina Buff. *Work Desk October Calendar.*

"She told me once that she did not like night shift because she had difficulty sleeping during the daytime hours." Will Hewett also talked about the hard time Dee had staying awake. "She was trying to stay up until 2 or 3 in the morning. That way her sleep schedule wouldn't be messed up." She did not like having to leave the dogs alone at night either. However, it did allow her to observe what went on in some places without being detected quite as easily.

- Grasty, Karen. (nd). *FBI Questionnaire*. P. 10.
- Hewett, William L. (2-08-00) *Interview* by Monty Clark. P. 37.

The night shift on October 22nd was uneventful until the strange call from the River Pilot Café. According to Dee's notes the trip from the police station to the restaurant should have taken around five minutes yet when the partners arrived at the restaurant, not only were the owners of the missing cart not there, the whole restaurant was empty and locked. Supposedly the cart owners were requesting police drive them home, yet there was no one to be found but the workers waxing the floors.

It is not known if the police actually checked out the call to see if it had come from the hostess at the café. The call did not go to C-COM as reported in the papers. They had no idea as to the call until Dee called in asking if they had any further information. It was the first time Dee and Keith separated during the evening, driving in separate vehicles to the café. She was not supposed to drive according to the order Grasty, Horne, and Hardee had placed her under just days earlier – this was a call. Yet she drove, investigated by herself, drove with Cain in his vehicle to the lighthouse and then drove without him on a separate route back to the police station. Days later the golf cart left at the lighthouse was supposedly claimed by its rightful owner, but no information has been forthcoming as to its owner or the owner of the golf cart allegedly missing from the restaurant that night.

Jones had left a ferry pass for a narcotics drug agent to visit her on October 22nd to see what he thought of the drug traffic she was seeing. It sounds as if she was expecting some kind of drug activity to take place that night if she wanted his presence there with her to verify her discovery.

- Griffin, Anna. (6-02-02). Murder or suicide. *The Charlotte Observer*. P. 13A.

She did leave the police station and go to the ferry landing to call Scott Monzon from a pay phone. The call was short, lasting scarcely a minute. Witnesses saw her walk the dock, surveying some activity going on there.

Although he denied being on the island that night, we know the drug agent did present the pass Dee gave him at the ferry landing at Indigo. Also the daughter of Chief Grasty worked at Eb and Flo's at the time. She saw the man dressed in camouflage on the island before Dee was killed. She never came forward to testify to that fact. As a matter of fact, he was seen after the killing as well. It was not in the role of being an investigative officer later with the sheriff.

- Buff, Loy and Harriet. (8-24-06). *Interview* by Elaine Buff.

For whatever reason, it would seem that he was on the island but he did not want Davina to know that. Not finding him on the docks after the last ferry, Dee left the area. On the way to the lighthouse, she stopped a few seconds to tell the three vacationers in a golf cart that they were on the wrong side of the road. Then she went on to the lighthouse. Theoretically she was probably still searching, believing that her drug agent friend had gone on to where they were going to watch the drug traffic at the lighthouse. Or she was intending to have a cigarette at the lighthouse before returning to the station.

Officer Jones' last transmissions were captured by C-COM, the county communications center. Shift Supervisor Michelle Carter had advised SBI agents that she and Terri Clark, who had been the telecommunicator that night, would be available to assist with any questions regarding the radio traffic in reference to the investigation.

- *SBI report: crime scene on Bald Head Island.* (10-23-99). Pp. 1-5.

The dispatcher arrived at the hearing in 2003, ready to testify and both attorneys assured the hearing officer that she had nothing to add and dismissed her. The attorney for the Buffs at that time goes hunting with the man who was the then Attorney General and was keeping law records for both the man and his lawyer wife in his law office in Brunswick County while the Attorney General and his wife were in Raleigh. He abruptly quit representing the Buffs after winning the 2003 hearing.

Channel One is the primary one most Brunswick County officers used in 1999. Channel 2 was used by some officers because it was clearer to C-COM. Bald Head island was one of those areas. Its traffic, while clearer at C-COM, wouldn't be heard by those on Channel One. When Dee first said, "Show me out with three," she was on Channel One. She switched the channel to 2 when she was talking to whoever had the gun.

She knew that if she was transmitting on Channel 2 she would not be heard by anyone except C-COM and Keith Cain because unless the night is crystal clear or the people are close in proximity when they're talking to each other, the only people that are going to hear are C-COM and whoever is close to her. Only three people heard Dee's words that night about a gun: C-COM, Keith Cain, and a Holden Beach police officer on duty, Bill Jordan.

One of the reasons it is known that she had switched to Channel 2 was that Brunswick County Sheriff's Department Sergeant Randy Robinson, who was over road traffic that night, had just left C-COM and he never heard the traffic about the gun. There was no static such as was heard on the tape played on television. Her transmissions came across as clear as a bell, as clear as if she had been standing there in C-COM's building.

Dee's manner on the tape was criticized by some because she had not used proper police procedure that night in giving her badge number or position, yet she clearly said, "there ain't no reason to have a gun here on Bald Head Island." That let C-COM know which female on duty that night was sending the transmission concerning a gun being held on her.

This is something she would not have been doing if she were getting ready to shoot herself. It is the act of someone with a portable mike keyed discreetly, buying time, giving what information she could with a gun trained on her, trying to buy time until Keith Cain could hear her and could reach her. The fact that she moved from a keyed radio in her truck to a keyed portable radio outside could account for the squelch heard in the middle of the transmission that for a few seconds made a horrific blaring, jarring noise.

C-COM, knowing which officer was involved by her transmission regarding the island, had immediately asked for all further traffic to be suspended until contact could be made again with the officer, so Jones knew help would come if she could just get time on her side on way or another.

- Luper, Tim. (11-01-99). *SBI Laboratory Report: GSR. Agency File No.: 992665(ALA)*

Further conversation by the officer can still be heard even though it is inaudible, just as the analysis of the tape revealed. The button shown above on the right is what Dee would use to speak. There was no GSR found on the mike.

Keith Cain, however, kept saying that Jones' transmission had been hard to hear. "I … heard a mike key up but you couldn't quite make out what it was saying right off at first. I thought somebody may have been sitting on their mike … You had to listen real carefully, it sounds a little different on the tape than it did when you were standing right there but I realized it was <u>her</u> talking, and I heard her tell somebody, Sir, there's no need for guns on the island, or something like that. And then after that it mumbled down a little bit and I couldn't make out what *they* (emphasis mine) were saying. Then, shortly after that went *off.* (emphasis mine)"

- Cain, Keith. (1-25-00). *Interview* by Monty Clark. P. 19.

In the 2003 testimony, after he had worked for the sheriff's department for several years, Cain explained, "This one was away from the mouth, quite a ways. … It sounded like she was sitting on her mike." During the same testimony, for the first time, he added that he had had to switch out his radio that night because of a dead battery. He testified that he had had to get an older, big handheld one. One thing he did not want to do was look at pictures of the dead police partner.

- *Buff v. Village of Bald Head Island Police Department, North Carolina League of Municipalities and North Carolina Rescue Workers Cap Death Benefits Act.* North Carolina Industrial Commission. (10-23/24-03). P. 193.

District Attorney Rex Gore himself added to the mystery by speculating that the only way the gunshot would not have been heard by 911 operators was if Dee had "turned off the microphone

before shooting." That is exactly correct. Furthermore, C-COM
workers did not hear the shot.

- Reiss, Cory. (12-10-99). Bald Head officer shot self,
  DA says. *Morning-Star.* Pp. 1A.

During his Industrial Commission testimony in 2003,
Brunswick County Sheriff's Department Investigator David Crocker
made a point of stating that he had checked Dee's mike and it was
still working. "I keyed the mike to determine it was still working and it
keyed over the repeater, which indicated it was *still* (emphasis mine)
on Channel One."

- *Buff v. Village of Bald Head Island Police
  Department, North Carolina League of Municipalities
  and North Carolina Rescue Workers Cap Death
  Benefits Act.* North Carolina Industrial Commission.
  (10-23/24-03). P. 254.

If Dee did turn off her radio to hide the gun shot, she
certainly could not have turned it back on to any channel. The logical
conclusion is that someone did turn off her radio, shot her, and then
turned her radio back on to Channel One before they left her body.
They had no way of knowing she had had it turned to Channel Two.

Once he left to find Dee, Cain went the longest route to do
so. According to Grasty, it was customary for officers to park in the
cul-de-sac to take a break or do paperwork, watch last ferry traffic or
stop for a cigarette. If that was the case, since Cain knew his partner
smoked, it would be a good guess that she would do so there. It is
certainly very probable that he knew the drug agent was supposed to
visit Jones and they were going to the lighthouse. One of Dee's
faults was that she talked too much. Many of those she worked with
knew of her man problems. Odds are, Cain not only knew the drug
agent was supposed to come, he knew she was going to call
Monzon on the payphone at the landing when she left the police
station as well.

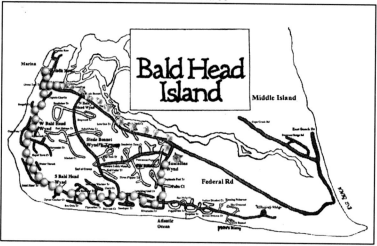

The police station was near Federal Road where the word
Muscadine Wynd is in the middle of the map. The lighthouse is
located at the upper left. The route Cain took is indicated by the line
with the large circles. It goes down, then follows the lower half of the
island and then curves up to the Marina and then back to the
lighthouse.

This was Cain's view of the lighthouse from the marina once he got
there. He described his route saying that he chose that way because
that was where most of the people would be found. The other,
184

shorter route he could have taken is shown by the lighter, popcorn dotted distance. Once he turned from Muscadine onto Federal Road, he would have had a straight route to where Dee was at the lighthouse. It has been estimated that it took between seven to fifteen minutes for Cain to find Jones. For whatever reason, the route Cain took in the most opposite direction gave her killers time to get away. It also protected him from running directly into them on what was generally a one lane road.

- *Buff v. Village of Bald Head Island Police Department, North Carolina League of Municipalities and North Carolina Rescue Workers Cap Death Benefits Act.* North Carolina Industrial Commission. (10-23/24-03). P. 195.

The testimonies of Brown and Cain further complicate the truth concerning who did what and why. All that is really known is that Cain was a trained Medical Responder. As such he should have been able to ascertain the condition of his partner. Once discovering that she was dead, his priority should have been to preserve the crime scene so her killer could be found. "I didn't know if I was – I don't know if I was too hyped up, too worried about my surroundings that maybe I'd felt in the wrong place (for a pulse.) Maybe I'd missed something because I wasn't just staring at her. At that time I was checking around the area, too. I didn't want somebody running up to me and popping me."

- *Buff v. Village of Bald Head Island Police Department, North Carolina League of Municipalities and North Carolina Rescue Workers Cap Death Benefits Act.* North Carolina Industrial Commission. (10-23/24-03). P. 227.

For whatever reason and whoever's fault, Brown had the body removed and somebody convinced Cain of the need to move Jones' gun not once, but twice. But it was not a "hot zone" as Brown termed it. Foy pointed out in court Cain had been walking around looking for Dee for ten to fifteen minutes and nobody shot at him.

185

Kent Brown and his wife came; nobody shot at them. Two EMS came in to pick up her body and nobody shot at them. "So nobody shot any of y'all while y'all were there?"

- *Buff v. Village of Bald Head Island Police Department, North Carolina League of Municipalities and North Carolina Rescue Workers Cap Death Benefits Act.* North Carolina Industrial Commission. (10-23/24-03). P. 236.

It has been noted that Dee's body was taken to the dock. The EMS sheet says an EMS covered the body yet employees from Eb and Flo's recounted seeing the body lying uncovered on the dock. Chief Grasty would receive a call from her daughter telling her about it. Neither Grasty would testify to that in court.

At least by 1:40 am the body was in the depot office because Gene Hardee told Grasty that the body stayed on the dock until Crocker arrived on the island at 1:40 am and the body was moved into the depot office. The small detail that the body may even have been left unguarded, much less out on the dock that long eluded Crocker when filling out the Gunshot Residue Analysis Information Form to send to the SBI. Where it asked: Write a brief description of subject's activity between the time of the shooting and the time of the GSR collection: Crocker wrote: 'Jones subject was taken to a secured area'.

- *Buff v. Village of Bald Head Island Police Department, North Carolina League of Municipalities and North Carolina Rescue Workers Cap Death Benefits Act.* North Carolina Industrial Commission. (10-23/24-03). P. 233.

We know that Kent Brown was opening the Village Hall, cleaning the ambulance used to transport her body, taking the fire engine to the crime scene along with the fire volunteers. What we don't know is what happened to the body during all that time. At 1:20 am, her body was viewed by three policemen from the mainland. A ferry shipmate and captain and four EMS were with the body. Sylvia Timmons, Trish

Brown and two other EMS were there. Dee's body apparently was the best show on the island at the time.

Back at the crime scene, Keith Cain had been orphaned with an unarmed EMS. The immediate events with the pair are unrecorded. They spent time huddled in the crease of Keith's Blazer. We know that a full-time resident rode by the area on his golf cart. We know that he had been seen in the area by the dock and the crime prior to Dee's death. In the darkness and quiet, these men were alone with their thoughts.

Much has been made of test results, but in reality, would it really be so unusual to find GSR on the glove of a police officer? GSR is known to stay on clothing for some time as long as the garment is not laundered. It can also be transferred. Michael Martinez, forensic scientist, warned that great care should be taken when collecting or preserving an area suspect of containing P-GSR. He saw the photographs Davis took of Crocker first examining Dee's head wound and then her gloves.

"A series of photographs taken from both of Photographs #12 reveal that an individual was in direct contact with the area around the gunshot wound to the head and was again shown removing the gloves worn by the deceased. In addition, the same batch of photographs show that the hands were not bagged upon arrival at the morgue."

- Martinez, Michael. (2-20-01). *Report. P. 4.*

As to whether Dee may have already had GSR on her gloves, you may pick a testimony. Consider this exchange between Monty Clark and Keith Cain as to what Cain may have known about Dee's having fired a weapon recently.

> MC: Have you ever gone to a firing range to practice with Dee?
> KC: No.
> MC: Do you have any knowledge of her ever going to a firing range or shooting?

KC: Maybe qualifying maybe. I don't know about on her own.

- Cain, Keith. (1-25-00). *Interview* by Monty Clark. P. 46.

In an exchange with the Buff's lawyer, Karen Grasty advised that Davina and the other officers had qualified on the firing range shortly before her death.

- Grasty, Karen. (8-29-01). *Interview* by Henry Foy. P. 2.

In a strange twist of fate, Crocker himself settled the GSR debate and exonerated Dee from the stand during the Industrial Commission Hearing in 2003 with three words. He was being questioned about the GSR results from the three men in the boat picked up that night near Bald Head Island. The GSR results from those men were the same as they were for Keith Cain as they were for Davina Jones. Crocker said of the three men's results: "They were negative."

- *Buff v. Village of Bald Head Island Police Department, North Carolina League of Municipalities and North Carolina Rescue Workers Cap Death Benefits Act.* North Carolina Industrial Commission. (10-23/24-03). P. 262.

Dee Jones had no more fired a gun that night than the three fishermen or her partner had.

Chapter Twenty Two

With Friends Like These

A verdict of suicide arose almost before Dee's body could get to the dock, as if it had been predetermined. Will Hewett showed up waiting in the dark recesses of the Indigo parking lot, not going on up to talk to his friend Gerry, Geraldine Hewett, the Indigo Plantation security guard, like he said he usually did. He saw a police boat leave and called her to ask what was wrong. She told him Dee had been shot. He asked how bad and she told him Dee was dead. As he said during the 2003 hearing, "if you knew Dee, you couldn't help but love her to death." He had been obsessed with her. However upon hearing that she was dead, had been killed, he did not seem overcome too much to talk. He never shed tears on the dock.

"There were – there were a large number of officers at the dock. They were waiting to be transported over. ... I knew probably half of them there. So it was comfortable for them to talk to me and me to talk to them." We know he talked to the SBI because he gave an interview and said, "I talked to the SBI. *I* went to *them*." (Emphasis mine.)

- *Buff v. Village of Bald Head Island Police Department, North Carolina League of Municipalities and North Carolina Rescue Workers Cap Death Benefits Act.* North Carolina Industrial Commission. (10-23/24-03). Pp. 496, 506-507.
- Hewett, William L. (2-08-00) *Interview* by Monty Clark. P 54.

According to him, it was these "seasoned officers whose opinions he respected who were talking suicide, but that's not what happened when he gave an SBI agent his own opinion on the dock. Hewett said he knew what had happened to Jones: she had committed suicide. He told the agent about Dee's statement during the recent hurricane that she was going for a swim and not coming back. He added that Dee had low self esteem and had trouble dealing with the public. He said that Dee was seeing a doctor for depression. She had been distraught and crying and talked to him four times on Friday. He added that he did not believe that any person shot Jones. "He just knew that Jones shot herself."

- Hewett, William. L. (10-23-99). *Interview* by S. W. Johnson.

Some friend. It seems more probable that the story of suicide was more likely told by Hewett to the officers on the dock just as he told the SBI agent. He was the one who supposedly knew her so well. He called himself her boyfriend; she didn't. If he loved her, it would have been more natural to have defended her name, to have shed tears, to have a least skipped a beat before telling anyone who would listen that she had killed herself. So if the suicide rumor got started quickly at Indigo, he was more likely the source; the reason he was there in the first place.

The only other thing he failed to tell them was how much he knew about navigating the waters in the area. "As far as small boats, you can take a small boat across there any time you want to. You've got 18 miles of beach, so you can land just about anywhere and be on and off and do just about anything you want. ... At high tide you don't ever have to know where you're going, you can just zip on through there."

- Hewett, William L. (2-08-00) *Interview* by Monty Clark. P 54.

Perhaps the fact that Dee had chosen Monzon over him had not been forgiven after all. In fact he had taken a gift to her house on Thursday. She had been under the weather with bronchitis ever since she had helped evacuate a large number of people from Bald Head during the recent hurricane. Hewett had ordered a blanket robe for her as a surprise. "I asked her if I could give it to her and she said she just didn't think she was ready to see me just yet." He had left the package on the porch.

- Hewett, William L. (2-08-00) *Interview* by Monty Clark. P. 31.

When Chief Grasty arrived at Indigo, Hewett was still there. His first words to her were, "You will see my cell phone number on Dee's pager because I was going to call her to see if she wanted me to come over to Bald Head to see her tonight. I guess I paged her about the time she died."

- Grasty, Karen. (7-28-00). *Email* to Martha Lee.

If Dee would not open the door of her house to him or to accept a gift from him, why would he think she would want him on Bald Head while she was on duty? Had one of the officers told him the time she died? How had he known that?

Later on Hewett told Monty Clark, "But as far as if she was capable of doing it, (committing suicide) I know she was upset, but I

191

also know that she was looking forward to things and she was working things out." He added, "I mean, she that she, whenever she would get upset she would say something ... but she never did anything as far as cutting herself or injuring herself or anything of that nature or actually trying to go through and stop at the last minute or anything like that. She would just make the comment."

- Hewett, William L. (2-08-00) *Interview* by Monty Clark. P. 29.

On the witness stand in 2003, he was unable to give a definitive answer as to whether he thought she committed suicide or not.

- Calhoun, Terry. (7-06-05). Officer's death wasn't suicide. *The State Port Pilot.* Pp. 1A.

Too bad his opinion changed or wavered. He had already done his damage.

Upon meeting SBI Special Agent Janet Storms, Chief Grasty asked her, "Did she kill herself?" District Attorney Gore would be quick to point this out in defense of his decision later. Grasty's explanation for the question was "I did because I'd already heard rumors about it [sic] see if she had heard anything about it."

- *Buff v. Village of Bald Head Island Police Department, North Carolina League of Municipalities and North Carolina Rescue Workers Cap Death Benefits Act.* North Carolina Industrial Commission. (10-23/24-03). P. 116.

We know that the source of those rumors may have been Grasty's daughter calling from the island. Storms said she herself had heard the suicide talk, that it was a suicide. This statement was made before there had been any investigation of the crime scene or anything else. No SBI agent had set foot on a boat yet, much less reached the island. Then Storms assured Grasty that the SBI would treat this as a "death investigation of a police officer."

- Grasty, Karen. (8-29-01). *Interview* by Henry Foy.

When officers were sending in evidence to be analyzed in the lab, there were some bothersome inconsistencies that also seem unprofessional, if not dangerously detrimental police procedure, especially for conduct by an SBI agent. For example, when Sam Davis sent 12 live rounds from Dee's gun, her palm fingerprints, pants, duty belt, ASP, pepper spray, cuffs, multi-pliers, badge and Glock magazine, he listed the type of case as 'homicide.'

Agent Storms sent in prints of a suspect in the case. She listed for type of case: *Self Inflicted death*. What good would checking fingerprints against latent prints found at the crime scene do in a suicide case? Why bother to send in the prints?

Davina's partner Keith Cain was asked to draw a sketch of

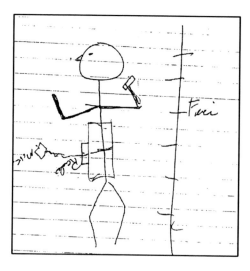

her body as it was when he found her that October night. His sketch shows that she was face down on the ground behind the trash pile when he found her. His sketch shows the approximate distance of the picket fence on her right from where her body was found. Her gun is under her right hand. Her legs were slightly bowed and she resembled a 'field goal.' The sketch shows her radio and microphone on the ground to her left side while still attached to her side. Her truck would have been diagonally away from her to her left.

This is the sketch of Dee done by SBI Agent Storms. She never saw the body as it was found on the island. She never set foot on the island until the day of the reenactment. Notice the difference in the way she has drawn the gun. It is now in a totally different angle from the way Cain had originally drawn it and drawn pointed toward Jones' head.

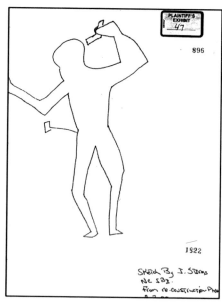

The drag marks from the death scene were dismissed by DA Rex Gore as being "most likely caused by construction materials and not Jones' body."

- Stites, Lisa. (6-07-06). DA calls it suicide. *The State Port Pilot*. P. 1.

If so, someone got hurt dragging those materials. Drops of blood, "spatters" moving toward where the body would be found were among the drag marks. As finicky as officials were about removing the blood of a dead police officer, surely they would have insisted that a mere construction worker's platelets be vacuumed up immediately on the very day it had fallen. At least the DA was aware of the marks; Crocker hadn't been.

It was possible to have had the drag marks processed. "Electrostatic myler sheets could have been placed over the marks to collect any foreign fibers left behind. This could then have been sent to a forensic laboratory for fiber identification and cross-compared to Davina Buff Jones' clothing."

- Martinez, Michael. (2-20-01). *Report. P. 7.*

Another chance to find the killer(s) evaporated when another decision was made. There was blood on the left side of Dee's pick-up and a bloody hand print on the back on the tailgate. The crime scene report not only noted their existence but also added that SBI Agent Tony Cummings, destined to become the right-hand man of Sheriff Ronald Hewett, dismissed them saying the blood was hers, so there was no reason to test it.

- *SBI report: crime scene on Bald Head Island.* (10-23-99). P. 5.

Cummings never had to explain how she was supposed to have been able to get blood on her truck once she shot herself yards away from the vehicle. She never moved again once that wound was put in the back of her head. It would have been impossible.

How her blood got to be back on her truck is a thorny problem. Keith Cain did reach in and turn off the engine, but he never, by his testimony, got her blood in the truck. He did not have that much blood on him when he went back to cover the EMS. Brown never got close enough to the body to get blood on him – he never left the back of Dee's truck. Without processing it, how could Cummings know whose blood it was?   Not all of the contact sheet pictures have been printed where they can be seen. Some seem to show a police jacket hanging out of the driver's side, seeming to hide what may be on the side door. The grainy pictures seem to show some dirt or grains of sand exploding across the hood of the truck. It doesn't look as clean as it does in the published pictures.

There are pictures of a blood smear found on the passenger door of Keith Cain's Blazer. This may have happened when he was placing the bloody Glock into his car. Processing decisions were made quickly. After all, there were press and cameras waiting on the mainland. Wade Horne told Grasty that she was on sick leave and did not exist. He named Ronald Hewett to be the little group's spokesperson.

- Grasty, Karen. (8-29-01). *Interview* by Henry Foy.

Robert Willis was left in charge of the crime scene. When Hewett, Horne, Grasty, and Hardee returned from facing the press, the crime scene tape was down, the fire department was washing down everything, all the blood, the drag marks, all were gone. Grasty asked Willis who ordered it. He shrugged his shoulders and said, "I don't know." She later said, "I asked everyone over there. No one would tell me or could tell me.

- Grasty, Karen. (6-28-00). *Letter* to Loy and Harriet Buff.
- *Buff v. Village of Bald Head Island Police Department, North Carolina League of Municipalities and North Carolina Rescue Workers Cap Death Benefits Act.* North Carolina Industrial Commission. (10-23/24-03). P. 111.

More details emerged. An employee from the Bald Head Island Club called the Fire Department wanting to know if the crime scene tape and blood would be removed or could be removed before a wedding party arrived at the chapel near the lighthouse the afternoon of Saturday, October 23rd.

- Grasty, Karen. (8-29-01). *Interview* by Henry Foy.

One might wonder why anyone would call the fire department about a police investigation. According to Grasty, Fire Chief Kent Brown was always "sucking up" to the developer. By that she meant that "He was always being accommodating to the power players, the residents, influential contacts, the developers, and the management of the Bald Head Island management group. Kent was power playing against Wade Horne, the town manager. What most people in government refer to as back door politics."

- Grasty, Karen. (8-29-01). *Interview* by Henry Foy.

That may help explain why Brown was the only officer with a subsidy allowing him to live on the island whereas the police and rescue chiefs lost theirs due to budget cuts a while back. Still others have placed the wash down decision at the feet of Wade Horne.

Two teenagers were brought over from Southport to clean up the area around the lighthouse compound where Keith Cain had looked for his partner. So any potential evidence leading down to the wooden dock hard by the back of the lighthouse was lost. However, 73 tourists did get to climb the lighthouse that Saturday afternoon so $219.00 was made and the Crake wedding party was not inconvenienced by a crime scene nearby. Every sign that Davina Buff Jones had been killed there had been successfully erased.

As a reporter noted, "Crime tape was taken down before Sunday morning, and tourists walked around the area, climbing to the top of the lighthouse Sunday afternoon."

- von Kolnitz, Cece. (10-26-99). Bald Head officer met 3 people, then was slain. *Morning-Star.* Pp. 1A.

District Attorney Rex Gore remarked that "The crime scene was cleaned *eventually*" (my emphasis), "after the SBI agents in charge cleared the scene about 1 pm. The fact was that it was hosed down after it was released. They had processed it."

- Stites, Lisa. (6-07-06). DA calls it suicide. *The State Port Pilot.* P. 1.

Actually they had processed as much as they intended to process. We know from first hand accounts that the island was never completely searched – far from it. We know that the canvass of the island amounted to asking people as they left the island if they had seen or heard anything. We now know that they ignored evidence that didn't fit with their suicide theory and then washed away what evidence had not already been bungled.

Brown had had his fire truck at the ready since the wee hours of the morning after he had cleaned the ambulance and left Dee's body on the dock and Keith Cain in the dark at the lighthouse with a defenseless EMS.

At the time the washdown was taking place, Norman MacCloud was entering Dosher Memorial Hospital apparently looking for Dr. Reschley, Dee's personal physician. The doctor described the drug agent as being very 'distraught' when MacCloud saw him and told him that Dee had shot herself. Earlier that morning, the doctor's secretary had told him she had heard that Dee had been killed during a drug deal that had gone bad.

- Reschley, Keith. (11-14-03). *Disposition.* P. 3.

MacCloud managed to pull himself together to explain that it was suicide for two reasons. First, the location of the gunshot being behind her right ear (incorrect) and second, they'd found "hair in the lock of Dee's gun."

- Griffin, Anna. *Fax* to Police Chief Karen Grasty.

Tanya Buff Hart remembers Norman MacCloud bringing a flower to put on the mailbox at her parents' house around lunch time and introducing himself as a Vice Narcotics Agent. He was the only police person the family dealt with in the several days following Dee's death. Loy and Harriet Buff had dealt with SBI Agent Janet Storms earlier in the morning. MacCloud acted as if his was an official presence.

> He came in and he was shaking his head.
> I said, "What is it?"
> He said, "She was under too much pressure at work."
> "What do you mean?"
> He said, "She was just under too much pressure at work."

- *Buff v. North Carolina Law Enforcement Officers and Rescue Workers Death Benefit Act and North Carolina Contingency and Emergency Fund. P. 63-64.*

Loy Buff testified that MacCloud introduced himself to him as the head of the county's drug division. He began talking on the family's house phone and telling people he was a friend of the family. He disclosed that he and Davina had spent a fair amount of time together discussing personal and professional problems, adding that she had been VERY depressed. "He seemed to indicate that he possibly knew more about her current circumstances than anyone else."

- Buff, Loy. (9-12-07). *Interview* by Elaine Buff.

He announced that all indications were suicide. According to a family friend at the home who witnessed MacCloud's conduct, "He seemed pretty confident that he was correct in his assessment of the situation and confident that he should tell you (the Buffs) of the suicide, rather than homicide of Davina." She further attested, "It came as a slap in the face ... that this conclusion had been reached in such a short period of time, without a complete investigation. What really seemed odd was that he came ... just hours after her death, and offered this information. His actions were somewhat callous and without explanation and seemed inappropriate to those who observed this whole scene."

- Workman. (1-15-03). *Email* to Loy and Harriet Buff.

He would cause such consternation in the house that another family friend who was mayor of Yaupon Beach called Ronald Hewett and told him he needed to remove that officer from the house.

Before being ordered away, MacCloud drove Dee's sisters and a family friend to Dee's house to retrieve photograph albums. On the way the sisters saw a white dove sitting beside the road and took it as a sign from Dee that she was all right. Then they wanted to know about their sister's wound. He told them that "...he was there and knew where she was shot." He said the bullet "entered here." Using his right hand, he pointed behind his right ear at the base of his skull. "It exited here." Using his left hand, he pointed at his left temple. He told Tanya that he met Ronald Hewett at Sunny Point. On the way from the Sunny Point Terminal by water to Bald Head Island, MacCloud had told his boss that Dee was having emotional problems.

- Hart, Tanya. (8-27-07). *Interview* by Elaine Buff.

The evening of Dee's memorial service, MacCloud appeared at the funeral home and motioned for a reporter from a local television station to speak with him. He told her he was helping set up the sound system for the service.

"You know what happened, right?" She explained she didn't know what he meant. He lowered his voice. "She'd killed herself" he said in a matter-of-fact way. He added that Dee had been having problems at work and had filed a sexual harassment case. Not only had her supervisors blown it off, they had written her up for trying to get legal action. "The island chief put her on probation – whatever that means."

The reporter asked him if Bald Head Island had a history of drugs.

"No complaints of drugs on Bald Head Island. Believe me, if there was [sic] drugs on Bald Head Island, I would know."

- Zink, Jody. (1-13-03). Email to Loy and Harriet Buff.

According to Grasty, Dee had been at MacCloud's house on Thursday night before she died, talking about undercover drug work. We know Dee was expecting him Friday night on the island and he had presented that pass at the ferry landing on the mainland. An eye-witness put him, dressed in camouflage, on Bald Head Island before Dee was shot. Yet MacCloud told Tanya Buff Hart that he had been with Sheriff Ronald Hewett on a raid on Turkey Trap Road near Holden Beach where he "broke" his foot.

- Hart, Tanya. (8-27-07). *Interview* by Elaine Buff.

When he was interviewed by Monty Clark for the Buff family, MacCloud said he was helping serve a search warrant when he broke his foot. "I'm in the hospital at Dosher (in Southport – Turkey Trap Road is near Holden Beach) getting x-rayed when the stuff with her happened. Me and my boss, all of a sudden it goes out and he looks at me and says stay here. I looked at the nurse and said, 'Give me two 800 milligram Motrin and stuff that ankle in that damn boot.' I went over there. I was in terrific pain. I had tears in my eyes. I went on the second boat."

Clark asked if it were after midnight.

"Probably. (He was seen on Bald Head before midnight.) We got over there and set up and stuff and then we found out it was Dee." Supposedly he had already learned that in the hospital – that was why he told the nurse to stuff his broken foot back into the boot.

He told Clark that Gene Caison told his boss that it looked like she may have killed herself. She had made up a fabrication to protect her family and she had killed herself. "I took a shower, dressed halfway decent, took the F.O.P. car (inaudible) went over to the family and took notes."

- *Buff v. Village of Bald Head Island Police Department, North Carolina League of Municipalities and North Carolina Rescue Workers Cap Death Benefits Act.* North Carolina Industrial Commission. (10-23/24-03). Exhibits Part II. Pp. 840-841.

How his broken foot got healed in such a short time was never explained. No one noticed a limp or a cast during his visit at the Buff house within hours of his breaking it. It was certainly heroic on his part to be able to walk, if not almost impossible to function normally on a broken foot. He had neither a limp nor a cast at the memorial service that the reporter noticed while talking to him either.

MacCloud was never asked why he felt he needed to take notes at the Buffs' house. No one saw him doing that, though he checked with the family almost compulsively two or three days, as did Will Hewett, and then they both disappeared.

Robert Willis reacted to Jones' death with writing directed toward the residents of Bald Head Island:

"We do not need 'Police Officers on Bald Head Island,' so some of you have said.
"We do not need 'That many Police Officers on Bald Head Island,' so some of you have said.
"We do not need 'Police Officers with guns on Bald Head Island,' so some of you have said.
Well, what do you say now!   10-30-99

From the sentiments expressed in these four edgy lines, Robert Willis apparently did not believe that Davina Buff Jones took her own life.

The gun that once was Davina Buff Jones' service revolver and used to murder her had been in a box in the possession of David

Cox. At the 2003 hearing that Glock was ordered to "be maintained in the custody – possession – control of – Captain David Cox."

- *Buff v. Village of Bald Head Island Police Department, North Carolina League of Municipalities and North Carolina Rescue Workers Cap Death Benefits Act.* North Carolina Industrial Commission. (10-23/24-03). Pp. 174-175.

Yet this same service weapon was cleaned and put back into service on Bald Head Island.

- *Buff v. Bureau of Justice Assistance Public Safety Officers' Benefits.* (1-18-03). P. 21.

Then the news broke in local papers that the village management had been selling ten surplus Glocks, one of which had belonged to Dee Buff Jones. Supposedly the sale had been halted because the selling process had not followed all the requirements of a village resolution. The price had been $125.00 each and sold with a proper serial number. Alina Medina, village clerk in charge of selling the guns, was dismissed and it was handled as a personnel matter and therefore discussed in closed session. The new village manager said, "Whether it was by accident or intentional, I have no idea."

- Ives, Millard. (5-20-03). Bald Head Island's gun sale investigated. *Morning Star.* Pp. 1B, 3B.

The *Southport Pilot* added that the SBI was investigating the sale.

- Peterson, Sarah. (5-21-03). Terms of resolution: SBI investigates [sic] Bald Head gun sale. *The State Port Pilot.* P. 18A.

Henry Foy, still attorney for the Buffs at that time, sent a letter to the Bald Head Island management on May 22.

I do not know whether or not the weapon which caused Officer Jones' death was included in this lot. However, if it was, it should have never been sold because it is evidence, certainly in one on-going civil action that I am involved in. It is further my understanding that weapons used

203

in the commission of a crime are to be destroyed.

- Foy, Henry. (5-22-03). *Letter* to Village of Bald Head Island

By May 28th news came that all of the guns that had been sold had been recovered. The District Attorney had made the directive after the SBI investigated the sale.

- Peterson, Sarah. (5-28-03). Handgun sale issue dropped. *The State Port Pilot.* np.

The affair gives rise to the speculation that the sale was a ruse to get rid of one more tangible trace of Dee as surely as they had barred the flowers and wreaths and black ribbons from where she died in the early days after her death and washed away her blood.

Chapter Twenty Three

So Good the SBI Uses Them

After the wash down, Grasty said, "I raised hell. They sent me home. Wade Horne and Mayor Kitty Henson called me in and told me to go home and shut up."

- Calhoun, Terry. (7-13-05). Former BHI chief: 'I know she was murdered.' *The State Port Pilot.* P. 6A.

Grasty's health would prevent her from ever taking a major role in fighting for a better investigative job on Dee's behalf. When she left her office for good, she turned over the investigative file to her successor Chief Ken Snead. That file consisted of five notebooks:

1. Tips sheets – contact sheets of people coming and going off the island
2. Investigative – contained incident report & all notes related thereto
3. Photographs
4. Interviews, etc. EMS reports
5. Miscellaneous

When she later tried to give him more information about the case, Snead told her he did not want it, to send it to the SBI. Wade Horne had told him the matter was close.

- *Buff v. Bureau of Justice Assistance Public Safety Officers' Benefits.* (1-18-03). P. 43.

Gene Hardee wanted to follow up on three suspects he thought were important and was upset when he discovered they had not been investigated at all. Wade Horne denied him the resources to go to Charlotte to interview these men.

- Calhoun, Terry. (7-13-05). Former BHI chief: 'I know she was murdered.' *The State Port Pilot.* P. 6A.

The family was never given any of Dee's belongings except her radio mike. At the PSOB hearing, a family member testified, "The drag marks were never identified – did they come from her shoes? We don't know where her clothes, shoes, or anything belonging to her are. ... We can't find out from anyone if her clothes or shoes or anything belonging to her are still in existence.

- *Buff v. Bureau of Justice Assistance Public Safety Officers' Benefits.* (1-18-03). P. 20-21.

The family has since learned that the shoes have 'disappeared.' No one – no hearing officer, no private investigator – no one has ever been able to find the shoes Davina wore that night.

Dee's death has been ruled 'undetermined' by the hearings. That means that all evidence in the case is supposed to be kept forever, if necessary. Yet the shoes have disappeared. Why would someone want Dee's shoes? If the toes show wear that matches the drag marks, you no longer have a suicide theory. Where are Dee's shoes? Why have the authorities in charge of her things never been made to either produce her shoes or explain where they are?

Sheriff Ronald Hewett, David Crocker, and Larry Jones told the Buffs that Davina had been so upset on the night she died, she had torn up her personnel file and threw it into the garbage. Actually there were two personnel files on each officer; one was kept in the Village business office; the other was in the Police Chief's locked office. Both were under lock and key and not accessible to officers.

- Grasty, Karen. (8-29-01). *Interview* by Henry Foy.

The truth is Dee had once again been given the chore of completing another self evaluation of her good and bad points. She had transferred her notes to the actual report she was intending to turn in to the chief. She had torn up the notes she had used to make the report and thrown them into the trash. We have that information from Gene Hardee.

> - *Buff v. Bureau of Justice Assistance Public Safety Officers' Benefits.* (1-18-03). Pp. 73-74.

These same three, Hewett, Crocker, and Jones had come to the Buff house to tell them that Rex Gore was going to announce his decision the next morning. They would not let them see the autopsy pictures which they had brought with them, but added that the family could come to their office at any time. Crocker added he "didn't think it was appropriate for the family to observe the photographs."

> - *Buff v. Bureau of Justice Assistance Public Safety Officers' Benefits.* (1-18-03). Pp. 72-73.

They did not tell them that they had not seen them either. At least Crocker testified he had not seen them. Neither would Gore. But they did show them Garrett's autopsy drawing with Crocker explaining that Garrett actually had not drawn it correctly. "It was closer to her right ear." How would he begin to know where the wound was or decide what the family should see when *he never saw the autopsy pictures himself?* The private investigator for the family had to argue with them later about the location of the head wound because Gore and Crocker still did not know where the fatal head wound was. That testimony during 2003 hearing came after Crocker admitted that Dee's shoes, (the missing ones), shirt and the blood smear on the back of her truck were never examined. Of course, had the Buffs looked at the autopsy pictures, they would have asked even more questions.

The other non-challenged remark in his testimony was that he had known about Jones' mental issues beforehand. How that was possible no one ever made him explain. Jones and he were not friends or close associates.

Dee's sister Tanya was present at the Buffs that night and did back him up on his comment about the wound being nearer Dee's right ear. "I saw her in the funeral home and I know that it was closer to what Garrett had drawn." The family and the men argued for about twenty minutes on the subject during which Hewett went outside twice to talk to his wife Julie on the phone.

Crocker's response. "Sometimes he makes mistakes, too."

When Tanya said that she had seen the wound, all three policemen's mouths dropped open.

Hewett said, "I thought she was cremated!"

Tonya answered, "She was but we got to view her Saturday night." All three men got nervous and suddenly changed the subject.

- *Buff v. Bureau of Justice Assistance Public Safety Officers' Benefits.* (1-18-03). P. 71-73.

Curiously, Tanya got the same response at the funeral home. The owners were friends of the Buffs, but they got quite nervous and changed the subject when Tanya began to question Bill Newman about the head wound. At first, they had told Tonya when she had called about viewing the body they didn't know when the body would be sent back. She got the feeling he knew where Dee had been shot, but didn't want to divulge that information. They were even so upset about handling the arrangements, they forgot to ask about printing the usual programs they have at funerals until Tanya asked about them to get the programs printed.

- Hart, Tanya. (8-27-07). *Interview* by Elaine Buff.

The chart below shows the drawings with the head wound and show who was correct and will end the speculation and lies once and for all. Garrett's sketch, except for it being upside down, is correct, not that of Hiltz.

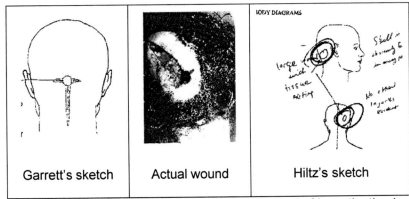

Garrett's sketch	Actual wound	Hiltz's sketch

- Hiltz, Douglas. (10-23-99). *Report of investigation by Medical Examiner.*
- Garrett, C. L. (10-23-99). Autopsy of Davina Buff Jones.

This is what they did not want the family – or the public – to see. This is what the hearing officers time after time saw and realized. Davina Buff Jones was murdered.

Forty (40) hair samples were sent to the lab. "There were no hair and fibers standards submitted. So, only did cursory examination of the tapings collected from the above items." (The hair samples.)

- *Buff v. Village of Bald Head Island Police Department, North Carolina League of Municipalities and North Carolina Rescue Workers Cap Death Benefits Act.* North Carolina Industrial Commission. (10-23/24-03). Exhibits Part I. P. 346.

Her pants were sent to be examined and Storms called SBI lab technician Luper to tell him that Jones "could have been on her knees."

- *Buff v. Village of Bald Head Island Police Department, North Carolina League of Municipalities and North Carolina Rescue Workers Cap Death Benefits Act.* North Carolina Industrial Commission. (10-23/24-03). Exhibits Part I. Pp. 336, 347.

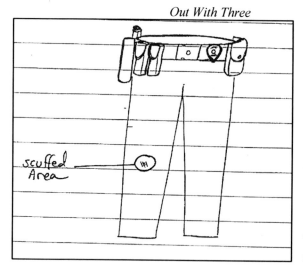

scuffed Area

Luper found that the blue uniform pants "revealed the presence of scuff marks on the right knee area and the presence of mineral material embedded in the fabric of the pants. Abrasions were noted also. The pants and Dee's pullover shirt were returned to Chief Ken Snead at Bald Head Island. Not twenty miles from the Buff house. Snead also had possession of Dee's gun. Yet the family was never notified of where any of their daughter's possessions were being kept.

- *Buff v. Village of Bald Head Island Police Department, North Carolina League of Municipalities and North Carolina Rescue Workers Cap Death Benefits Act.* North Carolina Industrial Commission. (10-23/24-03). Exhibits Part I. P. 343.

Another curious situation became evident during the hearing. The gun itself, Davina's service revolver, did not have her finger

prints on it. That fact was overlooked later on by the District Attorney and the Sheriff in giving all of their statements to the press.

During the 2003 hearing, testimony offered by Grasty discussed the lack of Dee's own fingerprints on her service revolver. "... she would have handled it every day and she would have checked it every time she went on shift to see if it was properly loaded and – magazine loaded and whatnot. So my knowledge of handling a weapon, it should have had her prints on there." The surprise was that fingerprints were taken off of Dee's gun. They were not hers; they were not Cain's. They were unidentifiable.

- *Buff v. Village of Bald Head Island Police Department, North Carolina League of Municipalities and North Carolina Rescue Workers Cap Death Benefits Act.* North Carolina Industrial Commission. (10-23/24-03). P. 167, 332-333.

By Saturday morning, a curtain of silence had fallen over the whole affair on Bald Head Island. Village Manager Wade Horne issued a memo to all department heads directing them not to answer any questions to the press. Council member William Leineweber proclaimed, "We've supported the police and the paramedics because they've been here to support us." Another translation of the Horne directive was that "...their job would be in jeopardy if they talked to the media."

- von Kolnitz, Cece. (12-14-99). Doors closing, but shooting probe goes on. *Sunday Morning-Star.* Pp. 1B, 5B.
- Officer's death termed a suicide. (12-10-99). *The Charlotte Observer.* P. 4C.

Two reporters found the silence order reached even further. "Workers at the café (River Pilot) near the lighthouse were silent about the incident during the past week, saying they could not talk about the case." Now we know that Bald Head management was telling everyone not to talk. Brunswick Sheriff's Department officials had told others not to talk. Strange behavior for a simple suicide case.

- von Kolnitz, Cece and Victoria Cherrie. (11-01-99). Bald Head residents seeking closure. *Morning-Star.* Pp. 6A.

Tanya Buff Hart, visiting the lighthouse on Saturday, October 23, 1999, found that workers there had also been ordered not to talk. They were told they would be fired if they did. Those who had known and been friends with Dee went home once they discovered their friend had been murdered.

- Hart, Tanya. (8-27-07). *Interview* by Elaine Buff.

This no-talk order would still be in effect in 2002 under a new village manager. "The village manager told Chief Snead who had told his officers they are not to discuss Dee's case with anyone. Her orders came form the city council and THEY gave said order under Billy Berne whose Bald Head Island City Council ... pays Wade Horne as an advisor of some kind – Wade is STILL on the payroll!!" If this was truly a suicide, as they would have you believe, it seems like they went to a lot of trouble to keep it under wraps. As late as October of 2007, a worker at the lighthouse went out of her way to assure a tourist that she knew nothing, no, no, no about the police officer who had died there!

- Doe, John II. (9-24-02). *Email* to Loy and Harriet Buff.

Publicly Horne alleged that the Brunswick County Sheriff's Department and the State Bureau of Investigation were the primary investigating units in the case. In return, Hewett insisted that both of these bodies were merely assisting the Bald Head Island Police Department, who was supposed to handle and release all information on the case. In private, Hewett and the SBI were not giving the Bald Head Police any information about the case. Gene Hardee was being bombarded from all sides for news, but he could not give them what he did not have. When the Buff family hired a private investigator, Gore, Hewett and the Bald Head Police tried to keep him running in circles looking for information as well.

While Grasty was still on the payroll, she twisted slowly in the wind, too. Marion Warren, an assistant District Attorney told her not to talk. He sent her a letter that said in part, "In order to maintain the *integrity* (my emphasis) of your current investigation, I would request you hold and not distribute reports, statements and/or investigative notes."

- Warren, Marion. (11-05-99). *Letter* to Karen Grasty.

Meanwhile the very county Warren served was saying publicly all information about the case would come from Bald Head Island.

At the same time, Reid Page, Jr. was trying to obtain information for his Bald Head Island publication, the *Gazette*. To his credit, he seemed to have been truly doing his job trying to uncover the truth about Dee's death. He asked questions time after time, regardless of the cold shoulders he received from village officials. Grasty answered what she could but that, under the circumstances, was minimal. Reid was not to be put off. He sent more questions, demanded answers more heatedly. Relations and communications between the two became quite strained. "As it stands, in my opinion, this entire matter is being handled in a most unprofessional, fragmented, disjointed and ineffective manner," he declared in a fax to her on December 1, 1999. Even in the dark, Page had correctly assessed the situation. The problem was, he didn't realize the stone-walling and deceit was more widespread than the local police department. Grasty was getting the blame, but it was not hers.

In his growing disgust, Page fired off another fax two days later to a fellow Bald Head Island resident Jay Walker, owner of Tri-Tech in Southport, who would later employ Norman MacCloud after he was unceremoniously dismissed by Ronald Hewett.

I believe in a country that is free – the people are absolutely entitled to know the truth and facts on everything. If this is wrong then the very foundations of America will someday collapse.

I've also had far more than enough of lying people in government positions who are power and money mad and controlling to the extent that freedom is a fleeting thing.

This comes from strictly a novice, but I believe she was murdered and those who did it must be found. I also would not at all doubt that big money drugs were involved.

What Reid Page, Jr. never knew was that Wade Horne ordered Grasty not to respond to Page's numerous requests for information. However, her response to Page that whether Dee's blue lights and take down lights were on was irrelevant leaves one baffled. Of course such information would be relevant to the case. Maybe that was something else about which they never wanted the truth to be known.

When Gore made his suicide decision, Page Jr. wrote to thank him. "Thank you for your news release on Dee Jones and for your cooperation. Your conclusion appears to me to be a list of brilliant work. We will pass the word verbatim far and wide." For such a good reporter, he turned out to be mollified by a bunch of half-truths and rumors and unfounded speculation. One can only hope that eventually the newspaper man realized he had been duped with a sleight-of-hand dog-and-pony show put on for the benefit of saving Bald Head Island's reputation and the drug trade's pocket books. If not, maybe this book will spell it out. (Mr. Reid is currently not allowed on Bald Head Island.)

- Page, Reid. A. Jr. (12-10-99). *Letter* to Rex Gore.

Chapter Twenty Four

Closing Ranks

October 14, 1999, a group of officers went over on the ferry for a meeting with acting Chief Gene Hardee. Dee took the opportunity to ask two of the three officers hired after her if they had been put back into training. Neither of them had heard anything about it. On her notes for the meeting Dee wrote, "Problems within the department – AGAIN."

- Jones, Davina Buff. (10-15-99) *Police Meeting Notes.*

The officers all returned to the landing together to wait for the ferry ride home. Dexter Ludlum commented in front of the others that Dee was "infected with cooties and one must be careful." The remark hurt her feelings and she walked off amid the laughter of the others and waited for the ride by herself.

Hardee stopped Jones at Indigo on the Southport side and talked with her about the councilman's complaint from Sunday about her speeding. Taussig's complaint claimed the offense had occurred on 10-12-99, a Tuesday when Dee had not been on duty. Hardee requested that Dee write a supplement to her statement about the incident as to her estimated speed.

"I never looked due to the road conditions, the blind spots on the road there."

He said it was *important* that she guess her speed. She answered that she couldn't have been going more than 33 mph, if that much.

"Write the supplement, Dee!" He revealed that he had already asked one of the paramedics what he thought her speed had been. The paramedic had estimated it at somewhere between 30 and 35 mph. Hardee was currently awaiting the written statement of that estimate. He added that he could argue the merit of the case due to the incorrect date but Wade Horne would dismiss that as an oversight.

He said that on Monday (10-18-99) they would measure from that "pipe hump location to where I saw this man at Timbercreek." Lt. Hardee said that they would go through the supplement she would write over the week end. After proofreading and making corrections, they would present it to Wade Horne. He then asked her what she thought would be an appropriate action on his part to discipline her.

After she thought about it, she responded, "Three days unpaid leave?"

He replied that he was thinking of two days. He knew it would be a financial burden, but he could possibly work around that. He didn't elaborate. He once again told her to keep their conversation between the two of them, otherwise he would be unable to help her.

- Jones, Davina Buff. (10-15-99) *Journal entry.*

Dee's initial description of the fire response referred to a yellow card medical call. C-COM notified her of a medical emergency at the ferry deport with no further information as to the nature of the call. She responded by turning on her blue lights and ran her manual siren. (She unlined 'manual' in her report.) The paramedics arrived about a minute after her. Officer Cain notified her that a man she referred to as 'the big man in the yellow shirt' had complained to him about her speed in response to this call. Dee had passed him at Timbercreek. His golf cart tag read "TC-9A." He was associated with response to medical calls on Bald Head.

Later the same day there was a second emergency call concerning a young lady who had fallen out of a golf cart and was having convulsions. A man had reported this in person at the station.

Dee had driven the man and his wife back to the scene behind the responding ambulance. After paramedics and Officer Cain had left the scene to take the girl to the ferry, the same man in the yellow shirt approached Dee.

"Who was the guy in front of the ambulance on the earlier call?"

"I was."

"No," he replied. "You were behind the ambulance."

"I was driving the pick-up in front of the ambulance."

He got loud with people around listening, asking why she had to go 50 miles an hour, faster than the ambulance?

"You need to contact Chief Grasty and the Village Manager if there is a problem."

"I will!"

Officer Jones then walked across Federal Road to interview the gentleman who had come to report the incident. Meanwhile, Taussig continued to discuss things with Fire Chief Kent Brown and Brown's wife Trish. Dee then drove her interviewee and his wife back to retrieve their golf cart and to finish the paperwork about the incident.

- Jones, Davina Buff. (10-10-99) *Incident Report.*

Cain's version of the incident said that Mr. Johnson came to him complaining, charging that "the officer driving the truck was going too fast, driving 90 miles an hour with lights and siren going and he could hear it coming from a mile away." Cain told him Cain would have a talk with the officer. Reports later had Taussig apologizing, so where the name Johnson came from is unclear.

- Cain, Keith. (10-10-99) *Incident Report.*

The rough draft Hardee demanded that Jones write contained the following information. To get from Middle Island to the

217

site of the emergency, Jones had to cross an area where piping crossed the roadway. She had to slow down almost to a stop because of the rough terrain, her speed dropping to 1 to 2 miles per hour. From there she approached Timbercreek. The area at that time had large trees which posed blind spots for drivers. She judged her cautionary speed here to be between 17 and 23 miles per hour. As Jones passed the entrance to Timbercreek, the man in the yellow shirt was stopped in his golf cart waiting to enter North Bald Head Wynd. He waved and she waved back. In her opinion, due to conditions of traffic, limited visibility, road conditions and citizen safety, her speed did not exceed 33 miles per hour.

- Jones, Davina Buff. (10-10-99) *Incident Report Addendum.*

This is the Timbercreek area as it appeared in October, 2007. It would have been in even more primitive conditions in 1999.

Gene Hardee and another man took the pick-up truck, went out and tried to replicate the speed Taussig accused Dee of and

218

found it impossible. "There was no way that she could [sic] got to fifty miles an hour in that particular area."

- *Buff v. Village of Bald Head Island Police Department, North Carolina League of Municipalities and North Carolina Rescue Workers Cap Death Benefits Act.* North Carolina Industrial Commission. (10-23/24-03). P. 151.

Under questioning, Taussig admitted that Dee's speed was more like 15 mph. Hardee said, "I never wrote her up. I called in about it. ... (inaudible) ... when it came out she was driving 90 mph. Then it was 50 mph. Then 30-35. ... actually apologized for it. He did it at somebody else's request. I told her, tell me exactly what happened and we'll see how to answer this thing." Since the man was last seen talking to Kent Brown, one wonders if that was who told him to complain.

- *Buff v. Village of Bald Head Island Police Department, North Carolina League of Municipalities and North Carolina Rescue Workers Cap Death Benefits Act.* North Carolina Industrial Commission. (10-23/24-03). Pp. 858-859.

So Taussig later apologized, but it was too late. The damage had already been done. It can only be hoped that all who saw fit to complain about Dee's 'speeds' to emergencies would have someday lay waiting, needing her to hurry to their aid.

Jones talked to Beverly on the phone about her growing disappointment in the way she was being treated, especially since she had contacted an F.O.P. lawyer for advice. She also recounted the recent incident with Taussig. He was aware of her sexual harassment complaint. She was afraid and told her sister that they were trying to use any and every thing to fire her.

Laura Atkins testified that Keith Cain had "let Dee know they were trying to get rid of Dee and Dee should be careful." He neglected or forgot to tell that in any of the court proceedings, too, once he went to work for the sheriff's office. She waited for him to come to her aid the night she died. He wouldn't even try to help clear her name once she was dead.

On November 10, 1999, Beverly, Dee's younger sister, wrote Cain a letter, thanking him for all he had done and wishing him well in getting over the tragedy. She asked that he meet with her sister Tanya and her when she was able to come from her home in Charlotte to Southport. They wanted to meet with him and asked that he tell them anything he could about Dee's last day with him. "God bless you, Keith! ... Thank you again for being my sister's friend and partner – it is our honor. ... We love you and look forward to meeting you. Please feel free to call us anytime." Beverly added her home phone number at the bottom of the letter. She never got a response.

- Atkins, Laura. (10-28-99). *Telephone interview* by Janet Storms.
- *Sadler, Beverly Buff. (November 10, 1999). Letter to Keith Cain.*

Closing the Sexual Harassment Suit

William Fairley, attorney for Bald Head Island did investigate Davina's complaint against Ilvento. In doing so, he interviewed Dee, Mike Ilvento, Sylvia Timmons, Robert Willis, Kent Brown, Gene Hardee, Karen Grasty, Heather Hardee Josann Campanello and the mother of the little boy at the center of the emergency call on the island. On the application for legal defense aid, Dee had written "Paramedic for the Village of Bald Head Island 'finger-tickled' this officer between the legs on a medical call."

- Jones, Davina Buff. (nd). *Application for Legal defense.*

Ilvento claimed that he had only been concerned about the manager at Eb and Floe's during that call. He did not remember Dee being there, much less speaking to her. He denied having any interest in or having made any inquiries about her. Concerning the incident with the child, he charged that Jones had picked up the child incorrectly to cradle the child before the child was placed on the gurney. Jones then assumed a position at the child's head at the end of the gurney, immobilizing the body's head with her hands. He denied any contact with Jones' torso or between her legs. He confirmed the presence of Kent Brown, Robert Willis and Jones on the scene. He also named Helen Rozar as being there, which Jones had failed to do in her account of the incident.

- Ilvento, Michael. (nd). *Interview* by William Fairley.

Fairley interviewed Gene Hardee on September 26, 1999. Hardee said he had not known of the allegations until he had ordered Dee to write a letter about it. She had been reluctant to do so. He discussed it with Chief Brown and "had rather substantial differences of opinion with Brown over what was and was not said by Brown to Jones."

- Hardee, Gene. (9-26-99). *Interview* by William Fairley.

Fire Chief Kent Brown told Monty Clark that he never talked to Dee directly about Ilvento, becoming aware of the situation at a meeting in Wade Horne's office when Horne, Hardee and Brown had discussed the Ilvento situation over the speakerphone with Karen Grasty at her home. According to Brown, he made the decision to watch Ilvento for any activity of sexual harassment but he did not verbalize that at the meeting.

- Brown, Kent. (2-11-00). *Interview* by Monty Clark. Pp. 4-5.

Fairley found Brown to be "not tremendously helpful in terms of recollection of the details of the specific calls." Chief Grasty did talk to him but he had not believed it to be 'significant' and had not even talked to Ilvento about it. He denied ever talking to Jones. He added that he had not talked to his wife Trish and she had not talked to Jones. Fairley observed, "It is clear, from having spoken to the chiefs and acting chiefs of the Police and Fire departments, that a great deal of distrust, if not animosity, exists between these two departments."

- Brown, Kent. (10-22-99). *Interview* by William Fairley.

Heather Hardee and Josann Campanello told Fairley that while Ilvento did not act unpleasant during the committee meeting when Jones was present he was unimpressed. Jones was uncomfortable during the meeting until Ilvento was called away. Jones did ask if Ilvento could be replaced on the committee. Campanello began to lecture Jones about the departments needing to get along until Jones said there had been inappropriate conduct.

Then both women had urged her to report the matter up through her chain of command and to be sure that it received the necessary attention.

- Hardee, Heather and Josann Campanello. (10-22-99). *Interview* by William Fairley.

Robert Willis told Fairley about the jokes within the police department about Jones and Ilvento. At the time she was the only single female on the force besides the chief. He claimed Jones laughed about it. He denied that he had told her that Ilvento was interested in her or if Ilvento messed with Dee Ilvento would be sorry. Willis said Dee's attitude toward Ilvento had changed after early March. She intimated she was angry or annoyed with Ilvento. Willis said he never inquired as to the reason for this.

According to Willis, the Eb and Flo call was uneventful. During the Chandler Building incident, the child was placed on the ground. He did recall Jones squatting at the child's head and using her hands to immobilize the child's neck while the collar was being attached. Willis was standing to the child's left when the second collar was finally placed on the child and affixed. He had a direct view of that procedure although he did not specifically recall having watched every bit of the process of attaching the collar. He indicated that, until the collar was placed on the child, Jones was squatting at the child's head and Ilvento was on the child's right affixing the collar.

Willis did say that as they went to their vehicles Dee told him Ilvento had touched her. "That son-of-a-bitch touched me!" He said he had inquired into the details of the touching during that conversation but had sensed it was not a significant matter to Jones. Willis, therefore, had not reduced the report to writing nor did her report the allegations to any of his superiors. He further indicated that Jones' job performance had been criticized on any number of occasions including direct discussions with the Village Manager

Wade Horne relating to her job performance. Willis indicated that he had personally spoken with her about it and had undertaken efforts to improve areas in which she was deficient, which tended to center upon her relations and interactions with the public.

- Willis, Robert. (10-22-99). *Interview* by William Fairley.

Sylvia Timmons was an EMS and a Village Council member, so her testimony is as interesting as that of Robert Willis. While she did recall the incident at Eb and Flo's, her memory was 'very spotty – indicative that nothing unusual happened.' She also did not recall having even attended the incident at the Chandler Building. She denied any involvement in the call involving the child. However she could remember to say that Ilvento was a kind of "touchy/feely kind of fellow who routinely hugs" Timmons when they met. She herself had never taken offense at any such actions but could envision Ilvento touching someone's shoulder or arm in a "casual" sort of way. She said she had never heard of any interest shown toward Jones by Ilvento.

- Timmons, Sylvia. (10-22-99). *Interview* by William Fairley.

While Timmons may not have had a problem with Ilvento's ministrations, others did. Females from as far away as the government complex at Bolivia didn't welcome his 'friendliness.' "There were several of us who could have filed complaints against him." So Dee wasn't the only one who found him less than tolerable.
- Doe, Jane*. (7-24-07). *Telephone interview* by Elaine Buff. P. 4.

Too bad they didn't file charges. It may have saved Dee's life.

Most baffling as well as interesting is the mother of the child at the center of the controversy. When interviewed by telephone, this lady told the lawyer that she remembered a man with glasses (Kent Brown) and a short, stocky man with a dark moustache (Ilvento). She did not remember any female officer responding to the call. Neither did she remember a female officer directly in front of her for any
224

length of time during the episode. Such poor luck to have terrible memory and pitiful eye sight. But maybe lots of free vacations on an exclusive island.

As we know, Ilvento had told SBI Agent Storms he had not touched Jones, he had not liked her, she was too cocky. He had worked back-to-back shifts during the time Jones was killed. He had called and told Kent Brown he would take a polygraph. The charges against him were "bullshit!" and he had gone to her funeral only to "pay his respects."

- Ilvento, Michael. (10-26-99). *Interview* by Janet Storms. Pp. 1-3.

After finishing the interviews, Fairley wrote a report to present to Wade Horne in which he listed testimony that seemed to support Dee's side and that which seemed to support Ilvento's. Then he went on to add that "... there are numerous other accounts from *disinterested* (emphasis mine) individuals that rather dramatically contradict certain aspects of Jones' version of the story." Two accounts he noted were those of Robert Willis and the mother of the child. He noted that no other witness said the child was against Jones' torso. Actually, each witness said the child was somewhere different:

Willis: deckboards
Parent: lying on the backboard
Ilvento: on gurney

Each of these positions would have made it impossible for Ilvento to have touched Jones. Willis said that Jones was not upset over the incident. While Jones told Heather Hardee that Ilvento had made comments, Jones nowhere said in her statement Ilvento and she had ever had direct conversation.

The recollections of Willis and the parent tend to support Ilvento more than Jones. "It is also somewhat illuminating to note that Kent Brown never heard Ilvento mention any interest in Jones at any time, in fact Brown reported Ilvento denied any interest in Jones when he was asked by one of the EMT's if he might be interested in her." This seems to be a strange comment if no one was supposedly making remarks about one to the other as Willis had claimed.

"The most immediate question that would have to be answered is how an act such as the one described by Jones would not have been noted by the parent when the act would have taken place not more than eighteen inches directly in front of her face."

Perhaps the most important question would be how the lawyer could expect the parent to be a viable witness about anything when the woman didn't even see a female on the scene.

Fairley continued his opinion that if the town wanted to take action against Ilvento it would have the burden of showing such actions had taken place. "There is not evidence to do so."

"I believe that it is impossible to say, by the greater weight of the evidence, that the acts alleged by Jones did in fact occur. It would, therefore, be my recommendation that the town take no disciplinary action with regard to Mike Ilvento."

Furthermore, Fairley made several recommendations to Wade Horne. First he suggested that the town's procedures for dealing with allegations of this sort be reviewed. "It is clear that communication between employees and supervisors were not adequate."

Fairley traced the series of instances from its inception pointing out problems with its procedures. It went from Jones to Grasty to Brown "but Ilvento was never told of the allegations and consequently a matter that might possibly been resolved between Jones and Ilvento was never given a chance to be resolved."

Then he called Robert Willis onto the carpet. "Additionally, I would point out that, when a complaint regarding sexual harassment was made to Corporal Willis, Jones' immediate supervisor ... it was never reported to either of his superiors." Did anybody realize that this fact may have skewed his testimony against Dee? He had already gotten into trouble because of what he had not done.

The attorney counseled, " ... the town has a legal obligation to investigate the matters and that the town's failure to do so may give rise to a Title VII claim ... such allegations should be reduced to writing by the recipient thereof and passed up the chain of command to the Village Manager for formal investigation." This was the crux of the whole problem; if Dee's story had been found supported, they would have had such a lawsuit.

Fairley closed with the following observation: "In my judgment there are significant problems existing between the personnel in Fire and Police departments. There is rampant distrust on both sides."

- Fairley, William F. (11-03-99). *Investigative Report Concerning Mike Ilvento vs. Dee Jones*

Richard Hattendorf, the FOP lawyer Dee consulted said later, "It was my opinion at the time, and still is my opinion today, that Dee's employment security was set in motion by her assault complaint." They spoke again on October 18th after her meeting with Fairley. She had been reprimanded twice by that time. She told Hattendorf that she was afraid she was going to lose her job. "I told Dee that, in my opinion, her employer was likely to take just such a course of action but that she would be represented by counsel."

During the conversation Dee repeated that she loved working as a police officer, that she had finally found a profession that suited her. Though he did not tell her, the FOP lawyer "formed the opinion that Dee was likely a victim of retaliation by her employer."

- Hattendorf, Richard. (nd). *Memo: Chronological Summary of Dee Jones' Case* to Monty Clark

The dates on many of the interviews Fairley did are on October 22, 1999. Did he really do them on the day Dee was murdered? Grasty told Dee that Willis had already been written up when she was angry at Dee for having contacted the F.O.P. Dee didn't seem to know any investigating was proceeding in her case. Why was there such a gap in time between actions? Or was it just easier to close the case once Davina was out of the picture?

Even after all the trouble over Ilvento, even after the warnings Fairley gave Horne about future sexual harassment cases, the village management had a work session in 2005 where they were trying to formulate a policy, report, and complaint form concerning sexual harassment for employees that would "help avoid any problems during the complaint process as well as make the Village insurance carrier happy."

- Village of Bald Head, Work Session Meeting. (2-11-05). Retrieved 9-30-07 from http://www.villagebhi.org/government/council/pdf/vcm2005_02_11wk.pdf

Chapter Twenty Six

Loose Ends, Eye Witnesses, and a Confession

Some of the mysteries of that Friday night in 1999 have been answered. Several people reported seeing a low-flying airplane flying toward Bald Head Island late in the afternoon. Around 5:00 pm, Stuart Brown flew over Old Baldy to take photographs. Later he came forward, identified himself and offered the photographs to the police. It is not known if his work was viewed; none of it appears in any of the hearing evidence.

> I would like to state that I firmly believe that most, if not all, the investigators involved in this tragedy rushed to the conclusion that Officer Jones' death was a suicide. I heard this from one of the high ranking investigators with the Brunswick County Sheriff's Department within one hour of my arrival on the night of her death."

- Hardee, Gene. (4-30-04). *Fax* to Loy Buff.

What investigation there was, didn't stretch too far. Hardee told Monty Clark that the police didn't comb the island as the newspaper told its readers. "… they didn't even go to the two houses I asked them to."

- Hardee, Gene. (2-11-00). *Interview* by Monty Clark. P. 19.

George and Martha Hayworth lived across from the lighthouse. These were year-round residents at home the night of the murder, yet they were never contacted by police. "We've never been asked about anything."

- von Kolnitz, Cece. (12-07-99). Questions linger about Bald Head officer's death. *Morning-Star.* P. 1B.

Grasty maintained that "as it was explained to me by an assistant District Attorney, the District Attorney was being forced by the Sheriff and higher political figures to conclude that this was a suicide and for everyone to stop investigating the murder angle." Notice this casts no dispersions of any kind on those persons in the field or in the SBI labs doing their jobs. This is a local intervention.

- Grasty, Karen. (nd). *Letter* to A & E.

Even Wade Horne, who wielded tremendous pressure to keep Dee's death quiet and under wraps, had his own personal thoughts on the matter. "That's the mentality of this place. Settle it, close it out, because it's better for us to find that we've got a person who shot themselves, and disregard whether it's really true or not, because of the comfort level we're going to get by thinking ... that's the thought process that went on."

- *Buff v. Village of Bald Head Island Police Department, North Carolina League of Municipalities and North Carolina Rescue Workers Cap Death Benefits Act.* North Carolina Industrial Commission. (10-23/24-03). Exhibits Part II. P. 893.

One underlying tenet was that the owner of the island had placed its daily operations in the hands of his two sons with the stipulation that, if anything ever happened that brought embarrassment to it, the island would revert back to him. That has always been the rumor.

The law took its task to heart. Chief Grasty received a questionnaire from the Wilmington FBI on December 6, 1999 to help assist officers in investigating the death of Jones. This set of questions shows the 'neutral' level of investigative focus being conducted in the death of this police officer.

Did you notice any noticeable behavioral or emotional changes?
Were these changes related to anything else in her life at the time?
How would you describe Dee?
Generally speaking, what did others think of her?
How did she cope with problems in her life?
Did you know of any problems/difficulties/concerns she may

have been experiencing?

What type of stress was Dee experiencing?

 a. What type? b. When? c. How severe?

Did Dee have someone in whom she could confide?

 a. If so, who?

Did you ever hear Dee make any statements such as, "I can't take it anymore,"

"I'd be better off dead," etc.

 a. What was specifically said?

 b. Why?

 c. How often?

Were you aware if Dee was experiencing any of the following symptoms

(If so, indicate when, how often and how severe)?

 a. Sleep difficulties (trouble getting to sleep, recurrent awakenings, abrupt awakenings, awakening with anxiety, etc.

 b. Physical ailment (were they treated? By whom?)

 c. Persistent, recurring headaches

 d. Loss of appetite or lack of pleasure form favorite foods?

 e. Indigestion, heartburn, gas, cramps, etc.

 f. Vomiting?

 g. Bowel disturbances (diarrhea, constipation)

 h. Changes in sex drive, lack of pleasure from sex

- Grasty, Karen. (nd). *FBI Questionnaire.*

How many of these questions have anything remotely to do with being overcome and shot in the back of her head? This is a neutral investigative effort?

The preliminary autopsy report by Garret went to the State Medical Examiner's Office in Chapel Hill (OCME). This office is composed of 4-5 certified forensic pathologists who work full-time to review cases. If they don't like the cause of death or want to modify it, they can. Interestingly enough, that happened in Davina's case. As it happened, a Supplemental Death Certificate was added by Karen Chandler, MD, who on March 22, 2000, changed Dee's death to 'suicide.' Attached to her work is a "Case Encounter Form" on which was scribbled "they made her work with another officer. She went off by herself. She called in ... said sir, you're not supposed to have a gun on Bald Head island put gun down don't shoot me sir. Apparently told bf [boyfriend] she was going to off herself."

- *Buff v. Village of Bald Head Island Police Department, North Carolina League of Municipalities and North Carolina Rescue Workers Cap Death Benefits Act.* North Carolina Industrial Commission. (10-23/24-03). Exhibits Part I. P. 400.

The State Medical Examiner John D. Butts, MD was hardly any better in explaining the work of Chandler or of his own concurring decision. "I don't know for sure how she did but I believe that it is certainly possible for her to have done so."

Asked about the wound on her arm, he replied, "I don't know anything about a wound on the right forearm." He admitted that he had not been at the hearing, nor had he read any of the transcripts. At the time, Butts, who had been the Chief Medical Examiner since 1986, had a salary of between $143,612.00 and $250,432.00. One would think he could do a little better job before allowing a change in a cause of death.

- Butts, John D. (12-08-03). *Deposition.* P. 41.
- *Classification and pay actions.* Retrieved 10-17-07 from http://www.osp.state.nc.us/rtablecomm/spc-actions/07Meetings/classpayactions9-30.pdf

After the last ruling in the Buffs' favor in May, 2006, SBI Agent David Allen sent a letter to Gore after a so-called extensive re-evaluation of the case, "... the totality of information available does not support our requesting you change your ruling on the case."

- Little, Ken. (6-03-06). SBI reinforces suicide ruling in officer death. *Morning-Star.* P. 3B.

Who has the power to cover it up?

Consider pictures from the crime scene. There were problems getting photographs that give a real idea of what was really found that night as it was recorded by the police. There are contact sheets of the photographs taken during the time evidence was being collected but not all of the pictures were printed, or at least, were actually presented during the hearings. Then there is the question of why some of the photographs were printed and some were not.

For example, many people referred during the trial to the bloody hand print on the back of Dee's truck, but there was no picture of it found in the evidence files or the hearings presentation materials. The family's private investigator had a terrible time getting any materials from the Bolivia government complex or Bald Head Island.

It is difficult to blow up shots from a contact sheet to get really clear pictures, but we can see enough to make a point. Here is a shot of the passenger side of Dee's vehicle. The picture is grainy but it almost looks as if the symbol on the side of the truck on the left is not the same as the one on the right. Granted, that could be an optical illusion from the shadows and the poor quality of the photograph on the left. But the emblem on the truck on the left more closely resembles those found on the fire department vehicles than of those from the police department.

However, it is more difficult to explain away the next odd sets of photographs. The picture on the left is from the crime scene on Saturday morning; the one on the right from the re-enactment on the following Monday afternoon.

Both show a jacket hanging out of the driver's window. Also the truck on the right shows large black 911 numbers on the back of Dee's pick-up. Below, the back wheels appear to have been washed. These were not the only differences to be found in the photographs in the contact sheets from the crime scene.

In the crime scene photographs seen here that were provided to the hearings, it is quite evident that there is no jacket in the window and there are no 911 numbers on the back of Dee's pick-up. The numbers appeared between Friday night and Monday afternoon on the back of the truck. If they were originally on her truck, for whatever reason, someone removed them before the crime scene pictures were taken.

This jacket is shown in a series of photographs in the passenger seat in Davina's pick-up. This is not the one that is hanging out of the truck window.

Why were the photographs showing it hanging out of the door never printed? Why were the 911 numbers put on the tailgate of the pick-up between Friday night and Monday afternoon? Were they on there and taken off sometime before the pictures were taken at the crime scene because they had blood on them and the magnetic sign was cleaned and then put back on the truck? How much else has been rearranged or compromised in the photographs besides the shell casing and now the jacket?

When Lt. Gene Hardee arrived at the Bald Head Island crime scene with Sheriff Hewett, he had found Kent Brown, the island's fire truck and the volunteer fire crew on the scene. Hardee ordered Kent Brown to remove the fire truck and its volunteer crew. Apparently, Brown ignored that direct order because the fire truck was still in place when the highway patrol helicopter came to take overhead pictures at day break.

How do we know? The fire truck is clearly visible in the aerial crime scene photographs taken from the patrol helicopter. Dee's pick-up truck can be seen in the upper mid-horizon with both doors open facing towards the fire truck. The sun is rising. The fire truck is

no longer needed for its 'lighting,' if it was at all during the night. Yet it still sits where it will wash down the area before 12:00 pm. Apparently Brown wasn't taking his orders from the Bald Head Island Police Department during the hours on that Saturday following Dee's murder.

There was a witness within a block of where Dee died. Andy Adams was working on the island that week end. His brother Jerry and he had come over on the same ferry as Dee and Keith. They had seen Dee and the First Mate take the beer away from the three men.

Jerry had talked to Dee about the golf cart call at the River Pilot where he was waxing floors. He was the one who had described the way Dee had spun her tires when she had left the marina area. She was one of the few who could drive the straight-shift truck.

Andy had been working for a home owner on North Bald Head Wynd. Around 11:30 pm he was sitting at the front of the chapel drinking beer. The chapel is just out of sight in the picture above, down to the lower left hand corner. Close to midnight, he went around to the side on the right, away from the lighthouse to relieve himself.

He heard a loud Boom! He eased to the corner of the chapel and peered around in the direction of the lighthouse. He saw three men in a golf cart without its lights on leave the area going towards the post office from the direction of Old Baldy. "I had a bad feeling and went back to the house immediately."

Jerry called him between 12:30 – 1:00 am and told him not to leave the house because a policeman had been murdered. Andy Adams told Loy Buff he had not come forward sooner because he had not wanted to become involved. He only contacted the Buffs after hearing about the NC Industrial Commission Ruling. As the family certainly realized before the police pointed it out, Adams could have been seeking some kind of reward, but he never mentioned this to the family. He never asked for money when he sent them a notarized statement of his testimony. However, David Crocker

237

actually called the family's private investigator and said he had heard there was a reward for information concerning Dee's killer. Clark told him there was. Crocker said he could tell him who killed her: she did; now send him the reward.

In 2006 during the reinvestigation forced on them, the SBI located Andy Adams, handcuffed him, transported him to Raleigh and questioned him around the clock for three days until he recanted his testimony. They painted him as a drug addict and alcoholic and dismissed his story.

Below is the celebrated instrument given to anyone departing the island the weekend following Dee's murder.

SBI FILE 99-03464

I.D.   all persons (picture i.d.)

NAME_____

ADDRESS_____

TELEPHONE_____

SSN#_____

EMPLOYMENT_____

DATE OF ARRIVAL_____

REASON FOR DEPARTURE_____

DID YOU SEE OR HEAR ANY UNUSUAL ACTIVITY ON FRIDAY, OCTOBER 22, 1999 BETWEEN 11:00 P.M. & 12:00 MIDNIGHT.

ANYONE WITH ANY INFORMATION, PLEASE CALL (POLICE NUMBER)

- *Bald Head Island Investigative Canvass Sheet.* 10-23-99

Andy Adams' treatment was quite different from that accorded the three Hispanics that we know were on the island, all of who had serious, involved criminal records. They were never really questioned, much less held for any amount of time. The reason? Three men leaving the scene take a little bit away from a suicide scenario.

Three Hispanic men had crossed over on the ferry and Dee had helped take alcoholic beverages from them. They left on the 6:00 a.m. ferry on Saturday morning after filling out the investigative 'canvass' sheets for police.

Of course the respondents had more room in which to respond if they had anything to report, but that was basically what they were asked before they left the island. Rex Gore said the three Hispanics had been eliminated as suspects, the SBI reporting that they were good citizens, tax-payers, raising families and working hard. But Gene Hardee could not let it drop, even though Wade Horne would not finance his trip to Charlotte to investigate these three. When information was obtained on these three by other sources, their criminal reports painted quite a different picture.

One had a fairly clean record except for two speeding convictions. Between the other two, they shared a conviction list including: burglary, grand larceny, trespassing, weapons possession, throwing a missile into a dwelling, selling cocaine, burglary of a vehicle, assault and battery of an elderly person, strong-armed robbery, shoplifting and loitering, and pandering. One had been deported as a convicted felon. One had 5 social security numbers covering seventeen aliases.

- Calhoun, Terry. (7-06-05). Officer's death wasn't suicide. *The State Port Pilot.* Pp. 11A.

At least one had a history of trouble in the Miami-Dade area of Florida from 7-14-90 to 12-05-98. Seven days after being on Bald

Head Island, one of them had been ticketed in Fayetteville with a DUI.

Whether or not these three were involved in Dee's murder, it should concern Bald Head Island residents and future tourists to know that on any given night a trio such as this is free to roam the island and leave, being of no concern to county and state police. Better buy heavier locks and maybe use them. The residents really had more dangers to worry about that night on their precious turf than a police woman driving her vehicle going over 25 mph to an emergency call.

SBI Agent Steve Netherland appeared unannounced at the Buff residence and told Loy that the three were "law-abiding, family-raising tax-paying people."

- Buff, Loy. (9-12-07). *Interview* by Elaine Buff.

In 2006 Netherland explained to Buff that he hadn't actually gone to Charlotte to do the interview. SBI agents in Wilmington contacted the agency office in Charlotte. No, they didn't interview the men directly either. They called the employer of the men and talked to him over the phone. He said that the men were "law-abiding, family-raising tax-paying people." But Andy Adams spent three days in jail, constantly questioned until he recanted.

The most surprising fact in all of this is that there was a confession. Someone admitted to her murder. He bragged openly and loudly about it, not once, but many times in public, both in Southport and on Bald Head. This man, a contractor by trade, is a well-known resident of the island and has for many years openly threatened to kill anybody, police officers included, who might get in his way. He has a large drug trade in addition to being a contractor.

If someone wanted to get rid of Jones, why would the deed be done where her body could be found? There are alligators on the island, places where the body could have been taken out to sea

never to be seen again. If her death was to serve as a reminder and a statement to others, it had to be done where she could be found.

The gentleman we will call A. Crook* was the first suspect named by the Bald Head Police. His past includes several arrests for cocaine trafficking, including a two-year jail term for marijuana and cocaine delivery in Wilmington. South Carolina police warned Bald Head police about him immediately after Dee's death.

An informant told of A. Crook threatening the life of John Public* in Myrtle Beach, South Carolina because John Public was threatening to tell what he knew about his dealings with Crook in drug trafficking in Albemarle, North Carolina and Myrtle Beach. He wanted out of the business. Shortly after, Mr. Public disappeared. Mr. Crook advised that Mr. Public would never be found. His disappearance was to serve as a 'warning'.

- *Buff v. Bureau of Justice Assistance Public Safety Officers' Benefits.* (1-18-03). Pp. 42-43.

Supposedly Crook had cut a deal on subsequent charges in New Hanover with the SBI and/or FBI. True or not, he does seem to enjoy protection from somewhere high up the ladder of the law. His reputation on the island is known. He had no trouble clearly expressing his thoughts. A couple dining in the River Pilot Café overheard a conversation at the next table discussing Dee's death. Crook loudly proclaimed, "I had the bitch put down because she was getting into my shit!" Others have heard him make the same brazen statement. The cocaine found in the water near the Fort Fisher proves cocaine has been dispensed there in the water for collection.

- Buff, Harriet. (5-20-06). *Interview* by Elaine Buff.
- Doe, Jane*. (7-24-07). *Telephone interview* by Elaine Buff.

Crook told police that he went to bed at 10:00 p.m. the night Davina died. This has been disputed by eyewitnesses who placed him in his golf cart at the depot at the area of the ferry boat close to the spot where Dee was murdered near the time she was killed. He was also spotted in his cart at the US Army Survey Post BH-2 that was used as one of the crime scene markers afterwards by Bald Head Island Police.

As any visitor to Bald Head Island knows, there is a golf cart trail leading from the depot area to the place where Dee's body was found. The path is obscured by woods and can be used without discovery. It leads up to the back of where Dee's truck was parked. Beyond the second opening in the fence, her body was found several yards away on the left.

As we have learned, he or anyone else could have had access to her body while it lay uncovered on the dock.

All of this information was turned over to Detective Crocker and SBI Agent Storms. Mr. Crook was, of course, exonerated by the Brunswick County Sheriff's Department and still lives on Bald Head. The police list as many as three different addresses for him, one is on Middle Island from which there is easy access to Bald Head Island Creek and Fort Fisher. He has friends on the island in high political places. His name is readily seen in many places on the island.

Skoler noted an undocumented report of exoneration of Crook by polygraph test that was received after the report's closing or 9-01-05 without any indication of "when such investigative endeavor took place."

- Skoler, Daniel. (1-18-03). *Hearing officer claim determination. PSOB Case Number 2000-48.* P. 15.

Known as the 'drug dealer on the island,' Crook is known to hire Hispanics. It is assumed he still does.

Chapter Twenty Seven

Moving On

"It has been a very tough day on Bald Head Island. We are like a family here. This is a big loss." So said Wade Horne, Village Manager. Some family.

- Ramsey, Mike. (10-24-99). Officer dies in Bald Head Island shooting. *The Sunday Star-News.* P. 9A.

Public opinion was divided down the middle. If you were family or friend, you thought she was great and was murdered; if you were an island land owner, you really didn't care what had happened – you just wanted it to go away.

M. Lee, an island resident who knew Jones said, "She was perfect for this island because she was very friendly, but also very professional."

- von Kolnitz, Cece. (10-25-99). Slaying shatters peace of exclusive Bald Head. *Morning-Star.* P. 4A.

Another resident who had talked to Dee while she was on duty and considered her his friend said, "My personal opinion is that there's no way. She was a classy lady." Wayne Kester added, "I don't think that she would have killed herself."

- von Kolnitz, Cece. (12-10-99). Family, friends doubt suicide conclusion. *Morning-Star.* P. 1A.

Josann Campanello, the Village clerk remarked, "There didn't seem to be any concern about the woman who died, or the people who worked with her.

Reid Page, Jr. of the *Island Gazette* entered the affray with its Nov/Dec. issue in 1999.

I am so angry about this … I am angry about
wedding party comments such as 'Gee, I sure hope they get
those awful yellow ribbons down so it won't spoil our

245

pictures.' Another was heard to say, 'Well, of course this is awful, but I certainly hope there won't be publicity about it or all our property values will plummet!' Or worse yet, when the police set up a reenactment of the crime scene two days later, 'Can't you do this some other time? I need to get my mail?' Have we grown so immune to crime and death that all we can do is to retreat into our own little world of concerns? Does the death of a young woman mean so little that we would think to make a fuss over something so inane as not being able to our mail?

Let's stop being so petty and selfish. It is time we all stood up and said NO – not to those who think they can do such dirty business here with impunity.

The immediate family and Dee's friends were not the only ones to feel anger and frustration over the handling of her case as evident in the feelings voiced in a letter to the editor taking exception to Bald Head's mayor that all had moved on.

'The decision was made, people moved on,' said BHI Mayor Billy Berne. The rest of us out here, we didn't move on. We know something happened on your safe island that won't survive the light of day. Anyone who has lived here for any length of time knows that Brunswick County was used as a major route through the 80's and into the 90's because of its easy accessibility through waterways, rivers, creeks, and an ocean. People who knew Jones say she was zealous about ending drug dealing on Bald Head. Perhaps she surprised one of these dealers outside of Old Baldy that night in October, someone who also just might be a resident. Whether or not the residents of Bald Head want to know what happened that night, we do. Most of us don't believe for one second it was a suicide.

- Concerned Citizen. (6-19-02). *Letter* to the editor. *The State Port Pilot.*

Police Chief Grasty, at the time of Dee's death, described Dee as "well-like" by the other Bald Head Officers yet on the FBI questionnaire she added, "but to the best of my knowledge, the other officers also thought of her as being very aggressive and outspoken."

- Grasty, Karen. (nd). *FBI Questionnaire.*

At the time of Dee's funeral, Grasty said that, as a police officer, "Davina would do anything she was asked to do and would always go above and beyond the call of duty. You never had to ask her twice to do anything. She did what was expected of her and then some. She always wanted to do something to help someone or make sure people safe."

- D'Abruzzo, Diana. (10-27-99). 'The biggest heart of anyone ...' *The State Port Pilot.* P. 5.

This hardly sounds like the same officer who had become so inept by October that she would be in danger of losing her job. Some called the acts against her as placing her on probation. In 2004 Grasty characterized Dee as "a very eager and meticulous police officer."

- Peterson, Sarah. (7-28-04). Commission: Officer death was homicide. *The State Port Pilot.* P. 14A.

She told Ken Little of the Wilmington *Star-News* that Jones was aggressive and the subject of complaints but, "she was learning to exercise self-control and doing a good job."

- Little Ken. (10-24-03). Witness: Officer sought treatment for depression. *Morning-Star.* P. 5A.

Then on the FBI questionnaire, she wrote that Dee had "minor complaints and she took them as serious complaints."

- Grasty, Karen. (nd). *FBI Questionnaire.*

Those 'minor' complaints had turned quite serious; Hardee was up to his neck in piranhas wanting her throat. Combined with the Ilvento lawsuit, Dee was about to lose her job over the complaints and she knew it. So did Grasty.

Why did Hardee stay quiet? He was putting in time for his retirement. Grasty was working for her disability. She also hadn't testified that she had been called by her daughter from Bald Head Island. Her daughter had seen MacCloud dressed in camouflage that night before Dee died. He was already there when Dee was searching for him. The daughter had seen Dee's body lying uncovered on the dock. But the daughter was afraid and wouldn't testify and Grasty did not divulge what the daughter knew.

What about Cain, what did he really know? Immediately after the murder, he had called and told the Buffs he wanted to come and talk to them. But they were inundated with people and asked him to wait. He never went near them again. At a subsequent hearing, Cain ended up in the hall with a co-worker of both Dee and himself. He had not seen them since his partner's death. They asked him if he thought she had done this to herself and placed him in the position of having to find her. He lowered his head and barely said yes.

"I thought the two of you were friends. She would have to know you would be the one to find her. Why would she do this to you?"

"I don't know why, I don't know why she did it. But I think that's what she did." But he said it without conviction. He became distraught during the testimony and had to leave the room and he feared verbally that he would have to see Dee's pictures from that night. After several years with the sheriff's S.W.A.T. team, he left the area without ever having spoken to the Buffs, even though he attended the memorial service.

Extensive notes on all the calls and transmissions from that night were turned over to Randy Thompson, who is now the director of Brunswick County Emergency Services. He saw no reason to keep the information, even though it included information about several other pending cases at that time, so the material may no longer be in existence.

SBI Agent Janet Storms took Dee's journals from Loy Buff under the pretext of perusing them while visiting her sick father in the hospital and then never returned them. So she may have gotten Dee's last writings about the drug dealing she had just seen. If she had been writing about killing herself, Storms would have brought the journals out fast enough to be seen.

Had SBI Agent Storms found anything else in Dee's house besides her journals? Yes, she had, but it did not meld with a suicide scenario, so nothing much was made of it by the police. Dee had jammed sandals into the back door so the dogs could go outside while she was at work.

Going through the house to get the dogs, the Buffs and the officers saw something on Dee's kitchen table: a to-do list for Saturday, October 23, 1999.

She intended to buy heart worm pills for the dogs, laundry detergent, pick up the medicine the police tried to say she had quit taking due to the empty bottle they had found in the house. She was getting ready to replace the shocks on the truck. She had already gotten a price for the job. It didn't appear that she had left her house that Friday afternoon with the idea that she would not be returning to it.

Dee made notes for herself so that she would remember what she needed to do. There were other notes from other days that she left behind among her belongings. Notes from previous days included:

Wednesday: 10-20-99

    Caswell Beach PD
    Dr. appt. at 1:45
    Pick up/Deposit paycheck
    Fix resume at Daddy's   get leashes
    Get truck inspected
    Fill out application to Greensboro

Thursday: 10-21-99

    Shallotte
    Sunset
    Johnson Co. Sheriff Dept.
    Get drinks for PD
    Copy F-3 numerous times

- Jones, Davina Buff. (10-20-99). *To do list.*
- Jones, Davina Buff. (10-21-99). *To do list.*

Dee had ordered a copy of *What Southern Women Know (That Every Woman Should): Timeless Secrets to Getting Everything You Want in Life, Love, and Work.* The lady at the bookstore sold the copy after learning that Dee had died. When Harriet went to get the book, the lady had to order another copy for her.

    Davina Buff Jones left her dogs at home on Friday afternoon on October 22, 1999, intending to go to the drug store to get medicine for herself and then pick up medicine for her dogs the next day. She had no idea she would be dead before morning. She had no idea that when she died, two Southport policemen would load dogs onto the boat along with Chief Karen Grasty and go to Bald Head Island to help track down her killers. She had no idea that the Sheriff of Brunswick County would not let the dogs work once they had been taken off the boat.

- Doe, John III* (nd) Policeman. *Interview.*
- Grasty, Karen. (8-29-01). *Interview* by Henry Foy.

"This is certainly a terrible tragedy for the law enforcement community." Sheriff Hewett had made that comment two days after he had made that decision to stop the dogs on Bald Head.

- Ramsey, Mike. (10-24-99). Officer dies in Bald Head Island shooting. *The Sunday Star-News.* P. 9A.

SBI Agent Janet Storms thought she had struck a victory by getting Dee's journals from the Buffs. It had been so easy. They were trusting souls. But Storms wasn't as smart as she had thought.

Loy David Buff had just lost his namesake, told only hours early that his middle girl was dead. He was blind with grief, not yet in shock, moving solely on adrenalin. He picked up what he saw of his daughter. He grabbed some writing, some personal articles, and leashes for the dogs. He could not, did not do a good job of getting everything.

At the time he took it home. He thought nothing of it when the woman asked for it. Harriet and he could only begin to try and get their minds to understand one thing: one of their children, their blonde-haired little baby, the chubby little one who had waddled around in the snow, pulled on the dog when she was little, grown up to be a police officer – was no longer alive. Here was an SBI agent; someone you turn to for help in trouble. She was going to help find out who took your child. She was on their side. So when Storms asked for his Vannie's journals, the stuff he himself took out of his dead daughter's house with his own two hands, he gave them to her without a thought. He had no idea he would never see them again. The agent would deny she took them.

Were they that important to the case? *Oh, yes.*

"She kept a notebook and she documented *everything* (My emphasis) that ever happened with any of her calls, any confrontation she had, anything. She documented it all." If Will

Hewett was ever correct about anything he ever said about Davina Elaine Jones, he was right about that.

▪ Hewett, William L. (2-08-00) *Interview* by Monty Clark. P. 48.

It is true. Dee wrote about seeing workers peeing in broad day light. About Gene's snippy remarks to her when he felt she hadn't worked enough. When she stopped the man driving drunk on the golf cart with his little children and his wife complained about the alligator on the golf course. How the painter stashed marijuana in his van and hid it illegally in the woods there until he could sell it. How Dexter Ludlum accused her of having "cooties" in front of the rest of the police group and hurt her feelings. The cook-out when Grasty had been angry and raked her over the coals about her F.O.P. contact and MacCloud. How she just wanted to go away and start somewhere else.

How do we know about all of this from a dead woman? Because Loy Buff, still so stunned he could barely function, *did not get it all.* Storms may have gotten the journal entries about what Dee had seen earlier being unloaded from a boat, taken by panel truck and unloaded and stored in an outbuilding of a high ranking North Carolina official, she may have gotten the account she no doubt turned in on the job about the event, she may have come across more details about the suitcases of money MacCloud declared she never told him about and the pages most definitely there about the dirty deeds of Scott Monzon and what Dee thought of him. But Storms outsmarted herself: she *didn't get it all.*

What Did Happen?

Karen Grasty believes that Davina backed into the cul-de-sac that night to smoke and work on paperwork while she watched the traffic from the last ferry. The former police chief believes that Dee was approached and removed from the truck. Someone used her ponytail to help manage her until she could be maneuvered and shot from behind just outside of her pick-up truck. Then her body was dragged over to where Keith Cain found it.

- Buff, Loy and Harriet. (8-24-06). *Interview* by Elaine Buff.

If Dee was doing paperwork, was her interior light on and someone turned it off? Where was the clipboard and paperwork she had been working on? Is this where she had begun to notice the drug traffic going on at the lighthouse? Had the drug dealers been that brazen to carry on their activity with her sitting there?

"Fact is, after talking to the Buff family and after reviewing much of the documentation later shown to the Industrial Commission, I, too, concluded that Davina was likely murdered. ... Most of us who believe Jones was murdered also believe she interrupted a drug operation."

- Calhoun, Terry. (2-09-05). Will prohibition ever work? *The State Port Pilot*. P. 5A.

On October 31, 2006, Loy Buff received a letter from a man named Russell*. Russell was an inmate who had known a man in jail who he described as between 50 – 55 years of age and in bad health with heart trouble and diabetes.

This older man had been incarcerated for trying to extort money from a high Brunswick County official and a high state official with ties to the area. He told Russell that Dee had seen men unloading marijuana and/or cocaine from a boat onto shore into a panel van. Then it went to a specific lot belonging to the state official where it was unloaded into an out building. The official had supposedly acquired the lot by making a deal with a drug trafficker years earlier in return for a light sentence. Dee filed a report. Within days, she was dead.

The man said that she did not commit suicide but had been shot in the back of her head with her own pistol. He claimed he had wire-tapped the state official's phone in Raleigh. When Dee's report was turned in, calls were made to his office. The order was given to silence Jones. Then a call went from the Brunswick official to someone in Wilmington. The prisoner said there were tapes stored that could prove his story. He wanted to use them to work a deal to get himself out of jail.

Shortly after he made his request for a deal known, he was called to medical. Once there, they took his nitro pills and cancelled the rest of his medications. Within days, the man died of a heart attack, but his death was term 'natural causes.'

This prisoner did not ask for money when he wrote Buff. He did not ask for anything, as a matter of fact. How did the prisoner know these details about Dee? How did he know what she saw? Those details were never in a news article. Perhaps this story is completely false. It does remind us of Dee's journals. Did she see what this man said she did? If so, it was in her journal. If she saw it, she filed an official report about it, too. She was that kind of officer. If she did, someone in that police department turned her in to the powers that be and that was all it took. No more trying to force her out. She had to go permanently.

We know that MacCloud was on the island, keeping away from Dee, who was expecting him. Someone else may have been there that night, too. Will Hewett was the only one polygraphed who failed the test.

1. Were you present when Dee was shot?
2. Are you involved in any way in the shooting of Dee?
3. Did you plan with anyone to kill Dee?

- *Buff v. Village of Bald Head Island Police Department, North Carolina League of Municipalities and North Carolina Rescue Workers Cap Death Benefits Act.* North Carolina Industrial Commission. (10-23/24-03).P. 215.

Dee had turned him down to go back to another man who then left her for his ex-wife. "She was the first woman I ever forgave. … I've never forgiven anyone at all."

- Hewett, William L. (2-08-00) *Interview* by Monty Clark. P. 28.

Maybe he didn't forgive Dee, either. There is a gap of two and a half hours where he said he was at home watching television before he went to Indigo Plantation to see his friend. At his home he had a 15' scout boat belonging to a resident of Bald Head. He was supposed to be working on it. It had a 40 horsepower Yamaha engine and could make the trip from the Bald Head Marina to Southport in seven minutes. If one had the knowledge as he did to navigate from the public access within a quarter of a mile from his house over the flats in the river to the pier at the back of the lighthouse, the trip could be made in less time than that. Plus, such an arrival would place someone within yards of where the murder took place.

Hewett's yard where the boat stayed for months is thick with trees. Yet after keeping the boat during autumn's season of falling leaves, there were few leaves in the boat when the owner went to retrieve it. They alerted the police and Lt. Gene Hardee investigated. He, too, thought it curious to find so few leaves inside the boat.

As Will told the private investigator, "I know for a fact that there are people who come to the island, because I've seen them, and they are scary individuals. You don't know who's lurking around over there. That place is dark. It's grown up, little thin walkways, and everything. It's easy to do something over there and get away with it."

- Hewett, William L. (2-08-00) *Interview* by Monty Clark. P. 61.

Hewett had met Dee while he was working on the island. He knew it by heart. He also knew MacCloud having had worked narcotics for 5 years himself. He knew about A. Crook. A. Crook would have known Hewett's reputation as a "loose cannon" and his ability to do "anything without a conscience."

As for MacCloud, Dee had told him, "Come on over some time and let me see what you think of this shit." MacCloud declared that while Dee had told Monzon there were suitcases of drugs and money being passed around at the lighthouse, "She never said that to me.

- *Buff v. Village of Bald Head Island Police Department, North Carolina League of Municipalities and North Carolina Rescue Workers Cap Death Benefits Act.* North Carolina Industrial Commission. (10-23/24-03). Exhibits Part II. P. 844, 845.

That is doubtful. One of Dee's problems was that she couldn't be quiet when she needed to be. If she saw drugs on that island, she told MacCloud. That was why she had left him a pass at the ferry for that night.

She wanted to work undercover. She was looking to MacCloud to help train her, to help her make that big drug bust that would help her keep her job until she could get another one somewhere else. She certainly did discuss what was going on with him. She was looking for him on that Friday night.

"It appears that Jones had (or thought she had) an appointment with another police officer on the night of October 22, 1999, to discuss illicit drug activity and/or personal professional problems."

- Skoler, Daniel. (1-18-03). *Hearing officer claim determination. PSOB Case Number 2000-48.* Pp. 14.

As has been pointed out, he presented that pass at Indigo, which means he boarded the ferry or merely drove up, showed them his ticket and left with it. Jamie Grasty, the Police Chief's own daughter, working at Eb and Flo's, saw him dressed in camouflage on the island before Dee was killed. But she never testified to that fact. Nor did she testify to seeing Dee's body uncovered as it lay on the gurney on the dock. Nor did she testify that she called her mother and told her about Dee being dead.

Jamie may have seen MacCloud, but Dee didn't. Both Hewett and MacCloud knew she had been depressed, they could use that as a motive for suicide. They both knew she was deaf in her right ear. If either of them came up behind her, she would not have thought of either of them as her executioner. The only way to explain the curious workings of her radio from channel one to channel two to off and back to channel one is that it was done by someone familiar with police radios. We know Dee originally changed the channel from one to two. We know that the radio was probably turned off. "The only way the gunshot would not have been heard by 911 operators was if she had turned off the microphone before shooting."

- Reiss, Cory. (12-10-99). Bald Head officer shot self, DA says. *Morning-Star.* P. 8A.

One other thing these two men shared in common was that both of them had wanted to go to bed with Dee and she had wanted only friendship. "When either would come to her house, she would stay quiet and not let them in and they would leave."

- Hart, Tanya. (8-27-07). *Interview* by Elaine Buff.

So why was Jones Killed? She had made too many enemies by trying to uphold the law. Position and power and wealth meant nothing to her if you broke the law. She had sought to protect other women from being molested or harassed by a worker for the town and embarrassed the town. There loomed the real threat of a Title VII law suit. Finally, she lead learned too much about the drug business on the island and became a real liability for people in the higher echelons of wealth and politics. The mere irritation had become a cancer that had to be removed. And quickly.

They were the ones who had the most to benefit by the death. The last thing on her duty list was to check for footprints coming from Fort Fisher. Trouble didn't come from that direction; it was already there. First there were the complaints, louder and more numerous as the rookie refused to leave. Then they tried the no-ride-alone re-training insult. It was hard and embarrassing, but Dee wouldn't leave. She was moved to the night shift. But Dee wouldn't leave. Working the night shift gave the perfect opportunity to eradicate their problem. They couldn't let her leave now; she knew too much.

Who had the power to cover it up? People who won't let the family see the autopsy pictures of their own dead daughter. (When they did present themselves at Bolivia to see the autopsy pictures, they couldn't get in. In fact, the only one to see Rex Gore at all was Beverly, who posed as a student writing a paper about something else. Once he learned who she was, he ordered her out of his office.) People who have power change things at crime scenes and then clean them up quickly; oppose death benefits in hearings on up through state and federal levels where they are argued in hearings by attorneys from the Attorney General's Office; prevent dogs from working when they are brought in to help in the search for killers. Do they misguide in even more basic ways?

"It would be very unusual for an officer to approach three individuals in a poorly illuminated area without his/her service flashlight and the police unit's headlights pointed away from that area.

Was the flashlight moved?
Was the truck moved?
- Martinez, Michael. (2-20-01). *Report*. P. 5.

Martinez brings up interesting points. What may have

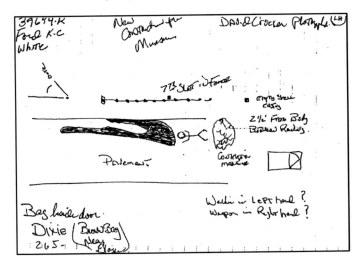

happened to Jones begins in those questions. We find answers

beginning in the crime scene diagram provided by Brunswick County

Sheriff's Department Detective David Crocker.

He was the only one to mention a brown paper bag found on

the scene, as he lists here, near Keith Cain's Blazer. On it was

written crudely 'Dixie 265.' This by itself would mean very little except

for a photograph taken of the Blazer. Keith Cain came into the

intersection and parked his vehicle at a diagonal when he first was

trying to locate Jones.

Once he found her body, he moved his vehicle so that his

lights would shed light on where her body was on the ground. So he

turned on his take-down lights to illuminate the area but once he

moved his vehicle, his lights would have been shining directly into

the golf cart and trash pile with Dee's body on the ground behind all

of this. It would almost seem to have been better to have stayed on the diagonal. Then he parked on the brown bag and white substance.

In the spot where he parked his car the second time, almost underneath his driver's door in this picture, the brown paper bag is visible along with some white substance and something else.

This blow-up of the brown paper bag shows the white substance, and blood drops. The notation for this picture states: "Photograph showing a trail of blood spots near the driver's door of Officer Cain's patrol vehicle."

- Crocker, David. (2-09-00). *Photograph Log*. P. 1

This is not blood from the EMS personnel carrying Jones away from the scene; they took her away between the two cars. This is not blood smeared by either Brown or Cain while they knelt. This blood was never mentioned anywhere in any report other than Crocker's diagram and this photograph.

>>>>>>>>>>>>>>>>>>>>>>>>>

Just suppose for a few moments that on October 22, 1999, the patrol shift begins as usual. The two answer the call about the van stuck on Middle Island. They answer the call about the missing cart at the café. They have seen a golf cart at the lighthouse so they leave the marina and drive the short distance there. The workers Dee talked to can see their vehicle tail lights through the brush scarcely a quarter of a mile away. They are there only long enough for Dee to jot down the Bald Head Island registration number of the golf cart. The two go back to the police station by different routes, getting back to the police station almost simultaneously. Dee would go the way her killers would flee the scene – Cain would follow the route he would re-trace when he searched for her later. Ironic.

Her visitor, whom we will call Dellenger Raines, has not yet arrived. After she has dinner and the last ferry bringing people from the mainland has come, Dee will go down to check for her friend, make a phone call and stop for a cigarette where she always does in the cul-de-sac at the lighthouse. Her partner lets her go because he has received the signal to let her go out by herself: the telephone call about a missing cart from the café. They didn't tell him they were going to kill her. Maybe they told him they were going to give her some experience at undercover work. Maybe he knew she was going to meet her friend.

Once at the dock, she still does not see her friend. She makes a quick call to her ex-boyfriend saying that she still wants to be friends with both he and his wife. Activity on the dock causes her to walk out and check, still scanning the dock for her friend. It is not like Dell to leave her hanging. Maybe he has been called elsewhere, but he usually lets her know if he's been detained. He knows the importance of what she has told, of the trouble she is in here. She has told him about the nights she has hidden her truck in the woods here and there on the island and just sat watching, observing what went on, taking notes.

She has told him about the lighthouse and what has been going on there. Maybe he is waiting for her there. Backtracking, she gets back into her truck and starts there. On the way the officer meets three people in a golf cart on the way to their week end rental. They are on the wrong side of the road. Jones rolls down her window and gets them going in the right direction in the correct lane. She continues on towards the lighthouse.

Turning into Ballast Alley, her lights stab into the darkness until she can see the base of Old Baldy. As she turns left onto Lighthouse Wynd she sees three Hispanic men. One of them is carrying a brown bag. Perhaps he tries to hide it. Perhaps one steps in front of the truck. Something is done to get her attention, to get her to stop. Just three men walking would not necessarily have brought her to a stop.

"Show me out with three. 10-4. Show me out with three. Stand by, stand by, please." She leaves her truck radio on, gets out. She carries her flashlight even though she has turned on her take-down and blue lights. Surreptitiously, as she nears them, Dee changes her portable radio channel from 1 to 2 and keys her mike because as she approaches them, one has drawn a gun. Maybe from inside the brown bag. She tries to stay cool and calm. Channel 2 guarantees that C-COM and her partner will hear her clearly. No one else can, but there is no one else to help her. When she keys her mike, it makes a loud squelch over the air. "There ain't no reason *to have a gun here on Bald Head Island, okay? You want to put down the gun? Come on, do me the favor and put down the gun."*

But they keep coming closer. They don't know that Adam and Precious are home sleeping, waiting for their momma. They don't care. Someone comes up behind her. She doesn't hear them. They know she won't. They have assurance. They're her friends. If she should turn and see them coming, she will think they are coming to help her.

"Please don't shoot me, sir," she pleads.

She is pushed down on her right knee, her radio is turned off. The coat from her front seat is draped over her head. Her Glock, taken from behind her, is placed against her head. Instantly her right hand goes up in reflex and she jerks her head. The bullet doesn't go behind her right ear and exit out her left temple like they planned. It is a dark place there at Old Baldy and the coat keeps the blood from splattering over the five men surrounding her but if obliterates their view. They may have insurance coming to help cover up their deed, but they don't have much time to look at their handiwork. One of the shooters turns her radio back on, putting it on channel 1, not realizing it had been on channel 2. One has come by ferry, but he will go back with the other so the two shooters strike out behind the lighthouse to the pier and the little boat waiting. The three Hispanics jump to action. One gets in the truck, the other two hold the body up

in the back, keeping it so the blood won't ooze any more than they can help until the truck has been backed up into the cul-de-sac just like she would have parked it. They fix the lights. Two drag her over behind the trash pile while one takes her flashlight and goes back to find the casing – or one drags her and two search. They put the gun under her hand, throw the flashlight into her front seat and toss the coat onto the driver's door. The three get into a golf cart and flee down Lighthouse Wynd past the post office, Village Hall, and the chapel where an island week end worker has been drinking beer and now hides terrified in the darkness as they race by.

All is quiet for several minutes except for the clamor on Dee's radio, back on channel 1, carrying the traffic as they look for her. Her blood trickles down the rough terrain. Two dogs whimper in their sleep miles away. A man in a golf cart ventures by the US Survey marker BH-2 surveying the results, willing to tell anybody anywhere that he had had her put down.

This book is written to tell all the details, to let the reader take it in and judge for themselves. Davina Buff Jones was killed by a single bullet, but she had been attacked for months by people who had wounded and gouged her spirit.

Rest easier now, Dee. We have brought your story out of the darkness, into the light.

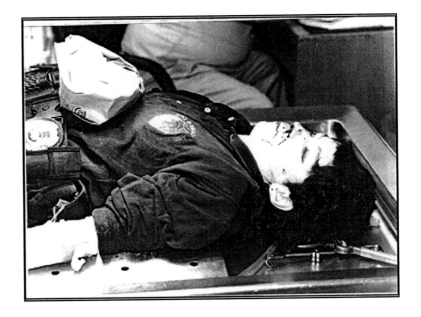

Davina Elaine Buff Jones

July 29, 1966 – October 22, 1999

"You will pay them back what they deserve, Lord, according to the work of their hands."　　　　　　　　*Lamentations 3:64*

In 2007 Harriet and Loy Buff made a pilgrimage to the place where someone left their daughter to die on the sands of Bald Head Island.

Aftermath:

Picking up the Pieces

Time has not been especially kind for the principals involved in the death and betrayal of Davina Buff Jones.

One of the first suspects to be exonerated by polygraph was charged on August 2, 2000, along with two others in stealing a $40,000.00 23 foot boat from the Bald Head Island Marina. It was run aground within Oak Island's jurisdiction. His mother and he moved from Bald Head Island.

- Three Charged in Boat Theft.(8-02-00). *State Port Pilot*. np.

Gene Hardee requested and received a demotion from lieutenant to corporal with a probationary period of employment and a pay cut. He had tired of being forced by Village Manager Wade Horne to break the law by continually illegally informing village council members of police information concerning the police investigation into Dee's murder. He stayed employed there long enough to qualify for his retirement. In private life, he became a private investigator.

- Horne, Wade. (11-29-99). *Memo* to Gene Hardee.

In December of 1999 Officer David Cox replaced Lt. Gene Hardee as acting chief. Then in March of the following year, Kenneth Snead Sr. was named the new chief.

- Perkins, Tommy. (3-01-00). Columbus deputy is Bald Head's new chief. *Morning Star*. P. 2B.

Wade Horne resigned as Village Manager in 2000 to 'spend more time with his eight-year old daughter and devote more time to his consulting business specialty coastal development. He left on April 28th wanting to stay until selecting a new police chief to replace Grasty. He had held the position of Village Manager for four years.

- von Kolnitz, Ceci. (2-22-00). Manager resigns at Bald Head. *Morning Star.* P. 2b.

Karen Grasty left her job as police chief, obtaining disability for her back. Her family relocated to the western part of the state.

Keith Cain had been treated for shock the night of the murder and had follow-up visits with the same Dr. Tonn who had declared Dee fit to be an officer. The time sheets show that Grasty covered the hours he missed to see the doctor. He was paid as if he had been on duty. Since much was made of Dee's visits to a mental health center, one wonders if these sessions with a psychiatrist will come back to haunt him or blemish his record as her visits were used against her.

- Grasty, Karen. (3-16-00). *Memo* to Keith Cain.

Cain resigned on March 16, 2000, to take a position with the Brunswick County Sheriff's Office. In his resignation letter Cain wrote, "I hate to leave the family I had at the Police Department, but I pray that some day the Police Department can pull together again and become the Department I once knew." In a note to Grasty at the bottom of her copy of his letter, Cain added a note including, "I will never forget what you did for me."

- Cain, Keith. (3-01-00). *Letter* to Lt. Gene Hardee, Chief Karen Grasty.

After working for several years on the sheriff's S.W.A.T. Cain left Brunswick County and is said to be living in the Charlotte area. Though he had immediately contacted the Buffs after the shooting and said he would like to come and talk to them, he never did contact them again.

SBI Special Agent Tony Cummings retired three months early as a special agent in charge of the SBI coastal district to be hired as Chief Deputy to Brunswick County Sheriff Ronald Hewett, replacing Charlie Miller. "Hewett said because the hiring decision was his to make, advertising the position was not required."

- Fulford, Edward. (11-08-01). SBI Agent picked as new chief deputy. *Brunswick Beacon.* P. 8A.

On December 13, 1999, a female officer on the force filed charges against Lt. Robert Willis for making unwanted sexually oriented gestures toward her "by placing his hands on her, rubbing her neck, playing with her hair, and kissing her." He had initiated this behavior around the time of Dee's memorial service. He had told her "if she did not smile that he was going to kiss her and he proceeded to kiss her." She told him such was not acceptable and told him to stop. She had discussed the situation with her family and the Village attorney William Fairley and was going to press charges. One has to wonder if she was influenced to take a stand because of what had happened to Dee. Willis left the police force at Bald Head. Some say he drove a truck for a while in another state. He returned to the area and joined the Southport Police Department for a while but was dismissed there.

Fire Chief Kent Brown received so much criticism concerning his decision to move Dee, he sought counsel from outside sources who upheld his decision to move her. But in the immediate days following Dee's death, he accompanied Robert Willis to check out some possible hideout locations. On his way back, he got a call from Mayor Kitty Henson who said she need him a.s.a.p. He went straight to Village Hall without removing the gun he had worn while with Willis.

Apparently someone saw him wearing the weapon in to see her and complained to Wade Horne who sent Brown a memo telling him he now had to get permission from Horne or the Police Chief before wearing his weapon in the future. Brown requested clarification on procedures in writing. He also asked Grasty for her reaction.

- Brown, Kent. (10-27-99). *Memo: Possessing Firearms* to Wade Horne

Grasty informed the fire chief that he could have solved the situation by having removed his gun after helping Willis. She told him there was a Procedural Manual at the police department that he could peruse at any time. She gave him the number to her phone and pager and told him to contact her or the duty officer or Gene Hardee. He had specifically mentioned concern when investigating arson scenes. She assured him that officers would be on hand to assist him in that event.

- Grasty, Karen. (11-04-99). *Letter* to Kent Brown.

In March of 2000 Village Manager Wade Horne brought unspecified charges against Kent Brown and suspended him without pay. Brown had taken emergency actions in Horne's absence following Hurricane Floyd. Horne had not approved. Durham lawyer Lee Castle represented Brown and 90 full-time residents signed a petition supporting Brown.

- Calhoun, Terry. (4-05-00). Emergency services case reviewed. *State Port Pilot*. P. 2.

Emergency service workers Mike Ilvento, Mike Tripp and Ted Lee resigned as a result of the situation. All of them found employment elsewhere and continued on with their lives. Mike Ilvento would return to the limelight later with Kent Brown.

- Calhoun, Terry. (3-29-00). Hearing set Monday on EMS suspension. *State Port Pilot*. P. 2.

Kent Brown left Bald Head Island to become the first EMS chief for Oak Island. He was replaced on the island by Chip Munna.

Mike Ilvento became an EMS for Brunswick County. On June 23, 2002, he was in an Oak Island restaurant/night club when a fight broke out. Resulting injuries caused 911 to send EMS to the scene. When they arrived, "Good Samaritan" Ilvento had been rendering first aid and began telling the arriving EMS personnel what to do and what equipment to get and use.

On July 3rd Kent Brown wrote the Brunswick County EMS Director Joey Folding complaining of Ilvento's behavior ordering squad members and police around in a loud and sarcastic voice. Brown claimed that Ilvento smelled of alcohol and at one point brought out an oversized knife and cut the button off the patient's shirt.

Brown further charged that Ilvento had been rude to females then and in the past and should not be tolerated. He requested that Ilvento not be sent to Oak Island calls in the future. "His presence continues to disrupt the atmosphere on emergency medical scenes and his arrogance and argumentative attitude will not be tolerated on Oak Island." Some time after Folding received Brown's letter, Ilvento was terminated as an employee of the Brunswick County EMS. He later sued. At the time of the hearing in 2003, Will Hewett testified that Ilvento was doing construction work in High Point, North Carolina. At one time, prior to Ilvento leaving the area, he and Brown came to fisticuffs in a local eatery.

- Nubel, Richard. (6-17-02). Libel claimed in EMS complaint. *The State Port Pilot.* P. 5.
- *Buff v. Village of Bald Head Island Police Department, North Carolina League of Municipalities and North Carolina Rescue Workers Cap Death Benefits Act.* North Carolina Industrial Commission. (10-23/24-03). P. 516.

Kent Brown resigned from his position at Oak Island at the request of Town Manager David Oles in 2002. Oles said Brown had misled him about a budget request for the town's emergency medical services. Brown had misrepresented state law and county intent to upgrade services, causing Oles to lose confidence in Brown's ability to lead, even though Brown had done a good job in his three-year tenure.

- Nubel, Richard. (6-05-02). Fire/EMS chief resigns. *The State Port Pilot.* P. 8.

SBI special agent Janet Storms was relocated to the western part of the state without the necklace and earrings Dee had been wearing the night she died that Storms almost 'forgot' to return to Harriet Buff when returning other items.

Even the pathologist working in the State Medical Examiner's Officer has moved to Texas. There have been new police officers, new police chiefs, mayors, council members on Bald Head.

The officer designation '4206' was not retired as promised. Dee's friend John Doe II was infuriated to hear an officer being called over the radio by that designation in 2001.

The high official named by a prisoner as being involved in her death has his supporters, but also his detractors. He is known on the island, according to John Doe II, as "Mr. Sleazy." The word from people in real estate circles is that he "is not to be trusted." The politico has had generous deals given to him without paying taxes or with the gifter doing the necessary paying. A property on the island came to him in 1996 at the price of $250,000.00. There was no deed of trust. He later sold this land to a fellow Democrat without a deed. This friend later sold it back to Bald Head properties. The deeds to either deal were not recorded until the same minute by the same lawyer. Now this friend has a bill he is trying to get passed in the state legislature that would make it more difficult to investigate elected officials by couching it as a way to protect elected officials from political witch hunts by the opposing political party. It is much easier to intimidate a three-judge panel than try to deal with federal investigative bodies.

Norman MacCloud received an early hour call from Sheriff Ronald Hewett while Hewett was in Raleigh. Hewett fired him saying that "he did not need to show up the next day. They no longer needed him." The other story about MacCloud that made the rounds was that he had stopped a woman for a violation and tried to solicit sex from her. According to a reporter, he wasn't too broken up about Dee's death to try to pick her up at the Indigo Plantation Press Conference on October 23, 1999. Either way he and several who worked for him were canned at the same time. He worked for Jay Walker of Tri-Tech in Southport.

According to people in the sheriff's department, dismissal comes through a phone call around one or two o'clock in the morning from someone doing the sheriff's dirty work, telling the unfortunate employee not to come in for work. They are no longer needed.

- Doe, Jane*. (7-24-07). *Telephone interview* by Elaine Buff. P. 7.

Speaking of grand jury investigations versus a three-judge panel, Brunswick County Sheriff Ronald Hewett is under a grand jury investigation that apparently began as a look at the use of re-election funds. It reaches back to 2000 and the process may continue into 2008. Deputies, past and present, various organizations funded by the Sheriff's works such as his cookbook, and other names not released by the public have been subpoenaed to testify.

It has just been announced that David Crocker will retire and go to work in the District Attorney's office as an investigator. William Fairley has been appointed by Governor Mike Easley to the district court bench in the 13th Judicial District, which includes Brunswick County.

Dee's case has been closed in Brunswick County. It is still open on Bald Head and her death there has been classified as 'Undetermined.'

Friday, October 22, 1999

(Times are approximate)

Time	Action	Proof
	William Fairley interviewed Fire Chief Kent Brown, Heather Hardee, Josann Campanello, Robert Willis, Sylvia Timmons, and the parent a child concerning Dee's sexual harassment lawsuit against BHI employee.	Fairley
6:00 pm	Jones and Cain caught ferry at Indigo Plantation	Cain
6:25 pm	Arrived at Bald Head Island	Cain
6:35 pm	Began shift work: checked vehicles: Cain the Blazer; Jones the Ford pick-up; checked oil and fluids in vehicles; tires, radio, lights, etc. picked up clipboards w/call & incident sheets; radios; flashlights: Cain, a stinger; Jones, a big mag light	Cain
7:10 pm	Left office to patrol together	Cain
	Catering van from River Pilot Café stuck at 829 Killigray Dr. on Middle Island	
8:50 pm	Jones called Monzon's cell from station & apologized	Monzon
10:21 pm	Investigated larceny of golf cart at River Pilot Café	
	Jones drives pick-up, Cain drives Blazer	
10:55 pm	Cain & Jones stopped at lighthouse to check golf cart they had seen earlier	Cain
10:56 pm	They returned to the station	Cain
	Cain went by way of West Bald Head Wynd; Jones by North Bald Head Wynd	
	Cain finished meal	Cain
	Jones checked cart registration & worked on resume;	
	At some point during the evening, Jones worked on self-evaluation	G. Hardee
	Jones left in pick-up truck	Cain
11:30 pm	Jones called Monzon from marina payphone – call lasted 1 minute	Monzon
	Jones saw a disturbance or some behavior on the dock that caused her to walk its length to investigate.	Witnesses
	(Trip to Old Baldy takes about 2 minutes from ferry landing by vehicle.)	Jones
11:45 pm	Jones stopped golf cart on wrong side of road, did not get out of truck.	3 in cart
11:48 pm	Jones reported: "Out with three. Stand by." on Channel 1.	C-COM
	Cain started to car on this transmission. He went in a direction away from lighthouse.	Cain
	Jones asked the men to put away the gun. She had switched to Channel 2.	C-COM Gore
	Someone turned off Jones' radio	Cain
11:53 pm	2 tram drivers saw the tail lights of Jones' vehicles and heard a loud "BOOM!" from one place while Andy Adams heard it from another. The tram drivers thought it was the construction site trash can lid slamming shut in the wind.	Tram drivers A. Adams
	Someone turned Jones' radio back on to Channel 1.	Crocker
	Andy Adams then crouched in the protection of the chapel's shadows as three men rush by in a golf cart running without lights away from the lighthouse.	A. Adams
	Cain moved down Muscadine to S. Bald Head to the Marina where he saw Jones' tail lights at the lighthouse.	Cain
	C-COM has been trying urgently to raise Jones over the radio.	C-COM
11:55	*(At least 7 minutes have passed.)*	C-COM

pm

	Cain found Jones' pickup backed in to the cul-de-sac, still running with park lights on	Cain
		C-COM
	He searched the lighthouse, bathroom, inside of the truck.	911 tape
	He found Jones behind the trash pile.	
	Cain checked her body and found no pulse, her eyes slightly open, blood coming from her head.	C-COM
	He called C-COM and asked for help, asked Coast Guard, Asked for K-9.	C-COM
11:56 pm	EMS Fire Chief Kent Brown paged out 10-18.	Brown

(Times are approximate)

Time	Action	Proof
12:04 am	EMS enroute from station 32	EMS
12:06 am	EMS Brown & wife Trish arrived on crime scene	Brown
12:08 am	EMS Mike Tripp & Danny Kiser arrived on crime scene	EMS
	Brown & Cain covered Tripp & Kiser as they did 'snatch & grab' on Jones' body	EMS
12:10 am	Trish Brown & Tripp took Jones' body to ferry landing	EMS
12:12 am	Trish Brown & Tripp arrived at the ferry landing	EMS
12:19 am	EKG Chest #1 done on Jones	EMS
12:26 am	EKG Chest #2 done on Jones	EMS
12:27 am	Doctor confirmed death asystole x3	EMS
	Tripp covered the body with a sheet	Tripp
	Kent Brown cleaned out the ambulance used to bring Jones to the dock so arriving police can be taken to the crime scene	Brown
	He set up a headquarters in the Village Offices.	
	Before G. Hardee arrived, Brown brought the fire truck and his volunteer fire department members to the crime scene.	
	During this time employees from Eb and Flo's were told to get to the ferry. They got to the landing where they view Jones' body on the gurney without the cover that had been placed over her by Tripp.	J. Grasty
12:40 am	Personnel arrived from the mainland, according to crime scene log (csl):	CSL
	Lt. Charlie Miller, Deputy Allen Britton, Deputy John Balduc, Kent Brown Patrolman Brian Wrenn	
12:50 am	Crime scene tape was secured	CSL
	Will Hewett appeared and waited in the Indigo Plantation Parking Lot	W. Hewett
	Somewhere during this time he talked to police going to BHI telling them that Dee has killed herself.	
1:07 am	Criminal Specialist SD Netherland contacted Special Agent PM Daly	CSL
1:15 am	EMS Sylvia Timmons with Jones' body	CSL
1:20 am	Shipmate Thomas McKellar with body	CSL
	Shallotte Police Chief Rodney Gause with body	CSL
	Sergeant Randy Robinson with body	CSL
	Lt. John Ingram with body	CSL
	EMS John Johnson with body	CSL
	EMS Brian Johnson with body	CSL
	EMS Trish Brown with body	CSL
	Captain Rodney Melton with body	CSL
1:24 am	Lt. Gene Hardee arrived on crime scene	CSL
	He told Brown to remove the fire truck and volunteer firemen from the scene but the truck was still there when the HP helicopter was taking pictures in the early morning hours.	CS Photographs
1:25 am	3 subjects stopped in boat running without lights coming from BHI off Ft. Fisher	C-COM

Saturday, October 23, 1999 (con't)

Time	Action	Proof
1:40 am	Lt. Crocker arrived and had body moved to depot office; performed gsr test	CSL CSL
	Sheriff Ronald Hewett & SWAT Team left Sunny Point headed for BHI	MacCloud
	MacCloud was supposedly with him, telling him that Jones has been emotionally upset.	
1:41 am	Det. Sam Davis photographed body	CSL
	EMS Michael Tripp with body	CSL
	EMS Danny Kiser with body	CSL
	EMS Kent Brown with body	CSL
2:00 am	Family friend Larry Jones notified Loy & Harriet Buff that Jones is dead.	CSL
2:30 am	Arrived on Bald Head: Corporal Robert Willis (Jones' training officer), Sheriff Hewett and the SWAT team,	
	BHI in-active Chief Karen Grasty arrived at BHI	CSL
2:50 am	Arrived on BHI: Det. Roger Harrington & Plt. Dexter Ludlum	CSL
3:15 am	Lt. Crocker secured evidence & body for transport accompanied by:	CSL
	Shallotte Police Chief Rodney Gause, Shallotte Police Office Carey Gaskins, and Topsail Beach Police Officer David Grasty	
	C-COM first became aware that Jones' body had been moved from crime scene	C-COM
3:30 am	Grasty & Hardee created a synopsis	CSL
3:35 am	EMS Chief Brown debriefed	CSL
3:45 am	Debriefing with SBI, Bald Head Island police & Brunswick County Sheriff's Dept.	CSL
3:55 am	Ferry arrived at Indigo Plantation Ferry Landing at Southport	CSL
3:57 am	Jones' body loaded into Southport Police Fire & Rescue vehicle & transferred to Dosher Hospital morgue by: Charles A. Drew, David A. Frye, Tammy A. Drew, & SBI SA Storms.	SBI Report
4:01 am	Jones' body arrived at the morgue. It was met by Coroner Greg White & Southport Police Chief Robert Gray.	SBI Report
	Hiltz completed the Medical Examiner's report and request for autopsy.	
	Jones was removed from gurney & placed in white plastic body bag.	
	White arranged for transport to Jacksonville for autopsy.	
	Body moved to holding station.	
	SA Storms took photographs of body.	
	Body bag closed.	
	White attached an ID tag to the outside of the body bag.	
	White secured the holding station.	
4:03 am	SBI SA's Daly, Netherland, Cummings, Netherland, Johnson, Bridges departed Indigo for BHI	SBI report
4:35 am	SBI SA's met with Sheriff at BHI Village Hall	SBI report
	Sometime after this meeting, the Sheriff closed down the command center that Brown had set up here.	Testimonies
5:10 am	Chief Grasty delivered Jones' bookbag to Daly	SBI report
5:15 am	SA Daly seized items from bookbag	SBI report

Time	Action	Proof
5:23 am	S. Davis & D. Crocker searched Rescue Unit #4273 parked outside the hall for relevant evidence	CSL
5:25 am	Hospital security secured and locked the area where Jones' body lay	SBI report
5:30 am	SA Storms interviewed the Buffs at their home	SBI report
5:38 am	SA Daly at crime scene: scribed GSP coordinates & security tape	SBI report
5:40 am	Lt. Gene Caison arrived on the crime scene SBI SA Steve Netherland on crime scene	CSL
5:46 am	On the crime scene: Lt. Crocker, BCSD Same Davis photographer, SA Wayne Johnson, & SA Aundrea Bridges.	SBI report
5:59 am	Chief Rodney Gause on crime scene	CSL
6:00 am	Storms went to Jones' house with Buffs.	SBI report
6:05 am	The Glock was seized from Officer Cain's Blazer	SBI report
6:30 am	3 Hispanics left the island on the 1st morning ferry	SBI report
7:00 am	Jones' magazine & live bullets were accounted for	SBI report
7:20 am	S. Davis located spent .40 shell casing SBI Supervisor Tony Cummings arrived on the crime scene	CSL CSL
7:24 am	Ship Pilot Sgt. Woodard on crime scene	CSL
7:29 am	Ship Pilot Tripp Gardner on crime scene	CSL
7:37 am	SA Storms seized items from Jones' body prior to autopsy transport Turned items over to Gene Caison	SBI report
7:42 am	Security Guard Steve Stout secured the morgue	SBI report
8:10 am	S. Davis photographed & sketched crime scene	CSL
9:00 am	Clothes & weapon taken from Keith Cain Travis Snead met ferry, collected Cain, stopped at Brunswick Hospital, then home.	CSL Interview
9:10 am	S. Davis processed left driver's door & left front quarter panel of Jones' pick-up, lifting numerous latent prints	CSL
10:30 am	C.L. Garrett, Jim Beddard-Drenir, SA Hans Miller met at Jacksonville for autopsy	SBI report
	Miller called back to BHI & said it looked like a suicide. Garrett BEGAN the autopsy. Before leaving, Grasty put Robert Willis in charge of crime scene, telling him to keep it in tact.	Testimony Testimony
11:00 am	McCloud told Dr. Reschley at Dosher that Jones has killed herself.	Testimony
	Sheriff Hewett, Chief Grasty, Lt. Hardee, Horne, & Cummings held a press conference at Indigo Plantation. BHI fire department finished washing down the crime scene.	Testimony Press Conf. Testimony
12:00 pm	McCloud at Buff's house announced Jones had committed suicide	Testimony
12:35 pm	S. Davis left the crime scene	CSL

Time	Action	Proof
1:10 pm	SA Daly transferred evidence seized by S. Davis over to Det. Donald Marlow of BCSD	SBI report
2:00 pm	MacCloud drove Dee's sisters & a friend to Dee's house to obtain pictures to use in memorial service on Tuesday. He had the only key to her house.	Testimony

Out With Three
Sunday, October 24, 1999

(Times are approximate)

Time	Action	Proof
10:35 am	BCSD members interviewed the three golf cart tourists who were going the wrong way	CSL
	The three people who actually heard Jones' Channel 2 transmission had to meet with authorities and be taught how to talk to the press. (Don't.)	Interview

Monday, October 25, 1999

(Times are approximate)

Time	Action	Proof
9:00 am	Evidence submitted to SBI lab	S. Davis
10:20 am	Subject interviewed at Southport marina	Crocker
11:20 am	Village attorney interviewed	Crocker
2:00 pm	SBI/BHIPD/BCSD recreated crime scene	Crocker
5:00 pm	Interviewed resident suspect	Crocker

Tuesday, October 26, 1999

(Times are approximate)

Time	Action	Proof
11:38 am	$50,000.00 reward for information notice sent out statewide	Poster
Afternoon	Village meeting held on BHI to discuss the situation – some residents demanded a suicide ruling so property values would not plummet	Newspaper articles Grasty
Evening	Memorial service held for Jones in Southport	Newspaper articles

Aaron, Robert. (nc). *Gunshot primer residue: The invisible clue.* FBI Laboratory: Washington, DC. Retrieved 11-20-06 from http://www.hackcanada.com/blackcraw/survive/gunshot.txt

Adams, Andy. (9-16-04). *Eye witness testimony.*

Aerial map of Old Baldy. Retrieved 10-20-07 from http://maps.google.com/maps?ll=33.861876,-77.990138&spn=0.11,0.18&t=h

Asystole definition retrieved 8-15-07 from http://www.en.wikipedia.org/wiki/asystole

Atkins, Laura. (10-28-99). *Telephone interview* by Janet Storms.

Atkins, Laura. (10-27-07). *Telephone interview* by Elaine Buff.

Bald Head Island. Retrieved 10-24-07 from http://www.city-data.com/city/Bald-Head-Island-North-Carolina.html

Bald Head Island Incident/Investigative Report. (3-29-99).

Bald Head Island Investigative Canvass Sheet. 10-23-99

Bald Head Island Police Department. (1999). *Performance record of Davina Buff Jones.* Industrial Commission Hearing Exhibits II. Pp. 1005-1007.

Bald Head officials accept DA ruling on officer's death. (12-12-99). *Morning-Star.* P. 1B.

Baldwin, Hayden B. *Crime Scene Processing Protocol.* Retrieved 10/05/07 from http://www.feinc.net/cs-proc.htm

Berman, Alan L. Ph. D. (5-28-02). *Psychological Autopsy.* Pp. 1-12.

Best Uniforms (2-02-99). *Invoice.*

Bishop, E. E. (10-25-99). *SBI Investigative Report: Firearms and ballistics.* File No.: 992665(ALA).

Bishop, E. E. (10-27-99). *SBI Investigative Report* File No.: 992665(ALA).

Bissette, Brenda. (11-01-99). *SBI Investigative Report* File No.: 992665(ALA).

Brown, Kent. (10-22-99). *Interview* by William Fairley.

Brown, Kent. (10-27-99). *Memo: Possessing Firearms* to Wade Horne

Brown, Kent. (2-11-00). *Interview* by Monty Clark.

Buff v. Bureau of Justice Assistance Public Safety Officers' Benefits. (1-18-03).

Buff v. Village of Bald Head Island Police Department, North Carolina League of Municipalities and North Carolina Rescue Workers Cap Death Benefits Act. North Carolina Industrial Commission. (10-23/24-03).

Buff v. Village of Bald Head Island Police Department, North Carolina League of Municipalities and North Carolina Rescue Workers Cap Death Benefits Act. North Carolina Industrial Commission. (10-23/24-03). Exhibits Part I

Buff v. Village of Bald Head Island Police Department, North Carolina League of Municipalities and North Carolina Rescue Workers Cap Death Benefits Act. North Carolina Industrial Commission. (10-23/24-03). Exhibits Part II

Buff v. North Carolina Law Enforcement Officers and Rescue Workers Death Benefit Act and North Carolina Contingency and Emergency Fund.

Buff family statement. (12-15-99). *The State Port Pilot.* P. 9.

Buff Family. (7-29-04). Happy Birthday, Dee! *The State Port Pilot.* Np.

Buff, Harriet. (5-20-06). *Interview* by Elaine Buff.

Buff, Loy. (nd). *Letter* to Richard Vinroot

Buff, Loy. (nd). *Letter* to William Bennett.

Buff, Loy. (nd). *Letter* to Senator Jesse Helms

Buff, Loy. (5-28-00). *Letter* to Attorney General Mike Easley.

Buff, Loy. (2-02-01). *Letter* to Senator John Edwards.

Buff, Loy. (2-19-04). *Notes: Davina's Benefits*

Buff, Loy. (3-08-04). *Notes: Davina's Workman's Comp.*

Buff. Loy. (7-11-05). *Letter* to Congressman Mike McIntyre

Buff, Loy. (9-12-07). *Interview* by Elaine Buff.

Buff, Loy and Harriet. (10-28-99). *Interview* by Janet Storms.

Buff, Loy and Harriet. (8-24-06). *Interview* by Elaine Buff.

Buff, Loy and Harriet. (11-13-06) *Interview* by Elaine Buff.

Butts, John D. (12-08-03). *Deposition.*

Byrd, Mike. *Duty Description for the Crime Scene Investigator.* Retrieved on 10-05-07 from http://www.crime-scene-investigator.net/dutydescription.html

Cain, Keith. (10-10-99) *Incident Report.*

Cain, Keith. (10-23-99.) *Interview* by S.D. Netherland.

Cain, Keith. (11-15-99). *Interview* by Gene Hardee.

Cain, Keith. (1-25-00). *Interview* by Monty Clark.

Cain, Keith. (3-01-00). *Letter* to Lt. Gene Hardee, Chief Karen Grasty

Calhoun, Terry. (12-15-99). Death is ruled suicide. *The State Port Pilot.* Pp. 1,9.

Calhoun, Terry. (3-29-00). Hearing set Monday on EMS suspension. *State Port Pilot.* P. 2.

Calhoun, Terry. (4-05-00). Emergency services case reviewed. *State Port Pilot.* P. 2.

Calhoun, Terry. (2-09-05). Will prohibition ever work? *The State Port Pilot.* P. 5A.

Calhoun, Terry. (7-06-05). Officer's death wasn't suicide. *The State Port Pilot.* Pp. 1A, 10A.

Calhoun, Terry. (7-06-05). Evidence refutes suicide theory. *The State Port Pilot*. P. 12A.

Calhoun, Terry. (7-13-05). Former BHI chief: 'I know she was murdered.' *The State Port Pilot*. Pp. 1A, 6A.

Calhoun, Terry. (7-27-05). Cold cases no longer. *The State Port Pilot*. Pp. 1A, 9A.

Calhoun, Terry. (2-01-06). Federal ruling: Officer was killed. *The State Port Pilot*. P. 1A.

Calhoun, Terry. (3-08-06). Federal ruling says Jones died in 'line of duty.' *The State Port Pilot*. Pp. 1A, 6A, 7A.

Carlson, Eric. (10-30-99). Sheriff expects 'Turning point' in investigation of officer's death. *Morning-Star*. P. 1A.

Carolclips. *Old Baldy*. Retrieved 5-25-06 from http://www.itip.dpi.state.nc.us/Caroclips/bald.html

Carter, Steve. (10-24-85). *Security Bank Memo* to Carl Dean.

Cherrie, Victoria and Cece von Kolnitz. (10-28-99). Single shot killed officer, autopsy shows. *Morning-Star*. Pp. 1A, 4A.

Cherrie, Victoria. (11-06-99). Town officials quiet about progress of investigation. *Morning-Star*. Pp. 1A, 8A.

Classification and pay actions. Retrieved 10-17-07 from http://www.osp.state.nc.us/rtablecomm/spc-actions/07Meetings/classpayactions9-30.pdf

Concerned Citizen. (6-19-02). *Letter* to the editor. *The State Port Pilot*.

Crocker, David. (nd). *Investigative report timeline*. Pp. 1-3.

Crocker, David. (nd). *Letter* to Ronald Hewett (Case update).

Crocker, David. (2-09-00). *Photograph Log*.

DA's statement. (12-15-99). *The State Port Pilot*. P. 9.

D'Abruzzo, Diana. (10-27-99). 'The biggest heart of anyone ...' *The State Port Pilot*. Pp. 3,5.

Davis, Sam. (10-23-99) *Davina Buff Jones Crime Scene Photographs*.

Doe, Jane*. (7-24-07). *Telephone interview* by Elaine Buff.

Doe, John*. (7-23-01). *Letter* to Loy Buff.

Doe, John II. (9-24-02). *Email* to Loy and Harriet Buff.

Doe, John II* (nd) *Email* to William Bennett

Doe, John III* (nd) Policeman. *Interview*.

Dover, Gigi. (2007). *Everybody knows*.

Dowell, Susan Stiles. Time Out. *Coastal Living*. Vol. 11, Issue 3. April, 2007. Retrieved 11-26-07 from http://www.baldheadisland.com/downloads/Press/Coastal_Living_april/coastal_living_April2007.pdf

Doyle, Jeffrey Scott. Gunshot Residue. Retrieved 10-14-07 from http://www.firearmsid.com/A_distanceGSR.htm

Easley, Mike. (8-14-00). *Letter* to Loy Buff.

Fairley, William F. (11-03-99). *Investigative Report Concerning Mike Ilvento vs. Dee   Jones*

Family hires investigator to probe officer's death. (5-23-00). *The Charlotte Observer.*   Np.

FBI Laboratory Report of bullet from victim. (12-02-99).

Foy, Henry. (5-22-03). *Letter* to Village of Bald Head Island

Fulford, Edward. (11-08-01). SBI Agent picked as new chief deputy. *Brunswick Beacon.* P. 8A.

Garrett, C. L. (10-23-99). Autopsy of Davina Buff Jones.

Garrett, C. L. (10-28-99). *Preliminary Report of autopsy examination.*

Garrett, C. L. (11-25-03). *Deposition.*

Gore, Rex. (12-08-99). *Letter* to Sheriff Ronald Hewett.

Gore, Rex. (12-09-99). *Fax* to David Cox.

Gore, Rex. (12-09-99). *Press Release.* Pp 1-2.

Grasty, Karen. (nd). *Letter* to A & E.

Grasty, Karen. (nd). *Personal writing.*

Grasty, Karen. (nd). *Letter* to Caddell.

Grasty, Karen. (nd). *FBI Questionnaire.*

Grasty, Karen. (1999). *Bald Head Island Guest Rules.*

Grasty, Karen. (4-07-98). *Memo: Telephone* to all officers.

Grasty, Karen. (4-08-98). *Memo: Radio Purchase* to Wade Horne.

Grasty, Karen. (11-17-98). *Memo: Police Department Turnover* to Wade Horne

Grasty, Karen. (1-14-99). *Direct order.*

Grasty, Karen. (3-17-99). *Memo* to Wade Horne.

Grasty, Karen. (3-18-99). *Memo: Performance Evaluation* to Wade Horne.

Grasty, Karen. (4-27-99). *Letter* to Kent Brown.

Grasty, Karen. (5-03-99). *Letter* to G. Wade Horne.

Grasty, Karen. (5-03-99). *Memo* to Wade Horne and Fire Chief Kent Brown.

Grasty, Karen. (5-04-99). *Memo* to Wade Horne.

Grasty, Karen. (5-12-99). *Memorandum Improper Procedure* to Officer Dee Jones.

Grasty, Karen. (10-13-99). *Email* to Wade Horne.

Grasty, Karen. (10-22-99). *Statement.*

Grasty, Karen. (10-23-99). *Interview* by Recording officer.

Grasty, Karen. (11-02-99). *Letter* to Kathleen (Kitty) Henson.

Grasty, Karen. (11-04-99). *Letter* to Kent Brown.

Grasty, Karen. (3-16-00). *Memo* to Keith Cain.

Grasty, Karen. (6-28-00). *Letter* to Loy and Harriet Buff.

Grasty, Karen. (7-02-00). *Letter* to Loy and Harriet Buff.

Grasty, Karen. (7-28-00). *Email* to Martha Lee.

Grasty, Karen. (9-12-00). *Letter* to Loy and Harriet Buff.

Grasty, Karen. (8-29-01). *Interview* by Henry Foy.

Grasty, Karen. (3-18-04). *Letter* to Loy and Harriet Buff.

Gregory, James. (10-25-99). *SBI Investigative Report* File No.: 992665(ALA)

Gregory, James. (03-01-00). *SBI Investigative Report: Trace evidence* File No.: 992665(ALA)

Gregory, James. (03-14-01). *SBI Investigative Report: Trace evidence: Clothes* File No.: 992665(ALA)

Griffin, Anna. (6-02-02). Murder or suicide. *The Charlotte Observer.* Pp. 1A, 12A, 13A.

Griffin, Anna. *Fax* to Police Chief Karen Grasty.

Hale, Charles. (10-26-99). *Eulogy for Davina Elaine Buff.*

Hale, Pat. (10-06-99). *Letter* to Dee.

Hardee, Gene. (11-15-98). *Memo Re: Building Security Check* to Chief Karen Grasty

Hardee, Gene. (9-26-99). *Interview* by William Fairley.

Hardee, Gene. (10-13-99). *Memo: Shift responsibilities.*

Hardee, Gene. (10-22-99). *Bald Head Island incident report.*

Hardee, Gene. (2-11-00). *Interview* by Monty Clark.

Hardee, Gene. (4-30-04). *Fax* to Loy Buff.

Hardee, Heather and Josann Campanello. (10-22-99). *Interview* by William Fairley.

Hart, Tanya. (8-27-07). *Interview* by Elaine Buff.

Hattendorf, Richard. (nd). *Memo: Chronological Summary of Dee Jones' Case* to Monty Clark

Hewett, Deborah. (1-22-99). *Recommendation.*

Hewett, William. L. (10-23-99). *Interview* by S. W. Johnson.

Hewett, William L. (2-08-00) *Interview* by Monty Clark.

Hiltz, Douglas. (10-23-99). *Medical Examiner's Certificate of Death.*

Hiltz, Douglas. (10-23-99). *Report of investigation by Medical Examiner.*

Hiltz, Douglas. (10-23-99). *Request by medical examiner for autopsy.*

Horne, Wade. (5-11-99). *Note re: grant money* to Karen Grasty.

Horne, Wade. (11-29-99). *Memo* to Gene Hardee.

Ilvento, Michael. (nd). *Interview* by William Fairley.

Ilvento, Michael. (10-26-99). *Interview* by Janet Storms. Pp. 1-3.

Inglesby, Henry. (11-16-95). *Recommendation.*

Ives, Millard. (5-20-03). Bald Head Island's gun sale investigated. *Morning Star.* Pp. 1B, 3B.

Jones, Davina Buff. (nd). *Application for Legal defense.*

Jones, Davina Buff. (nd). *Personal writings.*

Jones, Davina Buff. (97). *Personal writing.*

Jones, Davina Buff. (11-22-98). *Personal writing.*

Jones, Davina Buff. (99). *Bald Head Island Restaurants.*

Jones, Davina Buff. (02-99). *January Duty Notebook.*

Jones, Davina Buff. (03-99). *March Duty Notebook.*

Jones, Davina Buff. (3-11-99). *Journal.*

Jones, Davina Buff. (07-99). *July Duty Notebook.*

Jones, Davina Buff. (08-99). *August Duty Notebook.*

Jones, Davina Buff. (9-14-99). *Operations Report.*

Jones, Davina Buff. *Work Desk October Calendar.*

Jones, Davina Buff. (10-04-99). *Letter.*

Jones, Davina Buff. (10-04-99). *Journal entry.*

Jones, Davina Buff. (10-08-99). *Journal entry.*

Jones, Davina Buff. (10-10-99) *Incident Report.*

Jones, Davina Buff. (10-10-99) *Incident Report Addendum*

Jones, Davina Buff. (10-13-99). *Journal entry.*

Jones, Davina Buff. (10-15-99) *Police Meeting Notes.*

Jones, Davina Buff. (10-15-99) *Journal entry.*

Jones, Davina Buff. (10-18-99). *Interview* by William Fairley.

Jones, Davina Buff. (10-18-99). *Application for legal defense.*

Jones, Davina Buff. (10-20-99). *To do list.*

Jones, Davina Buff. (10-21-99). *To do list.*

Kiser, Danny. (10-23-99). *Ambulance call report narrative.*

Kiser, Danny. (10-23-99). *Interview* by recording officer.

Kokalis, Peter G. *Polymer perfection.* Retrieved 3-29-06 from
http://www.remtek.com/arms/glock/model/40/23/index.htm

LATTIMORE, BUCK, Chairman, N.C. Industrial Commission. OPINION AND AWARD for the Full Commission. (Filed 27 June 2005). I.C. NOS. 980154 & LH-0286, LOY BUFF, Father of DAVINA BUFF JONES, Deceased Employee, Plaintiff v. N.C. LAW ENFORCEMENT OFFICES AND RESCUE WORKERS DEATH BENEFITS ACT and STATE OF NORTH CAROLINA CONTINGENCY AND EMERGENCY FUND, Defendants.

Lee, Martha. (12-09-99). *Editorial* regarding the murder of Dee Buff Jones. [Letter to the Editor] *The State Port Pilot.*

Lee, Martha. (7-24-00). *Email* to Karen Grasty.

Lewis, Laura. (7-29-04). Family continues to defend slain Bald Head officer. *Brunswick Beacon.* P. 1.

Lewis, Laura. (6-15-06). Dad disputes DA's latest finding that BHI police death was suicide. *Brunswick Beacon.* P. 1.

Little, Ken. (nd). Commission: Officer's death not a suicide. *Morning Star.* Pp. 1A, 4A.

Little, Ken. (10-23-03). Lingering suspicion. *Morning-Star.* Pp. 1A, 4A.

Little Ken. (10-24-03). Witness: Officer sought treatment for depression. *Morning-Star.* Pp. 1A, 5A.

Little, Ken. (7-22-04). DA to review Jones hearing report. *Morning-Star.* Pp. 1A, 6A.

Little, Ken. (11-02-05). Bald Head death still disputed. *Morning-Star.* Pp. 1B, 3B.

Little, Ken. (7-03-05). DA willing to re-examine officer's death. *Morning-Star*. Pp. 1A, 6A.

Little, Ken. (7-22-05). DA examines '99 Bald Head shooting again. *Morning-Star*. Pp. 1B, 3B.

Little, Ken. (6-03-06). SBI reinforces suicide ruling in officer death. *Morning-Star*. Pp. 1B, 3B.

Luper, Tim. (10-27-99). *SBI Laboratory Report*. Agency File No.: 992665(ALA

Luper, Tim. (10-28-99). *SBI Laboratory Report: Latent prints* Agency File No.: 992665(ALA).

Luper, Tim. (11-01-99). *SBI Laboratory Report: GSR on 3 in boat*. Agency File No.: 992665(ALA)

Luper, Tim. (11-01-99). *SBI Laboratory Report: GSR. Agency File No.: 992665(ALA)*

Luper, Tim. (11-01-99). *SBI Laboratory Report: Pants*. Agency File No.: 992665(ALA

MacLeod, Norman. (2-10-00). *Interview* by Monty Clark.

Martinez, Michael. (2-20-01). *Report.*

Mama Sue. (8-22-86). *Letter* to Dee.

Mishoe, D. C. (10-29-99). *SBI Laboratory Report: Latent prints.*

Mishoe, D. C. (10-29-99). *SBI Laboratory Report: Latent evidence.*

Mishoe, D. C. (12-01-00). *SBI Laboratory Report: Latent evidence.*

Monzon, Scott. (10-24-99). *Interview* by Gene Caison.

Monzon, Scott. (2-10-00). *Interview* by Monty Clark.

Noles, Jamie. (10-25-99). Interview by police of record.

Nubel, Richard. (10-27-99). Service is held for slain officer. *The State Port Pilot*. Pp. 1, 9.

Nubel, Richard. (6-05-02). Fire/EMS chief resigns. *The State Port Pilot*. Pp. 1, 8.

Nubel, Richard. (6-17-02). Libel claimed in EMS complaint. *The State Port Pilot*. P. 5.

Oath of office for police officers. Basic law enforcement training commencement exercises. (12-08-98). Wilmington, NC.

O'Connor, Tom. *An Introduction to crime scene analysis*. Retrieved on 10/05/07 from http://faculty.ncwc.edu/TOConnor/315/315lect04.htm

Officer's death termed a suicide. (12-10-99). *The Charlotte Observer*. P. 4C.

Page, Reid. A. Jr. (12-10-99). *Letter* to Rex Gore.

Panel agrees officer did not kill herself. (7-04-05). *The Charlotte Observer*. Np.

Perkins, Tommy. (3-01-00). Columbus deputy is Bald Head's new chief. *Morning Star*. P. 2B.

Peterson, Sarah. (5-21-03). Terms of resolution: SBI investigates [sic] Bald Head gun sale. *The State Port Pilot*. P. 18A.

Peterson, Sarah. (5-28-03). Handgun sale issue dropped. *The State Port Pilot.* np.

Peterson, Sarah. (7-28-04). Commission: Officer death was homicide. *The State Port Pilot.* Pp. 1A, 14A.

Phillips, Adrian A. (7-19-04). *Judgment of Industrial Commission.*

Ramsey, Mike. (10-24-99). Officer dies in Bald Head Island shooting. *The Sunday Star-News.* Pp. 1A, 9A.

Ramsey, Mike. (10-24-99). Friends call her 'dynamite stuck in a little package.' *The Sunday Star-News.* Pp. 1A, 9A.

Ramsey, Mike. (10-27-99). Hundreds pay tribute to fallen officer. *Morning-Star.* Pp. 1A, 6A.

Ramsland, Katherine. *The medical examiner.* Retrieved on 9/28/07 from http://www.crimelibrary.com/criminal_mind/forensics/crimescene/4.html

Re-enactment. Jones Murder October 22, 1999 (10-25-99). SBI.

Reiss, Cory. (12-10-99). Bald Head officer shot self, DA says. *Morning-Star.* Pp. 1A, 8A.

Reisz, Charles Jr. (12-11-99). If it was suicide, what prompted it? *Morning-Star.* P. 14A.

Reschley, Keith. (nd). *Medical records of Davina Buff Jones.*

Reschley, Keith. (10-24-99). *Interview* by G. W. Johnson.

Reschley, Keith. (11-14-03). *Disposition.*

Rollins, Robert. (1-20-04). *Psychiatric autopsy: Ms. Davina Jones.* Raleigh, North Carolina.

Ross, Robert. (07-07-00). Bald Head Island tape analysis.

Ruling contradicts suicide finding. (7-22-04). *The Charlotte Observer.* Np.

Sadler, Beverly Buff. (October, 1999). *Davina "Dee" Elaine Buff Jones: Reflections on her life and death.*

Sadler, Beverly Buff. (November 10, 1999). *Letter to Keith Cain.*

SBI report: crime scene on Bald Head Island. (10-23-99). Pp. 1-5.

Scott, Andy. (5-18-99). *Letter of thanks* to Police Chief Karen Grasty.

Seymour, Jody. (1997) *Your child first* from *Finding God between the lines.* JudsonPress: Valley Forge, PA., p. 9.

Shooting death still unresolved. (11-03-99). *The State Port Pilot.* Pp. 1, 9.

Skoler, Daniel. (1-18-03). *Hearing officer claim determination. PSOB Case Number 2000-48.* Pp. 1-24.

Stites, Lisa. (6-07-06). DA calls it suicide. *The State Port Pilot.* P. 1.

Stone, Oliver and Zachery Sklar. (1992). *JFK: The book of the film: The documented screenplay.* Applause Books: New York.

Storms, Janet. (10-22-99). *Transcript of 911 tape.*

Storms, Janet. (10-23-99). *Report: Search of Davina Buff Jones' Nissan truck.*

Storms, Janet. (10-23-99). *SBI report: Seizure of personal items from Jones.*

Storms, Janet. (10-23-99). *Transportation of Jones' body/ Observation of coroner report.* Pp. 1-2.

Storms, Janet. (10-28-99) *Memo* about cocaine off Ft. Fisher.

Taussig, Pete. (10-15-99). *Letter* to Gene Hardee.

Teague, Matthew. (10-28-99). Police await lab results in death. *The News and Observer*. Np.

Three charged in boat larceny at BHI marina.(8-02-00). *The State Port Pilot*. np.

Timmons, Sylvia. (10-22-99). *Interview* by William Fairley.

Tonn, Henry. F. (12-30-98). *Psychological evaluation of Davina B. Jones*.

Tripp, Michael. (10-23-99). *Ambulance Call Report Narrative Attachment #1*

Tub, Jed. (11-01-99). *SBI Investigative Report* File No.: 992665(ALA).

U.S.Department Of Justice Office Of Justice Programs Bureau Of Justice Assistance Public Safety Officers' Benefits In The Matter OF: Police Officer Davina Buff-Jones Appeal Hearing PSOB Claim #00-48. January 18, 2003.

Village of Bald Head, Work Session Meeting. (2-11-05). Retrieved 9-30-07 from http://www.villagebhi.org/government/council/pdf/vcm2005_02_11wk.pdf

von Kolnitz, Cece. (10-25-99). Slaying shatters peace of exclusive Bald Head. *Morning-Star*. Pp. 1A, 4A.

von Kolnitz, Cece. (10-26-99). Bald Head officer met 3 people, then was slain. *Morning-Star*. Pp. 1A, 4A.

von Kolnitz, Cece. (10-27-99). Bald Head probe awaits lab report. *Morning-Star*. P. 6A.

von Kolnitz, Cece and Victoria Cherrie. (11-01-99). Bald Head residents seeking closure. *Morning-Star*. Pp. 1A, 6A.

von Kolnitz, Cece and Victoria Cherrie. (11-05-99). Evidence builds case for suicide. *Morning-Star* Pp 1A, 8A.

von Kolnitz, Cece. (11-11-99). Jones' death not in Bald Head report. *Morning-Star*. P. 2B.

von Kolnitz, Cece. (12-07-99). Questions linger about Bald Head officer's death. *Morning-Star*. Pp. 1B, 5B.

von Kolnitz, Cece. (12-10-99). Family, friends doubt suicide conclusion. *Morning-Star*. Pp. 1A, 8A.

von Kolnitz, Cece. (12-14-99). Doors closing, but shooting probe goes on. *Sunday Morning-Star*. Pp. 1B, 5B.

von Kolnitz, Cece. (2-22-00). Manager resigns at Bald Head. *Morning Star*. P. 2b.

von Kolnitz, Cece. (5-22-00). Officer's case not closed for all. *Morning-Star*. P. 1A, 4A.

Walton, James L. (10-16-98). *Recommendation for Bald Head Island Police Position.*

Warren, Marion. (11-05-99). *Letter* to Karen Grasty.

Weather history. Retrieved 8-15-07 from
http://www.wunderground.com
/history/airport/ksut/1999/10/ss/DailyHistory.html

Willis, Robert. (nd). *Poem.*

Willis, Robert. (10-22-99). *Interview* by William Fairley.

Workman. (1-15-03). *Email* to Loy and Harriet Buff.

Zink, Jody. (1-13-03). Email to Loy and Harriet Buff.

*Designates fictitious name to protect witnesses.

1590702

Made in the USA